Inside the IMF

An Ethnography of Documents,
Technology and Organisational Action

Richard H. R. Harper

Rank Xerox Research Centre
Regent Street
Cambridge

ACADEMIC PRESS

San Diego   London   Boston
New York   Sydney   Tokyo   Toronto

Copyright © 1998 by ACADEMIC PRESS

Academic Press, Inc.
525 B Street, Suite 1900, San Diego, California 92101–4495, USA
http://www.apnet.com

Academic Press Limited
24–28 Oval Road, London NW1 7DX, UK
http://www.hbuk.co.uk/ap/

ISBN 0–12–325840–5

A catalogue record for this book is available from the British Library

Typeset by J&L Composition Ltd, Filey, North Yorkshire
Printed in Great Britain by WBC, Bridgend, Mid Glamorgan

98 99 00 01 02 03 EB 9 8 7 6 5 4 3 2 1

Table of Contents

Preface

As I glance over the pages of this book so I am reminded of how much time has passed since I first set foot in the Fund. In some respects this would not matter, but my concern in this book is to report on how ethnographic findings can be used to improve the design of organisational work practice and supporting technologies. Such claims will not hold much water if, by the time the ethnographic findings are published, the organisation in question has moved on. And, indeed, the Fund has changed since I first started this research: the fiftieth anniversary of the Bretton Woods conference came in 1994 and this led to a report outlining how the Fund (and its sister organisation the World Bank) ought to develop and change and, even as these recommendations were being implemented (see the *IMF Survey*, August 8th, 1994), the Mexico crisis later that same year forced the Fund to "bolster" its surveillance activities even more. Meanwhile, and throughout the mid 1990s, the Fund has wanted to make its activities increasingly transparent to the public at large, and this has led it to make available a number of its policy reports and various statistical data on the *World Wide Web*. These changes, however, have not altered the fundamental elements of what I will call the social organisation of the Fund. These have remained the same, since the essential purpose of the Fund has not altered, nor have the organisational processes set up to achieve those purposes. It is these that lie at the heart of the book.

Besides, one needs to bear in mind that though my argument is that ethnographic findings can be used to guide organisational and technological change, it is not in their published form that they get so used. Instead, it is in the form of reports and presentations that are undertaken nearer the time of the research that ethnographic research has its influence. It is in the often hidden, private world between researcher and the organisation studied that the real work of using ethnography for practical ends gets done. Given the importance of this "hidden work", I spend some time discussing it in the pages that follow. But nonetheless, it should not be forgotten that a book is a different sort of object to the materials shared between ethnographer and the studied organisation. So in this case: the book has not been written for the Fund, but for a wider audience. Amongst other things, I have written this book so as to be informative to a general public seeking to understand what the Fund does and why. The perspective I offer is of course limited, being sociological, anthropological and ethnographic, and therefore needs supplementing by the perspectives of other disciplines. As it happens, there is very little on the Fund from any discipline, though as this book was being drafted, this has begun to change with the publication of Louis W. Pauly's extremely readable *"Who Elected the Bankers?"* (Cornell University Press, 1997). My text has also been written to illustrate to ethnographers themselves how their trade can be developed and revitalised. For the truth of the matter is that this trade has been a faltering enterprise over the past few decades and, even though there has been something of a renaissance of it (especially in British sociology), findings from the ethnography of organisations rarely circulate beyond the confines of the sociological and anthropological communities. Its revitalisation and development will only occur, I believe, if the materials that derive reach out beyond these narrow communities to those outside, whether the latter are concerned with the design of document technologies, the interface between technologies and organisational structures, or simply macro-economists wanting to understand how ethnographers view their trade. For those who have invested in this book, I hope that the enjoyment they get from reading what follows is as great as the labour that went into its completion.

Richard Harper
Cambridge, July 1997

Acknowledgements

Ethnographers always depend on the willingness of people to allow the intrusion and the (all too often arrogant) questioning of the ethnographer. In this case, I am indebted to a great many people. I cannot thank them all by name. But there are some I wish to express a public thanks to.

To begin with, I must thank Mr Richard Erb, Deputy Managing Director of the IMF for allowing the study to be undertaken. Mr A. Wright, too, Special Advisor to Mr Erb, was extremely supportive and helpful in opening the doors of the Fund. Once within, I would like to thank all those who opened yet more doors. These individuals included Mr J. McLenaghan, Mr A. Tait, Mr M. Deppler, Mr S. Nsouli, Mr W. Beveridge, Mr J. Pujol, Mr M. Allen, Mr P. Chabrier, Mr B. Short, Mr S. Rouai and Mr. P. Guilmard.

Beyond these individuals, I want to thank those who had the patience to describe their work to me. Amongst these tolerant individuals were Mr L. Wolfe, Mr P. Duran, Mr. T. Bayoumi, Mr G. Bell, Mr C. Brachet, Ms. S. Eken, Mr M. Valavi-Shadman, Mr A. Furtado, Mr. Z. Yucelik, Mr M. Miller, Mr. N Arya, Mr. P. Joyce and Ms V. Wertman.

There were several members of the Fund whose help through the research cannot be exaggerated. First, Terry Hill's quixotic faith in Xerox research provided myself and William Newman, also of RXRC Cambridge, with the initial opportunity to discuss the idea of the project with Mr A. Wright and other senior staff at the Fund. Once the research had commenced, Terry continued to offer his advice and help. Second, from the first day of my fieldwork, Gertrude Long, Chief Archivist of the Fund, was given the onerous task of being my guide and introduction. Her insight, conviviality and encouragement were all vital in helping me complete my work. Amongst those she introduced me to was Mr Chris Yandle (since retired, like several of those I met). It was Mr Yandle who guided me through the inner world of the Fund and who patiently corrected my misunderstandings (he was not able to correct them all). My meetings with Mr Yandle also led me to Mr John Hicklin. Like Mr Yandle, his curiosity about and interest in the research were invaluable and helped me gain much insight. My research also led me to a fifth individual, Mr Warren Minami, Director of the Fund's Bureau of Computer Services. Mr Minami was immediately struck by the possible utility of my research, and provided funding to allow the research to continue further than originally planned. This led me to meet Ms Christa Dub, whose charm and industry helped me move my initial research findings towards a form that could be more readily understood by the Fund at large. Mr. I. McDonald, of the Fund's External Relations department, was also crucial in this, as well as supportive of my wish to publish the findings.

There are, of course, some individuals whose help, though central to the research itself, cannot be thanked directly. I am thinking here of the mission team to "Arcadia" and Arcadian authorities themselves. For obvious reasons I do not want to identify these individuals, but their graciousness in allowing me to watch their every working hour was immense.

All of my research, not only on mission, would not have been possible without the excellent administrative help of Ms S. Christian and Ms M. La Plain of the Fund, and Ms. C. King, of RXRC. Lastly, I would like to thank the staff of the Concordia, where I stayed throughout my research in Washington.

These then are the individuals within the Fund (with one exception) for whom I owe a considerable debt of gratitude. But this project also involved many other people outside of the Fund. In particular, it owes a great deal to William Newman, Principal Scientist of RXRC, Cambridge. It was William who made the first contact with the Fund and whose letters and presentational skills resulted in the Fund opening its doors to me. Once those doors were opened, it was William who gave his closest attention to the findings that I brought home and whose vigorous debating skills forced me to think again and again about what it was I was uncovering. It was William also who led me to think seriously about the very complex and difficult relationship between the naturalistic observation of the world and the design of computer based systems.

I need to thank William also for being one of the three research managers who were able to provide funds for the project. A second was Mark Weiser, of Xerox's Palo Alto Research Centre (PARC). Mark did so because he hoped that I might provide his researchers with "stories about the real world". I hope this book conveys a sense of that real world. Bob Anderson, Director of RXRC, provided the last part of the funding, in the hope that I might be able to demonstrate the utility of sociological ethnography for design purposes.

Once my findings had been worked up into something like a presentable form, numerous people were willing to add critical commentary. These included Peter Brown, of the University of Canterbury,

England; Stefan Senders, of Cornell University, New York; Dave Randall, Manchester Metropolitan University, England; Ken Starkey, of the University of Nottingham, England; and Paul Luff, of the same institution. I also need to thank Marina Jirotka, of Oxford University and Liam Bannon of the University of Limerick, Ireland, for advice and general guidance on the book.

The drafting of this book also lead me to renew my acquaintance with former teachers who, as in former days, read my writing only to find it wanting. In particular, I am extremely grateful to Dick Werbner, of Manchester University, England, for his guidance in correcting at least some of my mistakes. Rod Watson, also of Manchester, helped me structure the whole work, and his strident guidance helped me finish it. Indeed, I cannot express how much my discussions with Rod helped me develop and refine my ideas.

Finally, within my own work place, many people help me develop my ideas and thinking. I cannot name them all. But alongside William Newman, two provided invaluable help. The first was Marge Eldridge. The second was Abi Sellen. Without Abi, the book could not have been written, for it was her tireless help in clarifying my expressions, sorting out my meaning and reminding me how arcane ethnographic argument can be that I have been able to write a book that reaches out beyond (I hope) the usual ethnographic readership.

As many of my colleagues will know, Abi Sellen is much more to me than a colleague, but she was not the only family member who helped in the completion of the book. My mother and father, Chris and Harry Harper, were continuously supportive in a variety of ways, not least with childminding two individuals who have joined this world while the "IMF Project" was underway: my children, Oliver and Madeleine. For those who are parents it hardly needs saying that these two have done their best to prevent me getting anything done. Still, they have reminded me how ephemeral research can be. I also need to thank my father-in-law for the title of the book, and a brother-in-law for astute comments in the limitation of my arguments. In all of these respects this is a family book.

Finally, acknowledgement is due to MCB Press Ltd for allowing me to republish pages 135–137 of L. Suchman & E. Wynn's 1984 article, "Procedures and Problems in the Office", which originally appeared in "Office, Technology and People".

Dedication

For

Abigail Jane Sellen

CHAPTER 1
Introduction

The International Monetary Fund's main building is situated a short distance from the White House in Washington, DC. From the outside, the building is nondescript, indicating nothing of the institution's importance in world affairs, nor about the activities undertaken within. From the inside, however, the building offers a much more spectacular and informative view. For one thing, it has an enormous atrium ensuring that nearly all of its offices have a window. Most face outward, towards the World Bank across the way on 19th Street, for example. But the remainder face in, meaning that the occupants can gaze across the atrium at their colleagues on the other side of the building. For those who do not have an office—an ethnographer for example—the landings by the elevators offer vantage points onto the atrium. Here the ethnographer can view the institution's staff in action: as they sit around conference tables in meetings, move from one office to the next, or crouch over their workstations keying in data. During my own ethnographic vagabondage in Washington, these landings provided me with havens in which I could wait in between interviews or could jot down notes from a meeting I had just finished. Sometimes I would simply rest here and watch the theatre of bureaucratic life before me.

There is of course much more that happens at "the Fund" (as it is known to insiders) than can be observed from the atrium. Day in and day out, huge numbers of Fund staff are on "missions", gathering information from their "member" countries, discussing policies with governments and making recommendations in "staff reports" to the Fund's Executive Board. The Board itself meets three days a week to discuss these and the many other documents presented for its review. This is the high profile work—the kind of work that gets commented on in the press and on television. But there is also the low profile work, to do with the mundane management and administration of an institution. In the basements of the building there are dozens of staff maintaining the computer systems. Nearby are rooms filled with off-set printers churning out the latest Fund publication. Meanwhile, more or less on a daily basis, large trucks reverse into the service gate on 20th Street to get loaded up with boxes of documents for the "safe repository" somewhere in Virginia. This is the Fund at work.

In this book I want to report an ethnographic examination of this work. Doing so is not simply a case of description, however. A key problem in ethnography is how to present what is observed in a way that does justice to the phenomena and allows some analytic insight. Just reporting on an institution would be merely a form of journalism (which has its place of course), but in ethnography the concern is to investigate in such a way as to produce a view that allows deeper understanding of the setting in question. There are, needless to say, many ways in which such a view can be constructed. In this book, I will not discuss all these possible approaches, nor will I offer a wholly new one. What I will do is alter and adapt an analytic approach that has become (in various guises) a standard within sociology and anthropology.

More specifically, over half a century ago, the sociologist Everett Hughes suggested that one effective way of examining society—of doing more than journalism—was to study the careers of individuals as they move through that society[1]. What the analyst does is to enquire into the different sets of concerns that are relevant at any stage within a career. Hughes suggested that by looking at these distinct elements of relevance within each stage, the "working constitution of society could be revealed". My approach is really an adaptation of this where, instead of focusing on the careers of people, I focus on the careers of *documents*. In so doing, what I hope to uncover is the working constitution of the Fund. Just how I hope to do so is more complex than I will elaborate on in this introduction. But since this is so crucial to the discussions that follow, let me introduce the reader to the way in which the concept of a "document career" can enable an unpacking of institutional life with the following remarks.

I am wanting to investigate such things as:

- how documents are oriented to in the Fund's work;
- how they are the outcome of that work;
- how they are used to assess work;
- how they can be the detritus of activities;
- how Fund documents allow for activities as diverse as telephone

---

[1]   See Hughes (1937).

calls and conversations, through to the disbursement of huge sums of money.

These might seem rather obvious things to list. And indeed they are obvious—but in precisely the ways that are of interest. For these kinds of activities or, if you like, these kinds of *doings with documents* are bound up with and can be explained by reference to the location of the documents within particular stages of their career. Such an explanation will also uncover the working constitution of the institution within which those documents have their career.

One can unpack this a little further with a simple contrast from the Fund. Let me describe and contrast what documents mean to the Fund's "Document Preparation Unit" (DPU) and a Fund mission team. The DPU deals with all those documents which have been reviewed, signed off and completed. In other words, it deals with documents once they have become finished products. The DPU is not concerned with what a document concludes (what recommendations, for example, it offers the Fund's Executive Board), but only with what *type* of document it is. Once a document has been identified, the DPU staff can commence a variety of courses of action. The most common is to select the appropriate distribution list and, on that basis, forward the document with that list attached to those who have the job of copying and delivering documents. But this job is made somewhat more complicated by the fact that within the category of documents for distribution are various subcategories. Some documents can be done "when there is time" (e.g. *briefings*) whereas others have to be done "right away" (e.g. *lapse of time* papers). There are many other categories too, each with more subcategories. For instance, certain *staff reports* are of immediate impact on the organisation. Their existence is announced in the *Executive Board Agenda*.

Now these various activities of the DPU are interesting for a number of reasons, but the only point I want to make here is that, for the DPU, a document has no contents. It is rather a thing to be evaluated in a certain kind of hierarchical fashion, and then it is a thing to be tagged, directed and stored. A document means nothing more to them than that.

Now contrast this with how a *mission team* views a document. A mission team is made up of a half-dozen or so Fund staff who are given the job of visiting a country and reporting on its economic position. A *staff report* is the outcome of their work. It presents a mission team's analysis of a member country's economy, an appraisal of that government's policies, and offers recommendations for the Fund's Executive Board. For a mission, a staff report is, unsurprisingly, more than just a thing to be catalogued. It is at once a representation of the mission's view, a justification for courses of action, and a political and diplomatic device (insofar as the recommendations once presented to the Executive Board will have political repercussions for the country in question as well as for the Fund and its relationship to that country).

I am not wanting to make too many grandiose claims here. All I want to suggest is that the DPU views documents (including staff reports), as much of a muchness: as things to be tagged. A mission views a staff report very differently: as something whose contents they spend a great deal of time mulling over. In other words, what this example shows is that the *same* document, when viewed with different purposes, is a very different kind of thing. It embodies different kinds of courses of social action.

What distinguishes these courses of action are the differences in perspective brought to bear by a division of labour. But this itself is bound up with and can be explained by what stage a document has reached in its career. So, crudely speaking, a staff report starts its career when it is first drafted by a mission team. At this point, certain sorts of concerns begin to show themselves. These have to do with how a team gradually works up and refines the contents of the document. At the next stage in its career, the document is reviewed. Here, there is a set of different and partly overlapping concerns to those of the mission team in the drafting stage. Once it has been reviewed, it is then delivered to the DPU. As I have said, by this stage, the contents of a staff report are no longer of concern. The staff in the DPU assume that all matters to do with its contents have been dealt with beforehand. Once the DPU has dealt with it, it goes on to what is more or less the last career stage I am interested in—its consideration by the Executive Board. I do not want to say anything about that stage now. My point is that within each of these stages there is a great deal of variation in the doings associated with a staff report, the interpretative schema brought to bear, the background expectations that allow users of those documents to act in expeditious ways, and so on. It is by examining these various doings, these sequential stages of action matrixed through time and a division of labour, that I hope to unpack the workings of the Fund.

Now, this approach will not let me cover every element of the Fund. But what it will provide is the mechanism that will allow the construction of an analytical view. However, my goal in this book is not just to create that analytic view. It is also to present that view as a resource for the discussion of future document technologies and hence the technology of future organisations. As this concern will be important later on, it is appropriate that I make some introductory remarks as to how reference to the ethnographic record may be useful for the analysis and design of new technologies.

It will be perfectly obvious that bound up with the courses of action at any point in the document's career will be the selection of various kinds of technologies. For example, the mission teams use electronic document editors for drafting their reports, but paper for review and discussion; the DPU prefers to use electronic forms for much of its work, but keeps paper forms for filing and storage. There are good reasons for this which I will not go into here. The point is that the medium of the document, or one might say the technology in which the document is embodied, changes through a document's career. This movement is not so much sequential as it has to do with how some document technologies are better suited for some tasks than others. This is another commonplace observation—we all know that different technologies provide us with different advantages and disadvantages given the particular job we want to do with some document. But if we look at the document career and courses of action within the stages of that career, we must also be concerned with the medium of those documents. Thus a perspective that looks at organisations through its documents is necessarily a perspective concerned with technology.

Now the point is that, insofar as organisations want to change (and most do), then their documents must change. Hence the technology of documents must change too. In addition, sometimes developments in technology may allow (or even force) change. But to understand what those changes might be, one needs to examine current practice. My concern here is to understand the careers of Fund documents, and this will mean detailing in part the ways in which various technologies are embedded in the stages of the document career. It is my contention that materials from this can be used to guide the design of work practice and technological office systems in the future, whether they be in the Fund or elsewhere. In this way, my arguments follow in the footsteps of others who have looked at the technologies of the past in an attempt to help define appropriate technologies for the future. However, my exposition differs from theirs in two respects. First, I use the present—rather than the past—to divine the future. Second, the tools I use come not from history but come from combining the concerns and analytic outlook of *sociological ethnography* with those of *information technology (IT) research*[2]. In this respect, this book reports on something that is rather new: an alliance between two disciplines—IT research and sociology—that have for a variety of reasons only recently begun to converge. As with the notion of the document career, this convergence is a key to the book and so it is worth spending a moment to say more.

In the past decade or so, practitioners within the disciplines traditionally associated with ethnography (namely sociology and social anthropology), have begun to explore the ways in which ethnographic findings, methods and arguments might find a more applied role. To the surprise of some, they have begun to find such a role in systems research. This is not due solely to their own efforts, however. For, at the same time as ethnographers have been searching for a new role, the IT research community has been looking for a new approach to understanding the social world. This search derives from growing dissatisfaction with psychological and laboratory-based methods for understanding what information technology is wanted and needed by people in organisations. It has resulted in a turn to what may be loosely described as social methods, and in particular ethnographic field work and associated methods of analysis.

The confluence of these two developments—from within the social sciences on the one hand, and within the design community on the other—is only now beginning to show itself in various publications and completed projects. What is becoming clear is that the use of ethnographic techniques in this new applied domain has enhanced the design of organisational systems, partly through improving the fit between needs and functionality, and partly through better reconciliation between requirements specification, user expectations and technical possibility.

Organisational ethnography is, however, relatively new (or rather has only begun to flourish after various faltering starts over the years),

---

[2] It could equally be "anthropological ethnography" but, for my purposes, the difference between the sociological and anthropological can be conflated.

and there is no text which reports on these developments in any depth, or which might provide a basis upon which future studies may be undertaken[3]. What there is (although this is not to undervalue this work), is an eclectic assemblage of conference papers and book chapters[4]. Some of these texts fulfil the needs I describe on a partial basis[5] whilst others provide an increasingly rich background through taking a management science perspective[6] or combine work from the philosophy and history of science (and sometimes social studies of science) with organisational theory[7], or look historically at technological determination of organisational work processes[8], or view the impact of the computer from the information sciences perspective[9]. There is also a growing literature on the developing use of social psychological approaches in systems design[10]. But there are none which report an in-depth ethnographic study and its investigations of how the present may teach us about the future. It is my purpose in this book to help fill that gap.

Needless to say, there are likely to be many ways in which this goal can be achieved, for it is far from certain how ethnographic findings might be used in design. But what I hope to do is provide a rich illustration of how an old trade such as ethnography (developed out

---

[3] For the best discussion of this see Wright (1994). For a review of the American literature, see Schwartzman (1993).

[4] I provide more details about a number of these in Chapter 3. For a review of the main ethnographic papers in the IT domain known as computer supported cooperative work (CSCW), where most of these have appeared, see Plowman et al. (1995). There are numerous edited books that present some of the many perspectives now being deployed in systems research and design. See for instance, Bowers & Benford (1991), Easterbrook (1993), Jirotka & Goguen (1994), Olson (1989), and Thomas (1995, 1996).

[5] See, for example. Bowers & Benford (1991), Luff et al. (1990) and Suchman (1987).

[6] See, for instance, Morton (1991).

[7] See Bud-Frierman (1994).

[8] See Yates (1989).

[9] See Anderson et al. (1993).

[10] See, for instance, Goodman et al. (1990), Hirschheim (1985), McGrath & Hollingshead (1994) and Sproull & Kiesler (1992).

of a mix of colonial concerns, a delight in the exotic and philanthropy) provides resources for an altogether modern technology.

Overview of the book

The next chapter will essentially be an opportunity to set up the empirical argument as well as saying something about why designers are interested in those empirical materials. Here, my concern will not be to draw attention to the search for better methods as part of design (a topic in the subsequent "methods" chapter) but to note how designers of IT now offer remarkably diverse, powerful and, it has to be said, fascinating technologies. I shall describe some of these technologies. I shall suggest that the technology is there, but the question is what one would want to do with it. I shall map out what one might call the answers to that by referring to the various ways documents—and indeed other information delivery mechanisms such as video—are conceived by those disciplines who have an interest in their nature. I shall note how much of the discussion of documents one finds in literary theory, in management science and organisational theory, as well as those who attempt to bridge these disciplines, tends to be of a too theoretical and somewhat abstract nature. This allows those arguments to spin-off into (often delightful) conjectures that bear little connection to empirical fact. I shall suggest that certain sociological conceptions, in particular as regards how documents are bound up with observable organisational praxis, can be a basis for better understanding of documents. I shall remark some more on the notion of the document career. With this approach, I shall contend that materials can be uncovered that allow some determination of what one might want to do with new technologies and what one might expect as the consequences of those technologies.

Chapter 3 will then present the methods used to investigate the Fund. Here the concern is not just to describe the *field work programme* used (focusing on the career of a staff report) but also to explain how ethnography has come to have a place in IT design. In particular, I shall remark on a domain of technology that has come to be called "computer supported cooperative work" (or CSCW) in which ethnography has become the main means for delivering knowledge about the organisational world. I shall discuss the vexing and obdurate problem of how to make ethnography robust enough as a method to prise open the kinds of issues made salient by design type concerns.

Chapter 4 consists of a sketch of the Fund, starting with its beginnings in the 1944 Bretton Woods conference through to its current organisational structures and processes. My main concern here will be to emphasise the Fund's role as a surveillance institution, and all that means in terms of gathering and analysing data, and exercising control over its membership.

I shall then begin in Chapter 5 the analytical part of my discussion with an outline of the organisation of the Fund's policy work or, as I put it, the organisation of the organisation. In particular, I shall pursue my concerns by treating the Fund as an information machine. Though this particular metaphor is well known and has been shown to be a trap that often misleads, I shall use it to draw attention to how the Fund is not just in the business of "policy analysis", but needs to have effective control over the flow of information (in other words, control over the how, when and by whom of information delivery). I shall begin to suggest that if one looks at the various stages within the document career, one will see that documents are part of the toolset that enables the assembly and interaction of the Fund's information mechanisms. Furthermore, part of the process of assembly and interaction results in the analysis of any and all countries being organised so that what an analysis "ought to be" is more or less "what was predicted beforehand". This is not meant to imply anything peculiar about the Fund's work, so much as to draw attention to the prospective and retrospective vision of adequacy that is part and parcel of how such things as Fund staff reports get used during their career. This has important implications for the nature of how facts are understood within the policy elements of the Fund, for the nature of adequacy and objectivity, and what is meant by a staff report "warranting action". Ultimately this has implications in terms of how the Executive Board has to invest trust in the information it is given by the mission teams.

In Chapter 6 I investigate some of the statistical information work that is undertaken at the Fund. Again I use the machine metaphor, but my main concern is to contrast statistical work with policy work. Key differences have to do with how information is or is not "authored" or "owned" in the two domains (i.e. statistical and policy), the importance of timeliness in the role and usefulness of information, and how one set of machinery involves extensive collaboration in information production and use whilst the other involves more autonomous and individualised working.

These discussions provide the background to more detailed discussions of the Fund's area department *desks*. These will form Chapter 7. A desk is a label for a number of individuals whose responsibility is to gather, analyse and represent information about particular member countries. For the sake of simplicity, I shall treat these individuals and their roles as more or less one under the title of *desk officer*. A desk officer is the main economist responsible for any desk. To outline the relationship between desk officers and their various doings with documents will require something of a panoramic investigation. I argue that one cannot really understand the importance of, say, staff reports and missions, unless one knows something about the materials and information desk officers collect in Washington. One cannot understand desk officers' contributions to the Fund's *World Economic Outlook* unless one understands the nature of policy analysis. Desk officers are not just "information traffic cops" as one described his activities to me, but individuals whose expertise involves transforming collected information into something like the interpreted stuff upon which policy analysis and decision-making can begin. I shall go on to contend that, in between missions, desk officers do not produce what they think of as "real" products, though they certainly do produce various briefings, background papers and other documents. I shall explain that they assume that it is only mission work that produces the documents that "really count". This difference shows itself both in the provisional and piecemeal nature of the data files desk officers keep on a daily basis, and in the attitudes desk officers have toward information they are required to provide for a range of documents during these periods.

To explain this I shall then describe missions, the subject of Chapter 8. The need for missions reflects fundamental features of policy information. Mission work involves the iteration and building up of findings; it involves the ability to negotiate and agree with country authorities over what are "reasonable" and "sensible" interpretations. Such agreements are crucial in a number of ways, and in particular for any attempt to understand current economic circumstance. This enables member authorities and the Fund to exchange and discuss practical advice and opinions and to determine benchmarks for assessment of economic policy. This last is essential for the Fund to warrant its policy decisions.

The chapter will report on the close observation of a single mission—the centrepiece of the ethnographic fieldwork. The purpose will not be to portray the country in question, but to characterise how mission teams are organised to do their work. In particular, it will describe how mission teams separate economic data into sectors and then allocate responsibility for collecting data for each to individual members of a mission. The data collection task will be described. It consists of an iterative process whereby a mixture of arithmetical, econometric, interaction and meeting skills are used to create data that are reconciled and measured against the data collected by others within a mission team. This process results in an overall "picture" of an economy being built up. This is shared with the local authorities, and, once agreement as to its adequacy has been made (which may take some time and reworking of the picture), the two sides use this to discuss policy. The outcome of these discussions as well as the agreed picture of the economy are used to create various documents, the most important of which is the staff report. This, along with an appendix, is delivered to the Executive Board when a mission returns to the Fund.

It is most important that the reader realises that in being a study of one mission, important elements of the Fund's mission process may have been missed. Each member country has slightly different problems and slightly different sets of expertise, and thus each mission team its own unique flavour and organisation. This is not to suggest that the Fund treats it members differently, but rather that each mission has its own particular characteristics. Only one mission was studied in this ethnography because of practical time constraints. Fund staff made it clear that observation of other missions would have provided useful supplements. Nonetheless, I have endeavoured to ensure that my analysis does provide a substantive insight into any and all Fund missions as well as the specific one reported.

Chapter 9 will pursue the fate of documents once they have been produced by the mission team and in particular as they go through the review process and eventually to the Board. The main focus will be on the career of *staff reports* with particular reference to the one deriving from the mission observed. Here issues to do with the nature of the relationship between the Fund and the members will be seen to be relevant, as well as issues to do with accountability for and ownership of a staff report by the mission chief. It will be noted that by the time a staff report is presented to the Board, a chief's oration is essentially a ceremonial display of his or her entitlement to claim ownership of that document. The chapter will conclude by emphasising that the

paramount function of staff reports is to act as instruments to cohere
and control the organisation.

The final chapter will consist of a synthesis and discussion. It will
develop and conclude issues to do with the boundaries of document-
using communities highlighted by reference to the document career. A
key concern throughout the book will have been with organisational
incumbents' perspective on action, and it will be suggested that key to
this is their understanding of the division of labour and time. These
provide a matrix of meaning enabling members of the Fund to act. This
conception of organisations is one that I shall suggest is basic to
understanding all organisational behaviour. The chapter will then go
on to discuss how the matrix of time and the division of labour is
connected to how staff reports have a certain temporal existence and
hence therefore also a certain shelf-life. As time passes, so the relevance of these reports declines. These facts, combined with the question
of the particular perspective brought to bear by the various communities of use, will be the resources for a discussion of the likely
potentialities of new document technologies within the Fund. Though
this discussion is not meant to be conclusive, it is meant to be illustrative of how the materials presented in this book can be used to
determine the future of organisational technology. The chapter will
finish with some comment on the mutual interplay of sociological and
systems design concerns, but will emphasise the goal of the book to
uncover important aspects of the relationship between the Fund's staff
and the documents they work toward, are guided by, and produce.

CHAPTER 2
What is a document?

We are surrounded by documents: by bits of paper lying on our desks, by memos from our colleagues, by articles, books, reports, newspapers and "Post-it" notes. Documents are embodied in all sorts of technologies, including paper, magnetic disc, microfiche and projector slides. And, to make things even more complex, documents move from one technology to another. In the case of my own documents, they start off in longhand on paper, at some later point are turned into electronic form for word processing, and then are turned back into paper when I print the final, "complete" version. I may then send copies of my work to others by transforming them into electronic data through the fax machine, or by copying them onto floppy discs for posting. When they are received, they are invariably turned back into paper for reading. Thus, documents are ubiquitous, but they are constantly going through technological transformation. Moreover, their ubiquity reflects the diversity of their functions: they deliver information, they store it, and they enable individuals to explicate their actions.

Yet (and partly because of this ubiquity), documents have a mundanity that might lead one to think that examination of them will lead to no new discoveries, no exciting developments for intellectual enquiry and research. Certainly in studying an institution that is at the centre of world affairs, one could ask "Why bother looking at its documents?" Surely it would be better to use a perspective that focuses, say, on the political relations that the institution has with other equally powerful institutions, or that looks at the patterns of power and control it has over those it deals with. This is the big stuff, the kinds of topics written about by "social theorists". But to disregard documents in this way would be a mistake. For over the past decade or so there has been an increasing realisation that it is just these sort of mundane artefacts, just these very ordinary things—the bits of paper, the memos, the reports— that are fundamental to organisations. As I shall show in this chapter, recent research demonstrates that documents are crucial to organisational life. Comprehension of them is therefore a vital component of any attempt to comprehend organisations[11].

Overview of the chapter

I want to approach the task of explaining how documents are key to organisational action in the following way.

First, I want to mull over some of the technologies currently used to support or mediate documents[12]. One needs to scope out the diverse forms of document media because, as I have said in Chapter 1, I want to offer my analysis as a template against which one might measure the suitability of certain types of document technologies. My concern in this book is not to spend a great deal of time enquiring into those possibilities (though this will be the focus of the last chapter). Rather, I want to set up my investigations in such a way that others with these central concerns can use this study as an empirical resource.

Second, I want to report recent research that has demonstrated that the physical manifestation of a document is crucial in determining the role of that document in organisational action. A particular concern of this research has been to underline the role of paper in organisational life.

Third, I want to move away from the technology of documents toward theories about the role of documents. In particular, I shall discuss views in literary theory, post modernism, organisational and management studies and sociology.

Fourth, I shall select from these various views the one I think is most useful, namely, one that emphasises how documents exist within the *praxis* of organisational action. I shall explain how this view needs some adapting for the research reported in later chapters of this book.

---

[11] The realisation has its parallels in the discovery that talk was important in organisational contexts over thirty years ago. The importance of talk was demonstrated most effectively in the now somewhat neglected *Language and Social Reality: The Case of Telling the Convict Code*, by D.L. Wieder (1974). For a more recent discussion of the role of talk see Boden (1994).

[12] Though I clearly will not be covering them all. For a review of the main papers in document systems see Furata (1992).

Document technologies: new and old

IT research laboratories (or "systems" research laboratories, as they are sometimes called) are curious places. Here it is not just the gizmos and computer-controlled contraptions that are odd and fascinating in equal measure, it is also the social relations one finds therein. One factor here is that these places are disproportionately populated by those with professional rights and status—namely, research scientists. Given that many of these individuals are powerfully motivated by the quest not just for fame but also for wealth, and given also that there are virtually no professional and institutional frameworks within which their work can be governed, the tension between these individuals and laboratory management, manifest in battles over altering working practices, rights to research outcomes, control over research projects and research funding and so on, is intense indeed[13]. The curious technologies only make the backdrop to these conflicts more exotic, sometimes a little strange and sometimes amusing[14]. But it is this backdrop—these strange technologies of research laboratories—with which I want to begin my discussions. These are not the kinds of technologies that will be discussed later in the book nor are most in a state to make it possible to predict in any concrete sense what role they might play in the future. But description of an example will give the reader a sense of what might be, and thus helps justify my belief that the central question for IT research is not "What sort of technology can we devise?" but rather "What do we want to do with technology?"

In our laboratory we have regular seminars. During one of these a colleague was making a list of facts on the whiteboard. As he did so there was a sudden squeak from one of the nearby computers and then a synthesised voice announced that a document was going to be printed. One of the graduate students in the audience flushed red and explained that his system had just mistaken the markings on the whiteboard for *instructions*. This was just one of many occasions when working prototypes have crossed over into our routine working lives in unexpected ways. But the partial irritation and amusement of the speaker notwithstanding, this particular technology is interesting

---

[13] See Harper (1992).
[14] Harper (1996a).

because it indicates that the kind of documents computers can support and interact with is becoming broader.

More specifically, the system in question, known as *Brightboard*, enables markings on whiteboards or indeed any markable office wall to act as a controlling mechanism for computer systems[15]. With this approach, video cameras placed judiciously around a building become the instruments whereby commands are conveyed from the user to the computer. A user can issue his or her command by making certain sorts of marks in view of the camera, for example on a whiteboard that a camera is focused on. Using fairly simple algorithms, the digitised image is then converted into computer-executable commands. This mechanism can be used to issue many different sorts of commands but, in the demonstration system, it was primarily used to issue document storage, print and distribution commands, the documents in question being whiteboard drawings and scribbles. In these ways Brightboard broadens what is meant by a document, extending it to include what is spread out over walls. In so doing, Brightboard also broadens what is meant by interaction between a user and a computer system. For it includes the use of video as the communication mechanism between them.

Of course, Brightboard was not the first system to stretch the boundaries in this way, nor is video the only new mode of interaction being explored with computer systems. There are many other equally interesting and at times odd interaction techniques[16]. Of the more well known are voice-based interaction systems, some of which are available on mass market personal computers. Without wanting to comment on any specific product, it is perhaps worth considering some of the limitations of these new modes of interaction.

One problem with voice command systems is that one needs to devise ways for the system to distinguish between ordinary conversation and conversation directed toward the computer. A system which reacts to sounds is not sensitive to users' intentions. Thus, if a user issues a command at one moment but shortly thereafter uses the same word or phrase in a conversation, the system will not be able to distinguish between them. Thus the vision of *Hal* the talking computer in the film *2001: A Space Odyssey* needs correcting: instead of an

---

[15] Stafford-Fraser & Robinson (1996).

[16] Some of the more interesting techniques that I do not have time to discuss are those which use context to determine the criteria in controlling systems. See Brown (1996).

apparently rational mind behind the voice, one is much more likely to get a system that keeps starting applications by mistake or finishing them prematurely. Instead of Big Brother knowing too much, Hal turns into an incompetent[17].

There are similar problems in using video-based interaction techniques for documents and markings in real world settings. For here a system cannot recognise the difference between signs that are intended for interpretation by the system and those that are not. Users are likely to find that they are issuing commands when they simply want to use the whiteboard. A clear parallel here of course is when someone scratches their nose at an auction and finds that the auctioneer has taken it as a bid.

The point I am wanting to make is that if such simplistic voice-controlled or camera-controlled systems were ever widely introduced there may be a curious impact on the *moral order* of the workplace: workers will be forced to talk less or in whispered hushes out of hearing of the computers; and they may be forced to be careful about making graffiti in view of the computers. The paradox of this is that the development of interface procedures which take advantage of what are sometimes called "natural" forms of interaction (namely such everyday practices as talk and writing on blackboards and whiteboards) ultimately can make interaction less natural. In effect, God the designer gives with one hand, and takes with the other. It is in this sense that the challenge for IT research laboratories is not to come up with startling new technologies, but rather to determine the implications and the value of technology in actual use, and on that basis determine whether it is really worth developing.

This then forms part of the context in which my own research finds its place: it is in some large part motivated by the need to find out what goes on in workplaces and to use that as a metric to determine what to devise technologically. But my discussion of Brightboard is also meant to indicate just how far IT research has come. Of importance here is the shift away from the original function of computers to compute in the arithmetical sense (i.e. for large mathematical tasks) towards the support of document-related activities. When word processing was invented by IBM with its magnetic tape devices, word processing applications were only a part, and a lesser part at that, of computing.

---

[17] Though one of my colleagues has reminded me that as the spaceship in question disintegrates, so Hal the computer becomes "crazed".

Since the merging of that technology with the personal workstation on the Xerox Star machine, however, word processing and text-related activities have become the largest segment of computer systems applications. What was once a technology (i.e. computers) designed for bespoke arithmetical and computational services is now a technology used primarily as a tool in the service of writing, corresponding and filing. But with this change has come a great deal of new potential, for now not only are people able to send text to each other over great distances and with great speed (via email for instance), but the very nature and organisation of the documents that computers can process has changed.

One way in which the nature of documents has changed is that electronic documents are much more than the electronic mirror of paper created with *interactive* editors (editors which allow the user to change and edit the text). Documents can also be *interactive media* in their own right. That is to say they can interact autonomously with other interactive documents. Thus documents can be linked to automatically updating databases, introducing the possibility of *active documents*—documents that are composed in part by individual authors and in part by applications that intelligently update and revise data subsets with them as changes are made elsewhere in the network. (Automatically updating spreadsheets within a text document is one obvious example.) This in part reflects but also extends what is meant by compound documents, documents that ally graphics, text, spreadsheet, video and audio into mosaics of interactive media.

The electronic domain also affords new kinds of *document databases*. In some senses this would appear simply to replicate the physical world of files and paper with a virtual one, but in fact electronic databases offer a number of entirely new possibilities.

First, new forms of searching procedures can be exploited. The most obvious are word search procedures, but more interesting are those that support different graphical representations of relationships among documents for the purpose of finding information. For example, documents can be searched and represented along temporal or semantic dimensions[18].

Second, documents can be related to each other in new ways. The World Wide Web uses a structuring language called HyperText Mark-up Language or HTML. This is an instance of a more generalised

---

[18] See, for example, Card et al. (1991).

standard called SGML (standard generalised mark-up language). Such a standard enables the structuring of relationships between documents so that those documents can be linked in new ways[19]. Although as any creator of their own Web page will know, construction of a *structured document* (as they are known) is a laborious process but, for some types of large document sets creating such documents is certainly worthwhile. Service documentation for aircraft is often cited as the proving example. Here standards like SGML are said to have saved manufacturers and airlines hundreds of thousands of dollars. With this technology (or with this standard, to be more exact), design and maintenance documents can be given a uniform appearance, so that users can find their way around; moreover, the appearance of all the documentation can be changed at a stroke by adjusting a table— there is no need to change the individual documents.

These structuring standards become particularly interesting when combined with certain communications technologies, such as those provided by the Internet. As it happens, HTML was designed as an instance of SGML that was specifically appropriate for the Internet[20]. What is interesting about this merging of technologies is not only how it allows the remote accessing of documents, but also how it has introduced vast numbers of people to a form of *hypertext.*

Hypertext is a label normally used to characterise a range of different types of systems, and there is some dispute as to what is a real hypertext system and what is not. For our purposes the following definition offered by one of the doyens of hypertext will suffice. Jakob Nielsen defines hypertext as:

consist(ing) of interlinked pieces of text (or other information). These pieces . . . can be scrolling windows, files, or smaller bits of information. Each unit of information is called a node. Whatever the grain size of these nodes, each of them may have pointers to other units, and these pointers are called links. The number of links is normally not fixed in advance but will depend upon the content of each node. Some nodes will be related to many others and so will therefore have many links, while other nodes serve only as destination for the link but have no outgoing links of their own . . . the entire hypertext structure forms a network of nodes and links. Readers move about this network in an activity that is often referred to as browsing or navigating rather

---

[19] See Barron (1989).

[20] For discussion and some history of this remarkable development, see Turner et al. (1996).

than just "reading" to emphasise that users must actively determine the order in which they read the nodes.[21]

The important point here is that users of documents are no longer required to go though those documents in sequential fashion. They can choose to work their way through documents as they see fit: backwards, forwards, middle out. Of course, users of such things as paper-based organisational documents will themselves choose to go through those documents in a variety of ways—there is no justification to the claim that paper-based documents force sequential reading. The point with hypertext is that it draws attention to how the order of a reading can be *actively constructed* by the reader and the technology can *actively support* that process. This is what is claimed to be the unique trick of hypertext. As we shall see, this is also what has excited many commentators.

As it happens, hypertext is the technology that forms the basis of some of the more advanced writing tools developed for computer supported cooperative work, CSCW. In particular, tools have been developed that offer users a range of hypertext and shared interactive editing capacities. *NoteCards* was perhaps one of the more well known, offering users a system of card-like windows linked according to users' preferences, along with a browsing facility[22]. *SEPIA* offers a more complex environment, allowing text to be entered under a variety of operationally defined categories (such as planning, arguing, composition)[23] whilst *ShrEdit* offers one of the most simple environments, allowing shared and private "work spaces" with virtually no prescribed structure. Most of these applications have not developed greatly and have remained research prototypes[24].

One CSCW application that has some hypertext like functionalities—though it would be difficult to define it as pure hypertext—is *Lotus Notes*. This has become quite common—and so is an exception rather than the rule as regards CSCW technology. It is therefore worth pausing to comment on. Although Lotus Notes is not specifically designed for reading (a key function supported by hypertext), its

---

[21] See Nielsen (1993), p. 2.

[22] See Trigg et al. (1986).

[23] See Haake & Wilson (1992).

[24] For discussion of these and issues to do with the basic organisation of these technologies, see McAlpine & Golder (1994).

flexible nature can allow it to support various aspects of authoring, writing and document management. Despite its sales success, very little research has been reported on Notes, however[25]. One reason for this may be to do with the diversity of its uses, in some instances to support individualised work, in other places to support distributed work. Another reason may have to do with how it has slipped through the disciplinary boundaries of what is called Human Computer Interaction (or HCI), a psychologically based approach to the use of computers, and CSCW itself with its concern with social organisation. Doubtless more research will be appearing soon.

The emergence of new document structuring, searching and retrieval tools with their various hypertext functionalities, combined with the development of more user-friendly document-structuring editors, has led many commentators to suggest that we are about to reach an era when Vannevar Bush's personal "Memex" (or at least something like it) is becoming a practical possibility[26]. Memex was a term used by Bush in a now famous *Atlantic Monthly* journal article published in 1945. In that article he suggested that in the future people would be able to easily access and search a vast library of microfiche slides. These slides would contain the world's scientific and scholarly knowledge. A feature of such a repository and associated technology was that it could support a personal Memex. In broad terms a Memex would be a desk that supported access to selected information (stored on microfiche) and would assist each reader in following a personal trail through the information. Bush argued that in these ways, or rather with this form of technology, a new information world beckoned. Now, microfiche is not actually the medium used for information storage but this vision is something that many hypertext researchers have been orienting to. Applications are now being developed to allow for the effective creation of large personalised electronic databases which will function

---

[25] Exceptions include Ehrlich & Cash (1994), Karsten (1995b), Orlikowski (1992, 1995) and Turrell (1995).

[26] No discussion of hypertext can go without mention of Bush's 1945 paper. See pp. 49–62 in Pylyshyn & Bannon (1989). In the same edited collection also see Bannon, "The pioneering work of Douglas C. Engelbart", pp. 301–306. Doug Engelbart and the Stanford Research Institute (or SRI) more or less invented such things as the mouse and many of the associated concepts that support WIMP systems (i.e. windows, icons, menus and pointing).

or rather offer the same kinds of opportunities as Bush's personal Memex.

Be that as it may, it would be a mistake to think of the contemporary technology of documents as microfiche or electronic technology—it also consists of wood pulp. As I said in the introduction, it might seem almost odd to want to say something about paper. After all, in comparison to its silicon alternatives, paper seems somewhat lacking in functionality. So much does paper appear to pale in comparison with electronic media, that predictions of the paperless office are now making a reappearance in the popular press. At least twenty years since the paperless office was first predicted, the emergence of the Web seems to have given renewed hope to those who continue to believe in the vision[27]. Presumably they are hoping that the failures of MIS (management information systems) and OIS (office information systems) "revolutions" to have an impact on paper can be forgotten[28]. Unfortunately, it is likely that some of the reasons for the failure of these earlier revolutions will also bear upon the changes brought about by the most modern computer document technology, including the Web. These reasons have to do with how paper provides a useful medium for certain type of tasks, offering "functionalities" that electronic systems do not. Understanding of these is interesting here not simply because of the curious continuity of paper as an artefact in office life, but because reference to these properties provides another angle on what documents do in organisational life.

More specifically, research is suggesting that paper documents provide an organisation allowing the reader of a document to impute the relationships between document sections. Although this research is still rather incomplete, the key seems to be that paper-based documents allow and support a certain form of embodied interaction. In a single phrase, paper allows users of documents to get to grips[29]. This is more difficult to do in, say, a hypertext environment, which makes the reading of hypertext documents quite different to the reading of paper documents. For example, Nunberg suggests that it is precisely the intangibility of electrical technologies which, in his opinion, will make it difficult for electronic documents to replace paper entirely[30].

---

[27] For discussion of this see Harper et al. (in press).
[28] See Hirschheim (1985). For a more recent discussion see Landauer (1995).
[29] See Haas (1996) and also O'Hara & Sellen (1997).
[30] See Nunberg (1993).

As Nunberg puts it, with paper, perception of content and the physical volume are inextricably intertwined:

A book doesn't simply contain the inscription of a text, it is the inscription. It is as fat as the text is long, it opens at the beginning of the text, and if we break off our reading, we are left literally in media res. (Nunberg, 1993: 18)

And further:

. . . there is no perceptible correlation between the boundaries of the texts we read on a computer and the physical properties of the artefact or the display itself. So there is inevitably a sense of disconnection between the text that is immediately present to the senses and the text that stretches out indefinitely and invisibly on either side of it—reading Proust in a (computer) window is like viewing Normandy through a bombsight. (*ibid.*)[31]

Other commentators have drawn attention to similar issues. Waller considers aspects of interacting with paper that may be fundamentally altered in the digital medium[32]. In particular, Waller cites the stability of text with respect to the printed page as an important basis for people's reading strategies. He speculates that this stability helps readers to build a "cognitive map" of the text as they skim the text, look back over it, and re-read sections. He suggests that electronic, dynamically structured texts are less likely to support such processes. Further, Waller points out that the process of navigating through text is fundamentally altered in the electronic medium, requiring more explicit articulation, as opposed to the semi-conscious process of flicking through paper pages. Finally, he turns to the importance of the linearity of paper-based documents, and the fact that this linearity is used by both authors and readers in producing and inferring cohesion from text. He points out that electronic texts— and especially hypertext—may result in the inappropriate juxtaposition of different portions of text. Readers tend to make inferences based on adjacent text, and thus may make inferences unpredicted by

---

[31] This particular analogy may be a little unfair to electronic documents since it would appear that Nunberg is assuming that the electronic version of Proust has no scroll bar. This seems unlikely.

[32] See Waller (1986).

the author. Thus the use of hypertext may undermine the commun-
icative intent of an author[33].

This is not to say that structured document technologies cannot
achieve the same powers of what one might call the rhetorical design
as is possible with paper. As Hendry has recently noted[34], a rhetorical
mark-up language may well be one route to solving this problem. And
as Seely Brown and Duguid have argued, it may well be that structured
documents will require the development of different rhetorical structures and means of interpretation[35]. This may make them different from
paper-based documents.

I do not intend to posit solutions to these kinds of problems and
questions at this point. My discussion of the technology of documents
has been intended to map out the diverse media of documents and to
draw attention to how the medium impacts upon use. In other words,
one can draw a line between the different kinds of things one can do
with different kinds of document technologies. With one medium
(hypertext), one can have access to vast amounts of information and
users therefore will want new browsing tools, information storage, and
manipulation facilities; with a second (such as a medium that allows
"reading" of whiteboard markings), individuals can use documents to
interact with systems, and this can spread out the human–machine
interface throughout the office domain; and with a third (paper), the
requisites of organisational work, most especially the delivery of
specific narrative structures, can be supported.

At the same time and by way of concluding this section, each of
these media (or technologies if you prefer) will interact with each other
creating the *context of* and the *resources for* document-related activity.
The next section investigates what that context and activity might
consist of.

Towards a non-technical conception of documents

So, having outlined something of the technology of documents, I now
want to say something about the ways in which documents have been

---

[33] Though one has to distinguish between what is simply badly authored hypertext
and problems inherent to that medium.
[34] See Hendry (1995).
[35] See Brown & Duguid (1995).

viewed from those disciplines and schools of thought that are not actually in the business of making or designing gizmos and gadgets. Rather, these disciplines attempt to place documents and their associated technologies within social practice, and seek to tell us what documents do. There are a number of these, but the first I want to deal with is literary theory.

Literary theory may appear well removed from our concern with documents in organisational life. But in fact it does have a lot to say on this topic. To understand this, one needs first of all to understand something about how literary theory approaches documents. In the work of de Saussure, and following on from that, Barthes and Derrida, the role, the nature and the meaning of documents or text (the preferred term), is to be treated *semiotically*. The semiotic view emphasises how language is a system of signs wherein the presentation of one sign implies the absence or shadowy presence of another sign. More significantly, it means there is no such thing as a "free standing text", or one that exists as a symbol of itself. Rather, each text is linked in one way or another to each and every other text in a system of "absences" and "presences".

The task for this school of thought is to unravel the interstices linking one text to all others and thus uncover the fabric of meaning holding together language, culture and society. This approach, called "critical theory", emphasises how certain types of meaning, constituted as they are by the intermingling of one symbol with hosts of others, come to *impose* themselves. This imposition is essentially controlled by the system of symbols and this in turn is controlled by those in power within society. If there was a transformation of power structures within society, so the systems of meaning would be transformed and instead of there being fixity through absence and presence, there would be diversity and plurality.

Followers of this school of thought within literary theory have developed a line of thinking that leads more or less straight to our door. George P. Landow[36], Jay Bolter[37] and Yellowlees Douglas[38] are amongst those who have been arguing that a new document technology has transformed what is an analytical programme—critical theory—into an empirical fact. That technology is hypertext.

---

[36] See Landow (1992).

[37] See Bolter (1991).

[38] See Douglas (undated) and Douglas (1992, 1993).

Let me explain by starting with Bolter. He commences his book *Writing Space* with the standard view that document technologies have been through a number of phases or eras. The first was the technology of the papyrus roll, in use from the time of ancient Egypt through to Byzantium; the second the medieval codex; the third the printed book; and the fourth, affecting us today, the era of hypertext. Hypertext is the most significant of these phases, we are told, because it has the power to alter the relationship between the reader and the text. No previous document technology has had this power[39]. According to Bolter:

An electronic book (in hypertext) is a fragmentary and potential text, a series of self contained units rather than an organic, developing whole. Elements in the electronic writing space are not simply chaotic; they are instead in a perpetual state of reorganisation. They form patterns, constellations, which are in constant danger of breaking down and combining into new patterns. This tension leads to a new definition of unity in writing, one that may replace or supplement our traditional notions of unity of voice and of analytic argument. (Bolter, 1991: 9)

As Ted Nelson puts it, quoted in Landow, "There is no Final Word [*sic*]. There can be no final versions, no last thought. There is always a new view, a new idea, a reinterpretation." (Nelson, *Literary Machines*, 2/61 48, in Landow, 1992: 58).

According to this view, what authors intend to convey and what they mean in their writing is obliterated by the freewheeling interpretative skill of the reader as he or she constructs new (hyper)texts out of the fabric of the authors' own. Thus Bathes' methodological dictum "Death to the author" is now replaced by a technological *fait accompli*:

Readers are now seen as breathing life into the texts they read, and reifying or concretising their possibilities—even reinventing the text by composing it in a creative effort [that is nearly tantamount to the author's own]. (Yellowlees Douglas, undated: 9; insert added)

The technology of hypertext has more than the blood of the authors on its hands, however. As Yellowlees Douglas writes: "(hypertext leads

---

[39] Presumably this is notwithstanding the longheld concerns of anthropologists to investigate the relationship between the ability to read and write, and the culture, intelligence and general ability of individuals. See Goody (1987).

to) bewildering questions and tasks which promise to redefine our concept of the reader's role." (Douglas, undated: 9).

In short, with this new technology, the relationship between the author and the reader, between documents and organisational action, is revolutionised. At least, this is what these authors would have us believe. For one of the lacunas in their work is the lack of empirical evidence to prove the case one way or another. This is also a problem which afflicts one of the founding fathers of their view, the theorist Derrida[40]. Hypertext is an extraordinary new medium, and applications based on hypertext such as the World Wide Web do illustrate new ways of managing and structuring documentation. But documents within the Web are not manifesting a form that allows the *blurring of boundaries*. Rather, documents in this particular hypertext world present a relatively fixed narrative structure. What the Web does provide, and this is something quite new, is ease of movement between, and access to, a vast range of different documents. This is not the same as allowing new readings of those documents[41]. I shall come back to this. In any case, my point here is that empirical issues to do with whether or how hypertextuality might transform the relationship between the individual and the text read in actual organisational circumstances has remained largely undiscussed in this work[42].

Some authors have begun to investigate what are the conceptual implications of hypertext for organisational life. J.R. Taylor and E. Van Every, in their delightfully titled *The Vulnerable Fortress: Bureaucratic Organisation and Management in the Information Age*[43], claim that technologies such as hypertext make the time ripe for a new view of organisations: instead of the model of bureaucracy as a hierarchical machine (as they describe it) they propose a hypertext model, one wherein managers undertake *hypermanagement* (1993: 204–208).

---

[40] See Gaver & Lee (1994).

[41] See Nunberg (1996).

[42] A similar lacuna can be found in another school of thought worth mentioning, namely *post modernism*. For a variety of reasons, post modernism has remained peripheral to academic life. For a discussion of why post modernism has remained peripheral to organisational analysis and especially main stream journals like *Administrative Science*, see Boje et al. (1996).

[43] Taylor & Van Every (1993).

To explain: Taylor and Van Every argue that driving the design and implementation of office automation systems in the 1970s and 1980s was the rational decision-making, hierarchical model of organisations. This ultimately derived from the sociologist Max Weber, but reflected also the model that lies at the heart of the computer[44]. This rational decision-making model turned out to be inappropriate for real organisations, exaggerating hierarchical systems of control, the adequacy and quality of information, and stopping organisations from the practical flexibility that enables them to cope in situations of complexity[45]. The result was that most systems introduced in that period were expensive—expensive in themselves and in the costly restrictions they brought to the organisations in question. Of course there were exceptions, American Airline's SABRE system providing a good example, but by and large the technology was a disappointment[46]. The tenor of Taylor and Van Every's assessment is generally accepted[47].

However, they go on to argue that as the systems of the 1970s and 1980s were being designed and introduced, so these systems began to provide a material basis for altering how one ought to conceive of organisations. This in turn led to an alteration to how one should conceive of the technology supporting organisations. In particular, the emergence of the economical personal workstation that could "augment" individual workers (a phrase harking back to Doug Englebart and Stanford Research Institute (SRI) meant that members of organisations could begin to communicate with each other in ways that transformed organisational relations. Irrespective of their geographic position, relations which had been previously functional and status-based could now turn into relations that had the characteristics of "conversation" and "intellectual exchange". Taking their lead from Zuboff, they argue that the new systems enabled individuals and organisations to become "informated"[48].

---

[44] See Weber (1947). For a good synopsis, see Merton (1957).
[45] A point they take from Scheil (1983).
[46] See Copeland et al. (1995).
[47] See Hirschheim (1985) and Landauer (1995).
[48] See Zuboff (1984). Zuboff's formulation is not the only one by any means. For an alternative analysis of how information alters organisational life, see Rule & Attewell (1989).

This, they claim, is the key revolutionary fact of contemporary systems. With new systems, members of an organisation can have a new means for making sense, for creating order and sharing purpose in a manner that makes redundant previous organisational structures. In particular, management by rule and status is no longer appropriate and instead needs to be replaced by management that cultivates and develops intellectual capital and "know how". Organisations need to become institutions that support the development of knowledge, rather than structures whose objective is, say, the most efficient completion of some pre-specified task. In this sense, organisational relationships are about creating and developing links as and when needed; such link-making activities, ad hoc, creative, flexible, transitory, are analogous to the creation and use of links in hypertext documents. Hence they arrive at the concepts of *hypertextual organisations* and *hypermanagement*.

Taylor and Van Every go to some lengths to avoid making the claim that organisations are or should be based on hypertext. Their thesis is that hypertext provides a metaphor for conceiving of organisational action, and that metaphors are crucial motivators in design and analysis—a point they take from Gareth Morgan[49]. In this sense, they are attempting to merge conceptions from the technological world with those from the organisational and management sciences, bridging the conceptual basis of diverse disciplines, and this makes their work particularly interesting[50]. But their arguments still lack a full empirical investigation of just whether hypertext will transform organisations. If the likes of Bolter and Landow simply get carried away with the fun of hypertext, Taylor and Van Every over-indulge in clever conceptual arguments. The result is the same: neither set of authors actually present empirical evidence either way. One is left persuaded by the possibilities described but unsure of the hard facts of the case: perhaps hypertext will become a technology defining a new document age; perhaps not. It is possible that hypertext will provide the new metaphor, but perhaps it will not.

One possible answer may come from some research in Japan. Ikuliro Nonaka and Hirotaka Takeuchi argue that certain organisations have been successful precisely because they have been adopting a form of hypertextuality long *before* the term was even coined. In their book,

---

[49] See Morgan (1986).
[50] For another interdisciplinary approach to the impact of systems, see Anderson et al. (1993).

The Knowledge Creating Company they argue that Japanese firms have been so successful in the post-war period because they are able bridge between the various boundaries that inhibit American and European organisations[51]. In particular, Japanese firms are able to learn from their customer base, from their research and development, and from the various echelons of the management structure—the senior managers being visionary and the middle managers more pragmatic—in such a way as to allow the various perspectives to coalesce and develop into "the best answers" for whatever product or service is being provided. This mixing bowl philosophy makes the source of knowledge in these companies a form of intertextuality, a blurring of narratives, a hyper-textuality. Although computer systems provide a living example of contemporary hypertextuality, Nonaka and Takeuchi's thesis is that it is the structures and processes of Japanese organisations that make them hypertextual, not necessarily their use of a hypertextual medium such as is provided in the computer world. This would seem to confirm Taylor and Van Every's view that hypertext provides the best metaphor for how organisations should organise themselves.

But a greater problem with their work still resides in the question of whether their theoretical constructions hold true empirically. It is not adequate to justify the claim that organisations need to become more hypertextual on the basis that some already were before the term was first used (in Japan). Much more research is needed to further corroborate or limit the applicability of this general thesis. What is certain is that hypertextuality, whatever its modality, is clearly something that needs to be thought about seriously. For it may be with hypertextuality—whether as regards the methods of work process and or the functionalities provided within the digital world—that organisations can reach out to the future. But as I noted earlier, just what this will mean for these organisations is as yet far from clear. A prior task is still to characterise the organisation of the organisation, and to grasp what role documents have in that.

One of the curious properties of organisational theory is its tendency to delight in the abstract, the theoretical, the idealised view of organisations. Taylor and Van Every, and Nonaka and Takeuchi, are following in a great tradition where theoretical suggestions are made as regards how to conceptualise organisation, but these suggestions end up needing correctives. These are delivered by those individuals more

---

[51] See Nonaka & Takeuchi (1995).

interested in the empirical than the theoretical. Irrespective of whether I am being unkind to organisational and management theory or even to the individuals in question, the point I am making is that with this perspective, there is a kind of "straw man" approach to arguments. This is not necessarily bad as long as the straw man enables more incisive observation and analysis of the real world.

The work of March and his various colleagues is of this kind and demonstrates just how useful this straw man approach can be[52]. His work was set up as an empirical corrective to what was (and is) called the "rational action" model of organisations. According to this model, everything that organisational actors do or try to do is governed by rational procedures of action. Observation of real organisational behaviour (undertaken by March) led to the discovery that this model was in many ways wrong. The character of organisational action is much more diverse than can be encompassed by the rational action model. The corrective that March developed led to a recognition that such things as documents are as much tools intended to achieve rationality in organisational life as they are manifestations of *irrationality*. This was quite a surprise for many within organisational studies since it was an assumption of their discipline that organisations were systematically organised elements of society. They were, after all, *organised*. March and his colleagues were not wanting to say that organisations were sites of chaos, however, so much as offering a corrective to the exaggerated faith in the rational organisation within organisations.

It is in this regard that the work of March provides us with a perspective from which documents can be understood. According to his view, organisational actors and, in particular, organisational managers, exist within settings of fluid political alliances, where the purposes and goals of individuals, of factions and cabals, coalesce and dissolve with the passing of time and the emergence of new, often competing goals and motivations. In these settings, attempts at rationality are best thought of as forms of "satisficing", where limited aims and bounded purposes are oriented to short-term, local purposes.

This view of the context of organisational action, where the role of technology is unclear, where the product of information systems is

---

[52] The first major publication was March & Simon (1958). Thereafter, March developed his own research, collaborating along the way with a host of others. See March (1987, 1991); and, for a good summary and collection of the main papers, see March (1988).

opaque, where the preferences of managers are diverse and problem-
atical and where alliances supporting one particular decision and one
particular rational course are only momentary and short-lived, is a view
of chaos knocking at the door of organisational coherence and structure. But one must not get the wrong end of the stick here: March's
view is not that organisations are fraught with diversity and incom-
mensurability. Rather it is a view offered as a corrective to the view of
organisational decision-making that exaggerates the basis of rationality
in that decision-making. Such exaggerations had been present in the
management sciences and organisational literature since the time of
Chester Barnard and his invoking of the moral goodness of organisation, right through to the time that March was first writing (the late
1950s). In other words, March's concern was to relate the analytic
conception of organisations to something like the reality that confronts
actual managers. This reality consists of a situation where practical
circumstances are such that it prevents managers from acting in the
ways they would ideally like or in ways proscribed by management and
organisational theorists.

   Now there might be some argument as to whether one would want to
make a contrast between the ideal and the practical, between the world
as it ought to be and the world as we unfortunately know it to be. Such
a contrast might give too much credence to the idealised view, implying that it is readily attainable, but for a few practical problems.
Leaving that aside, March is interesting since, according to his view,
documents are not instruments of organisational rationality or vehicles
for representing all the relevant materials in such a way as to enable
effective, objective decision-making. Rather, documents are devices
serving a range of local, short-term, political, ritual and symbolic
goals. Thus, documents are a means for ensuring post hoc accountability, a means of justifying a decision, a method for creating an
appearance of rationality and artefacts that are produced for ritualistic
and symbolic purposes.

   Despite the persuasiveness of his analysis, March's view does not
seem to have pervaded much beyond the management and organisational science schools. Managers in many organisations still treat
documents as embodiments of rational action and would appear to
lack any sense of the irony brought to bear on documents by March's
work. Similarly, this can also be found within sociology, and in particular the sociology of organisations. Here there is a fashionable view
that advanced technology enables new heights of surveillance and

supervision which results in late twentieth century organisations being the technological apogee of Weber's rational institution. There is no room in this view for ritual, for contingency, for the paradoxes of practical action that March uncovered[53]. Still, the work of March has been enormously influential in a variety of new schools of thought within management sciences and organisational theory and I now consider one of these.

One of the most influential thinkers in organisational theory in recent years has been Karl Weick[54]. In his work, the view of organisational rationality as situated in particular places and political circumstances (taken from March) has been merged with the sociologist Harold Garfinkel's view that social action consists of sense-making procedures[55]. This led Weick to develop a view which emphasises how organisations can be conceived of sense-making structures or, more exactly, as consisting of groups and communities who, in the process of making sense of their position, purpose and relationships, come to create the entity we commonsensically know as organisations. According to this view, organisations consist of mechanisms whereby shared meaning, common purpose and social coherence are achieved.

Weick's view is not just an ontology, a set of assumptions about organisations, as it is also the auspices for certain types of research. If March provided a framework whereby researchers could contrast the "is" of action from how it "ought to be", Weick set up a paradigm wherein researchers could specify the mechanisms through which meaning is created and sustained.

Documents are, perhaps unsurprisingly, very important amongst these mechanisms. Documents are devices whereby the "objectivity of action" is specified or rather, documents provide resources whereby objectivity can be achieved. This objectivity provides the materials which organisational actors can use to "see", "recognise" and "constitute" the rational basis for choosing one course of action over another. To put it in Weick's terms, documents are instruments that enable members of an organisation to coalesce into "loosely coupled" alliances. Organisations consist of these alliances.

Now it needs to be remembered that just as March built his argument against what had preceded, so too did Weick. His argument is not that

---

[53] See, for example, Dandeker (1990).
[54] For an introduction and overview of his work see Weick (1995).
[55] See Garfinkel (1967).

the "objectivity" of organisational rationality is constituted through such things as documents but that, in contexts where the rational basis of action is often difficult to determine, organisations only continue to survive through members coming to agree some kind of common perspective. In other words, if March was emphasising the irrationality of organisational action, Weick wants to draw attention to the basis of what rationality remains. His view is that there must be some sense of common purpose and shared goals, otherwise organisations would simply dissolve.

One instantiation of research into sense-making structures in organisations is Martha Feldman's *Order without Design*[56]. This presents an analysis of the somewhat curious position that "knowledge workers" find themselves in contemporary government institutions. According to Feldman, these individuals want to provide "clear and straightforward analyses or interpretations that could be used to make decisions or solve problems" (1989: 2). However, in practice they find it difficult to determine beforehand what purposes their research will be put to, and hence find it difficult to know what kind of research and analysis to undertake. For their work is made difficult by the fact that it is unclear what the auspices of some decision to be taken in the future will turn out to be. Hence, knowledge workers are in a bind: they are trying to prepare materials in the present for use in the future, but are unsure of what they will be required to deliver in the future.

Feldman's research is relevant at this juncture for illustrating how a perception of the nature of organisations leads to a view on documents. For Feldman, the documents that knowledge workers produce are not comprehensive surveys of all the information that in the end turns out to be relevant; they are instead collations put together on the basis of assumptions of what information is most likely to provide a suitable resource for what will turn out to be required. In this sense, documents embody what these workers are able to determine will be required, on the basis of their experience of the institutions. However, this sense-making or predictive work has a reflexive impact: what knowledge workers predict they will need turns into what they have in hand; this in turn becomes the basis for the decisions they make. Thus, although from the perspective of knowledge workers the future may be difficult

---

[56] See Feldman (1989).

to define, their efforts to make such predictions provide them with the very materials upon which their future decisions are based.

This view, at once paradoxical, to do with the present and the future, with the practical as against the ideal context of work, leads me to my old hunting ground, sociology. Sociology is at the moment (at least in my mind) somewhat obsessed with documents. This obsession may not always have existed. One of the two main authors I will discuss, Dorothy Smith, commences her *Texts, Facts, and Femininity* with the observation that texts have remained largely unexplored territory for sociologists[57]. Whether that was so when Smith wrote her book or not, certainly today the study of text is everywhere: if for Christians God is in the Word, for contemporary sociologists Society is in the Text[58].

But just what this means, just how society is writ large in the small confines of organisational memos, reports and analyses, or the more expansive and certainly more interesting bindings of novels and biographies, has been treated in a number of different ways. Amongst the numerous investigations of documents, texts or "inscriptions" as they are sometimes called, are those by Bruno Latour, who has undertaken an influential analysis of all things scientific and governmental. A second set have been produced by Dorothy Smith, who has investigated how text, reading and documents situate individuals within governed, organisational society. Although, of course, there is a great deal of other work being undertaken on text and documents from a sociological standpoint, their enquiries are representative of the main kinds of arguments in the discipline that are pertinent to my concerns.

Latour's work is far reaching and his publications deal with numerous and diverse topics. Perhaps his most influential paper went under the convenient title *Drawing Things Together*[59]. Here Latour argues that documents (along with other devices) enable individuals, groups and particular communities to "draw together", to "muster" facts and materials in ways that are persuasive. With documents or, more exactly, with documents put together in the right sort of way, individuals (such as scientists, government statisticians and technologists), can get their view of the world presented in convincing and powerful

---

[57] See Smith (1990).

[58] Although the word "Text" is sometimes substituted with such ugly terms as "Textuality", "Inscriptions" and "Topical Contextures".

[59] See Latour (1990).

ways. Indeed, it is through documents that certain individuals exercise a mechanism whereby their position, their perspective, can come to hold sway in the community at large. In effect, documents are a technology of power.

Now the arguments put forward to support his view are more complex than I can convey here, having to do with such things as how things get juxtaposed in texts; how "facts" of different orders (e.g. statistical surveys of populations and readouts from testing machines in laboratories) get systematically rendered as equivalent in documents; and how control of the production, access and distribution of documents is isomorphic with the locus of power. But essentially his arguments have to do with how documents create and sustain a concreteness in meaning. In this sense they are, according to Latour, "immutable" (1990: 45). But in addition, and adding immeasurably to their power, documents can be copied, circulated, distributed; they are, in a word, "mobile". Thus, to use his inimitable phrase, documents are a species of "immutable mobile" (1990: 44–45).

Now the physical technology of documents necessarily has an impact on their effectiveness as instruments of power, according to Latour. The introduction of international electronic data networks, for example, and thus the interchange of documents within the electronic domain at high speed, means that the instruments of power are now more expeditious than before[60]. If the determinations embedded in the documents of French government officials in the eighteenth century took some time to pervade down to the peasants of say, Languedoc, then in contrast, the findings of contemporary scientific experiments— and thus the status of the scientific experimenters—can be relayed around the world almost instantaneously. For Latour then, technology does not alter the *function* or *purpose* of documents but makes their operations more effective.

Recollecting the previous discussions on the increasingly varied modalities in which computers can now support documents, Latour's thesis has great salience. For if Latour is correct, these new computer forms will allow much more expeditious and tighter control over meaning. Those who have access to generate those meanings, the scientists, the government officials, international institutions—ones like the Fund no less—all of these will have greater resources to enable them to impose their views on others.

---

[60] As an illustration of this argument, see Bowker et al. (1995).

That said there are two other points worth noting. First, there is a difference between Latour's arguments and the hypertext protagonists (and post modernists). Whereas the latter two emphasise the competing nature of texts, documents and perspectives, Latour argues that this competition is dissolved in the process of organisational action so that one text, one document, one perspective comes to hold sway. His view is that though there might be some competition—and he lists the ways in which it can occur—the key fact of institutional life is that it is, in the end, driven out.

A second point is that Latour argues that the driving out of competition is important in achieving integration both within particular institutions and across them, in space and time. Latour argues that without the unification of meaning there would be a frenzy of disputation that would halt all practical action. Though we might abhor the silencing of competition, of debate and discussion, it is necessary for organisational life. This is the basis of stability, this is what makes the difference between a society of order and a society that suffers from the Hobbesian nightmare of all against all. Latour adds that social commentators should exert an influence over this to ensure that the most acceptable view is the one that wins out.

Both of these points one should accept. But Latour's work is not without its problems. Most importantly his view leads to the implication that society is merely a *social construction*. This implies that there is no such thing as a hard fact, a scientific discovery, or truth as against falsehood, since what defines these things is simply a question of who has control over defining them. This leads me to Dorothy Smith.

Although she does not directly discuss Latour's work, her view does offer a corrective to its flaws[61]. Her view is that society and institutions have the form they do because individuals within them *assume* that there is an order, a facticity, a truth, or a possible falsehood. Their assumption that these categories exist, and that they are real and substantive rather than mere social constructs, is the basis upon which those individuals are able to act. Assuming that there are such things as facts enables individuals to search for those facts; knowing of their existence enables persons to orient to modes of conduct that enable the discovery of them. This is the basis of science, of judicial proceedings, of hospital work; indeed of institutional life as a whole.

---

[61] For such a discussion see Woolgar (1991, 1993).

This view leads us back to March, Weick and Feldman. For it draws attention to how people can distinguish between such things as what is organisationally adequate and what is not; how it is they can explain and clarify their activities both to themselves and to others. It explains how people are able to *make sense* in the world.

This may sound very similar to Latour and his view that documents impose a certain order of meaning and a certain order of actions, and indeed it is similar. But the key difference is that whereas according to Latour the relationship between documents and the individual is *coercive*, the view Smith presents is one where documents are a *resource*. They are a resource because of two things. First, because documents are *self-explicating* devices. They show and tell the user just how they (the documents) are to be applied. And second, users are able to recognise what these instructions are because they are familiar with the settings in which those documents have a place.

The important point here is that users need to know how those documents are bound up with certain kinds of organisational practices. Users need to have some kind of *background knowledge*, or a set of *expectations* and *assumptions* which enables them to approach documents intelligently.

It is for this reason that newcomers to some organisational setting will have difficulty understanding "just what" some document is intended for, even though they may be able to read that document again and again. This is illustrated in my own case. Some time after I first started my study I was given a Fund *staff report* to read. However, I was not sure what I should look for, though I knew that for Fund insiders this was the document that really mattered. In my naïvety, I approached this staff report rather like I approach a novel, assuming that there would be a story—in this case the story of a member country. As it happens, there is something of a story but unless one knows something about how a staff report *reports* this story, and what are the big issues to users of such "stories", it is not a very gripping one. I was therefore bored.

By way of contrast, later on in my research I began to understand how Fund staff themselves approach staff reports. They know what to look for, which are the exciting bits, and which the boring. They also know how to use those reports to instruct them on how they should be read. To run ahead of the argument: users will tend to read the *staff appraisal* section of a staff report first since this contains the summary of important findings. This section occurs towards the end of the text.

Thus users have to flick through several pages to get to it. Once they have read it they will then know which sections of the rest of the report (if any) they should also read. It is in this way that staff reports self-explicate their use.

So Smith emphasises the cargo of background knowledge users of documents rely on, and how documents themselves support the task of their use through offering *instructions* to their readers. This is a corrective to the view that implies that documents simply deliver certain sorts of readings that are forced upon the reader. Instead, users engage with texts in a reciprocal relationship where the one informs the other. It is for this reason that Dorothy Smith talks of the *Active Text*.

Smith also emphasises the transformational process of the active text (i.e. the interaction between user and text). Through the engagement between text and user, both are altered. This is pointing toward how, in the reading of some document, what that document stands for, the user's concern with that document, and what the document does, also changes. Part of the power of a text to achieve such transformations has to do with the context of use. This context provides a resource whereby a user will know what to expect and how to use a text. A text itself will also affirm this knowledge of the proper context of use through its self-explicating character. So, for example, Smith argues that there are important differences in the organisation of personal letters and organisational texts. These are in part a reflection of how these texts are assumed and expected to be used and in part how these texts affirm and support those assumptions.

In simple terms, personal letters are assumed to report on the personal and unique view of some individual, and that is how they are written. In contrast, organisational texts are expected to be objective, authoritative and anonymous. They are also written in this way, so affirming the proper context of their use. Each of these kinds of text also carries its own kind of authority or weight. In different settings the importance of this power will vary. Smith is able to highlight many of these factors by reference to an interaction between two texts of this kind.

For example, she focuses on a letter written by a Mayor's office in response to a letter from the public sent to the local press. Both letters described police activity at a public event. She argues that the two documents, the letter and the response (also printed in the local press), were organised to support certain types of readings. The Mayor's was designed to use the personal letter as a resource to distinguish what could be seen as a personal, subjective view of the police action from a non-personal, objective view. In this way, the Mayor's view was organised to act as a corrective of the first. Now Smith makes no comment about which of the two documents was more true than the other (i.e. she has no concern with the verisimilitude of the descriptions of the police conduct offered in the two texts); her concern is with how the texts are organised to construct a certain order of reading. These readings are in part a reflection of what is expected to be an appropriate personal letter and what is expected to be an appropriate organisational one. From this view, a personal letter describing an event is treated as being just that, a *personal view*. A letter from the local authority, the Mayor's office, is viewed as an institutional document and therefore has no particular person or author, so much as it conveys the view of an institution. This is therefore an *objective view*. In such a fashion one letter, one kind of text, is juxtaposed against another and, in this case, one is viewed as more powerful than the other. The Mayor's letter counts, the personal letter does not.

Smith goes on to analyse the organisation of the two texts to see how they are constructed to support these kinds of readings. She is particularly interested in organisational kinds of reading (in this case exemplified by the Mayor's letter). These, she explains, "crystallise and preserve a definite form of words detached from their local historicity" (1990: 210). By this she means that these kinds of reading are somehow anonymous. They seem also to be split from particular moments in space and time: "(organisational) Texts speak in the absence of speakers; the meaning is detached from the local contexts of interpretations." (1990: 211). In so doing, such (organisational) documents separate the relationship between the individual and the organisation—bringing anonymity where there was (perhaps) at some earlier time identity and personality. "Organisational judgement, feedback, information and co-ordination (are transformed) into objectified textual rather than subjective processes." (1990: 214, inserts added). It is in this way that the two texts that Smith analyses have the relationship they do. For the one that corrects the other does so by presenting a narrative that is objective and anonymous. The other offers the subjective experience of a person. The former holds more weight than the latter; the objective supersedes the subjective.

Assessing documents in action

These discussions have covered considerable ground. I started with a review of some of the technologies currently available. Here I was particularly concerned to describe how the relationship between individuals and documentary forms is broadening. Wholly new ways of "interacting" with documents are on the increase. One of the more commonly available approaches centres on the use of hypertext. I noted that hypertext was of particular interest not only because of how the World Wide Web has made it familiar to millions, but because it offers new ways of interacting with documents. A notable feature is that it allows and emphasises non-sequential use of text.

But my review of the technology of documents was not only of exotic forms—exotic in the sense that they are new and may confront the user with the full force of strangeness—but also of the much more familiar technology of paper. I argued that paper is a technology of sorts, and has some remarkable features. Paper can be shown to allow a particular kind of engagement with documents—an engagement which supports the kinds of activities now recognised as of fundamental importance to organisational practice. Reading and "sense-making" are two examples of such activities. Paper and modern institutions, from this view, go hand in hand.

Having described some of the technologies of documents, I then discussed some of the main views one finds in those disciplines that have a concern with what documents do. I started my commentary with literary theory and the claim deriving from the work of Barthes and others that hypertext is a medium that will transform the relationship between the reader and the text. In brief, the claim is that documents tend to dominate the reader. With hypertext the reader is able to reverse this relationship. This, it is claimed, will constitute a radical change and will lead to as substantive a revolution as that deriving from the Gutenberg Press all those centuries ago[62]. I then discussed certain commentators who have attempted to investigate conceptually what might be the implications of this suggestion (i.e. a reversal of the relationship between reader and text). Here I reported on the suggestion that transforming this relationship will also transform organisations. Instead of

---

[62] Though just what this revolution consisted of, or even if the word revolution is appropriate, is much discussed. See Haas (1996).

being hierarchical and based on the imposition of certain orders of meaning, organisations will become more democratic and will encourage pluralistic perspectives.

I then argued that all of these discussions suffer from a lack of robust empirical investigation. I contended that if one looks at empirical materials—reported in the work of March, for example—one will find that the nature, role and purpose of documents is much more diverse than is supposed by those who have theoretically discussed the implications of hypertext. One particular role of documents is as a resource organisational members use to construct and determine a common ground between themselves. For this function, documents are not about coercing readers to accept a certain view, they are about providing resources to allow the creation of shared perspectives. Without this, organisations would dissolve. This contradicts those who urge a cacophony of perspectives in organisations whether it be through the medium of hypertext or the natural result of the dissolution of the "modernist narrative".

I then noted that research into how documents achieve this shared understanding points out how documents need to operate across time. For example, when analysts start to prepare a report, they may be unsure what the future context for that report will be. But they need to predetermine that future for the purpose of creating a draft. These "guesses at the future" end up being the resource whereby that future becomes a place of shared understanding or, in a phrase, an organisational reality.

I then turned to research in sociology which affirms the view that documents are tools in the construction of fixed and shared meaning. This perspective also draws attention to how documents need to drive out competing views. This serves to further refute those who believe organisations should allow a diversity of perspectives. For though this diversity might be theoretically desirable, it would be inimical to practical action.

Last of all, I examined a view that emphasises how the use of documents is always an interactive process, and that it would be wrong therefore to assume that the relationship is one way (i.e. with the text imposing itself on the user). Rather, the relationship is an active one with both the text and user contributing. The interaction in question involves constraints. These constraints consist of how documents are designed to be read in certain kinds of way to convey particular sorts of meanings. At the same time, users bring their own cargo of constraints as regards how they will read those documents. These derive from what they know of the relevant context of use, amongst other things. These two sets of constraints, provided by the text and the reader, interact such that the location of both document and user are transformed through the process of an active reading.

Conclusion: a view of documents within the Fund

I am convinced that arguments about borders between text, about the nature of navigation within a text, as regards the relationship between user and text, all of which are highlighted by hypertext and other new forms of document media, do draw attention to what is important in organisations and what may or may not be changed.

But these notions need supplementing by two things. First, there needs to be a recognition that the relationship between text and user is always *active* and *transformational*. Second, to understand how that relationship is active and what the transformation consists of, one needs to specify *the context* of that relationship. From this view, what needs to be investigated is what is brought to bear when someone uses a document. I would like to suggest that this is determined in large part by the juncture of organisational life in which that interaction occurs. This juncture determines what a user of a text expects and assumes will be relevant. It is on that basis that they *approach* a text. It determines also the ways in which the text needs to be organised to enable and support *preferred courses* of use. Organisational settings frame the relationship between text and reader.

So, for instance, it is my view that it might be appropriate at certain organisational junctures for the interaction between text and reader to result in the reader taking on board the view of the document. In this sense the text imposes its view on the user, albeit that I want to make it clear that the user is actively contributing to this process (a willing victim if you like!) At other points within organisational processes the reverse may happen (i.e. a reader will reject the view within a text) and here navigation between various texts and the creation of new narrative structures might be appropriate. One should not presuppose where these junctures might be, however. One needs to look at organisational locales to find them out.

Such an examination will uncover the nature of the transformation that occurs when text and user interact. Dorothy Smith's example of a transformation consists of how the use of a document provides a reader with resources to judge *adequate description*. More specifically, the reader and the texts in question are transformed because in the process of reading, one text is seen by the reader to be wrong and the other correct. But Smith's investigations are into only one kind of transformation. Consider that documents—especially within organisations—are subject to numerous processes, and these include such things as reviewing, acceptance, rejection, archiving and the like. It will surely be the case that within one of these stages a reader will be concerned with the "empirical adequacy" of a description. The review stage would appear a likely candidate for this. However, it may well be that once issues of empirical adequacy have been sorted out then other tasks, other questions, and other doings and transformations become pertinent. These may include such things as distribution, delivery, archiving and much more besides. In these other stages users will not have a concern with empirical adequacy. It is in this sense—how it is that when documents are used there is a before and an after, a changing of concerns, a movement between various states—that interaction with documents is transformational.

But it is in this sense also that I would like to suggest that the *working of an organisation* may be displayed. For what matters at any stage will vary and thus what the active reading consists of and the transformation that results will also vary. These differences will reflect the organisational context of those actions. But to understand that context will mean understanding the organisation and the various ways it *imposes* itself on the processes of active reading. Following a document through the various stages through which it goes—following its *career* in other words—will highlight the frameworks of organisational action as they are oriented to step by step, and phase by phase, by organisational actors.

One may begin to illustrate what this means by considering what some of the themes in such enquiries would be. This will also be a chance to foreshadow some of the arguments that follow in later chapters.

In the work of Smith one learns that organisational documents have a certain order of anonymity. In this she is merely repeating the often noted fact that institutional documents seem to have no author. They are instead the faceless products of bureaucratic machines. Yet, and as I have just noted, her discussion is based on the explication of a certain context and therefore a certain order of active readings. These are not all of the readings one would imagine organisational documents are subject to. In some ways the documents she analyses—in particular those generated by a Mayor's office—are the *products* of a certain institution, rather than documents that are still being processed *within* that institution. More specifically, hers is an analysis of the work that goes into the use of texts *subsequent* to other sorts of work that goes into the *prior production* of those texts. What I will want to suggest is that if one looks at the processes through which texts get transformed from mere drafts into the sanctioned, externally available documents— as is the case with such things as Fund staff reports—one theme that will show itself is how the original author(s) of such documents get shunted out of view and replaced by the identity of the institution as a whole. For I will want to suggest that responsibility for the adequacy of description, for appropriate revision and amendment, and, lastly, for the timely delivery of information, are those who author staff reports. However, if these issues are effectively dealt with by the time a staff report is accepted by the Fund's Executive Board, then their authorship disappears from view. To the extent that this is so, then from the perspective of those who participate in constructing documents in an organisation like the Fund, the notion of anonymity has a slightly more complex hue than the one Smith describes.

A second theme I will want to draw attention to has to do with the question of how the interaction between document and user leads to alternative perspectives, narratives, views (call them what you will), being driven out. I am thinking here of Latour's work and the process of *dealing with competition*. This sounds rather dramatic, or one might almost say sinister. What I am actually thinking of is how an institution like the Fund comes to hold a view on its member countries. This view needs to be constructed, or "worked up", if you will, until it is "just right". I will want to suggest that this process may play out in terms of such things as the career of a staff report (and associated documenta- tion) through the Fund. As a staff report goes through the various stages of its career, so what it "means", what it implies and what it stands for, gets gradually whittled down. One may characterise this as the tightening of the grip, a gradual fixing of meaning. Closely related to this is how time and more particularly the prediction of the future shows itself in this process. For Fund staff need to make intelligent predictions of what they expect to find on mission and these predictions turn into the building blocks of the descriptions they eventually gen- erate. In other words, their divinations into the future help them

determine what that future turns out to be. Again this sounds a little
sinister, but all I am pointing toward is how mission teams need to
know enough about a country to predict in a certain kind of way what
they will find. This is as crucial to the effectiveness of the mission
process as it is to the smooth running of the Fund as a whole.

There are other themes that will show themselves, but these give
sufficient ideas as to the kinds of materials that the programme of
enquiry I am pointing toward generates. But they also imply, it seems
to me, questions as to what role document technologies might play
within any of the stages of a document career. Related to that, they also
draw attention to how alteration of those technologies might impact
upon any stage.

So, as regards the whittling away of competing views, it may well be
the case that in the early stages of producing a staff report, when the
mission team is still gathering its data, knowledge about the various
ways a member country's economy may be viewed may be extremely
useful. Hypertext functionality may be one of those techniques for
providing access to those views, and there may be other technologies
too.

Then there is the case of achieving anonymity in Fund documents.
Here it may well be that the use of paper documents supports the
current procedures whereby Fund documents start off "owned" and
"authored" by someone. In particular, early stages of drafting where
the author(s) may be conspicuous may be supported by the use of
paper. This might create a geographical location for the document.
This might ensure that that document is kept *quite literally* in the hands
of the author(s). As a document works its way through the organisation, and as this authorship gradually slips into the hands of the
organisation as a whole, so that geographic and physical control will
diminish. The point here is that with electronic media, such geographic
control may be much more difficult to maintain.

These are perhaps simple and rather obvious examples, but they
point toward the kinds of issues that I will be looking into. I certainly
do not claim, however, that my research will enquire into every aspect
of the relationship between document and user, nor will it consider all
of the "functionalities" of the various document media currently
available. That is not my main goal. Rather (and this needs restating
after our sojourn into the nature of documents), my main purpose is to
describe the Fund, and my approach for doing this is to use the notion
of a document career as a prism whereby the working mechanisms of

the institution are made available. It is in this sense that the Fund's documents provide a means whereby I can better understand that institution. My purpose in this chapter, then, has been to give an indication of how I will want to proceed in the empirical chapters that follow. It has also indicated how the materials I present may be used and interpreted. In this respect, what I hope to have done is explain and outline a framework in which readers will be able to engage in their own appropriate, reciprocal and active reading of the text.

CHAPTER 3
Designing ethnography

In this chapter I want to consider the method I used to examine the Fund. The method is called ethnography, but this terms hides much. For ethnography is a label used by sociologists and anthropologists in a somewhat casual way—a catch-all phrase for a range of different things, just as long as they involve field work of one sort or another. Within IT research, the term is even more troublesome: as a member of the Fund once put it, "Ah, the E word", alluding to the fact that, as far as he understood, ethnography is something that whiz-kids from the research world use to transform what is "just" a means of looking at what people do in organisations into something that is a marvellous new technique that will revolutionise computer systems, particularly for the office.

Unfortunately, ensuring that ethnography is part of a research programme does not, by any means, ensure that the results which are generated solve all the problems the research sets out to investigate. Ethnography, as I shall argue, is simply one way of looking at how people do their work. It is a very valuable addition to the methods that have evolved over the years to understand and represent work. But it is not the answer to such things as the problem of requirements capture (i.e. how to get a perfect specification for a system). Nor is it the unique technique that will enable managers to understand properly "the culture" of their workplace. Nor yet is ethnography the trade that can ensure that systems are evaluated properly. Certainly ethnography can go some way toward these things, but it is like any tool: it is part of a toolbox—an artefact that has to be used alongside other tools.

Overview of the chapter

In this chapter I discuss two main issues related to the general problem of what ethnography involves: how to do it, and the analytical processes involved.

First, I want to discuss why ethnography has come to hold a place of such esteem in the IT research world and in CSCW (computer supported co-operative work) research particularly. Here I shall report on some of the debates and developments within the research community over the past twenty or so years, and also remark on the experiences and changing attitudes of organisational users of IT over the same period.

Second, I shall outline what I did during my sojourn in Washington, or to use a grander title, describe my *field work programme*. I want to offer this not simply because it is required in case studies (i.e. one has to report on how one did the research if only for protocol reasons), but because I think it is useful to illustrate a practical programme that has been developed for ethnography in IT research. I have been developing this programme for a number of years, and using it in a range of different settings. Although it is not the only way of undertaking field work, I am confident enough in it to claim that it is certainly one fairly effective way. Furthermore, one will scour the IT literature to find any information on what practical techniques others have been using (presumably they have been using some techniques). By and large, most discussions and reports of ethnography in IT say very little about what practicalities of the field work, treating those things as taken for granted matters that can be left aside. Most of the papers that do discuss ethnography are intended, as one of the authors of those papers puts it, for *aficionados*[63]. Exceptions to this are few, but worth reading. One paper I shall be remarking on comes from the Lancaster Centre for CSCW. *Ethnography in Systems Design* catalogues the types of ethnography undertaken within IT research (with particular reference to CSCW, naturally) and what processes are attendant on each[64]. I shall suggest this categorisation is very useful, but will offer my own programme as something that could be adopted for any of the kinds of processes that they describe.

Needless to say, the imbroglio surrounding ethnography and its role in IT research is not something that I can resolve in this chapter. Others have been investigating this topic and their work, too, needs to be referenced[65]. However, it is my belief that research such as is reported in this book will form part of the material that will enable some untying of knots in this area, but as yet we are on the path and are not quite

---

[63] See Anderson (1997).

[64] See Hughes et al. (1994).

[65] See, for example, Anderson (1994a, 1994b), Blomberg et al. (1992), Hughes et al. (1993b) and Shapiro (1994).

there yet. I do not want to give the impression that I am without strong opinions about the role of ethnography or how to do it. Yet one does need to be very careful when one starts discussing and reporting ethnography. It is not always quite what it seems. It is not as facile as it sometimes appears, nor yet as elusive and difficult to undertake as some methodological discussions pretend. But it is useful and can uncover important materials that need to be taken into account when systems are being designed, implemented and evaluated; it can make the difference between good and bad, between the nearly good and the just right.

To achieve these goals will require more than simply an adequate field work programme, whether that programme be the one I advocate or some other. Though my main concern in this chapter is with that programme and also with why one would be interested in applying it, I shall conclude with some discussion of the alternative processes of research and design into which ethnography can fit. I shall not comment conclusively on these processes since I believe much work needs to be done before one can confidently ascertain the powers of each, and hence the suitability of certain of these processes for specific design tasks. Nonetheless, it is appropriate to conclude on this question, since the processes in which ethnography will fit will be the next set of concerns that the reader will need to consider if, as I hope, I shall by then have persuaded them that there are good reasons for the ethnographic turn and systematic properties that can be relied upon in its undertaking.

The ethnographic turn: why has it come about?

In the introductory chapter, I noted that there has been a convergence of interests between ethnographers (from sociology and anthropology) who were looking for new places to ply their trade and IT designers who have been wanting to investigate new methods for requirements capture and evaluation. But this particular merging of interests is not the only one that has led ethnography—irrespective of what ethnography might mean for the moment—into something that has the status it currently does. For there were a number of other factors, an aggregation of other concerns, that have led to the ethnographic turn. There is no proper hierarchy of precedent or importance here, nor is it possible to explain all the reasons for the movements in question. All I offer

here therefore is a synopsis of what I believe are the most important of
these various trends and developments.

There are three trends one needs to be concerned with. The first trend
was the development of research into the social impact of computing.
This did not derive from sociology or anthropology, since these disciplines viewed that impact as little more than a continuation of trends
that were better explicated with reference to class structures and power.
One paradoxical consequence of this interest was that reference to
these classic concerns resulted in computing and computers disappearing from the view of those studies[66]. Be that as it may, the research I
am interested in came instead from researchers whose background was
largely in computer science itself with the odd management scientist
and social psychologist thrown in.

The second trend, which partly built on this, consisted of a set of
seminal publications that were a kind of clarion call for a new interpretative, loosely sociological/anthropological approach to requirements capture. These were combined with a claim from some that
one kind of "ethnographic approach" had all the answers. These
publications built upon and to some extent extrapolated ideas from
the much older *Socio-technical* approach to systems design and the
more contemporary experiences reported on *Participatory Design* in
Scandinavia.

The third trend has to do with the experiences and changing attitudes
of organisations themselves. For, whereas in the 1960s and 1970s
organisational managers took system designers and vendors at their
word, the burns that resulted made them more sanguine about what to
expect and, importantly, more open to new ways of determining what
they required. The Fund's experience is a case in point, and the Fund's
willingness to support the research reported here is a demonstration of
that new open mind.

Research into the social impact of computing

In the first twenty or so years during which computer systems began to
have a major influence on working life (from the early 1960s or there-
abouts), very few investigations were undertaken into the actual impact
of those systems[67]. Systems were designed, introduced, and then the

---

[66] See Button (1993).

[67] See Kling (1980).

users were left to it. Few bothered to assess what impact those systems might have. This is not to say that there was no contact between users and designers, but that this contact was minimal, occurring only briefly and at an early stage in the design process. More specifically, system analysts (though sometimes they were given other names) would be briefly sent into a setting to gather the procedural specifications of a system. Most of these requirements capture processes were of the most rudimentary kind. This is not to say that all of the systems that resulted were poor. Some were and some were not. The point is that determining what was required in work settings was not viewed as particularly difficult, nor was evaluating the impact of the systems once in place. Of greater concern was ensuring that the system could actually do what it was designed to do. Thus formal methods, which have their origin in this period and purport to be tools for the representation of user activities (amongst other things), are more accurately described as tools enabling designers to evaluate whether their systems will work in terms of their own (i.e. the system's) specification. This is quite distinct from evaluating whether the system helps users achieve their organisational goals.

Formal methods aside, the result of this general approach to requirements capture (that is to say, a superficial examination of work and the almost complete absence of post-implementation evaluation), was that designers of systems had little idea of what difference their technologies actually made. The systems were manufactured, delivered, and then forgotten about. Gradually, however, a small band of researchers (Rob Kling, Lynne Markus and others) began to uncover the fact that computers were having an impact in organisations and on work which was at once less consequential than expected but also more diversified[68]. One hope had been that with new computer systems, various mundane elements of work would be done away with, causing something of a revolution. In fact, the technology seemed to have very little impact on the amount of mundane clerical and administrative work undertaken in organisational life (although obviously impacting upon how it was done). It certainly did not cause a shift in the allocation of employment away from the administrative towards, say, the professional and creative. As regards use, the research showed that systems were deployed in more diverse ways than designers had thought, reflecting the specific contexts in which they were used. Further, users

---

[68] See Part II of Dunlop & Kling (1991).

were developing techniques to bypass elements of systems (so-called "work arounds") because those systems were ill-suited to the complex and often ad hoc organisation of work. Finally, computers were being used within larger patterns of work which, in part, were determining the nature of that use[69].

The result of this research was not simply to point out that system requirements had to be more effectively developed (i.e. that systems had to reflect the subtleties of work hitherto ignored). It also emphasised the fact that additional techniques for determining the *social consequences* of the technology needed to be developed, and these needed to enable prediction of what the future would hold. Such concerns as predicting the future and capturing and understanding the social life of workplaces were quite foreign to the traditions of systems design. Indeed, a question was asked at the time as to whether these should be part of the system designer's portfolio of concerns, or whether others whose trade was more suited to the investigation of these problems should get involved in the design and evaluation of systems.

This research was suggesting, then, that what was once a discrete world of technology design and manufacture should open its doors and let in new concerns, new forms of expertise and a broader vision of what computer system design for organisational work involved. This would involve looking at work practice in more detail, at the effects of systems and how to understand those effects. It was left to others, however, to develop what those new concerns might be.

Defining new sets of expertise

Central to the new concerns were ways of improving requirements capture. R. Hirschheim's 1985 book, *Office Automation: A Social and Organisational Perspective*[70] critiqued the rather rudimentary procedures then in use and argued for processes that could adequately represent the fact that "office work is largely unstructured, covert, political and symbolic" (1985: 10). The view Hirschheim propounded is not that workplaces—and offices in particular—were chaotic domains fraught with political friction, competing symbols and ritualised behaviour, so much as they were essentially social, and therefore

---

[69] See Gasser (1986).

[70] See Hirschheim (1985).

the processes therein were essentially social in character too. This makes them quite unlike the processes within, say, a computer machine—namely mechanical, causal and logical. As a result, requirements techniques that treat social processes as if they were mechanical were likely to misunderstand or at least misrepresent those processes. Most requirements capture techniques (including the previously mentioned formal methods) did precisely this. Hirschheim argued that what was needed were "interpretativist" techniques that recognised the social nature of work and which could merge this fact with the need for systematic description and predictive power. He illustrated this with what he called a hermeneutic analysis of role playing in organisations, a perspective that requires potential users of systems and those who will manage those users to sit down together and talk through what impact that system would have on their respective roles[71].

At the time of writing, Hirschheim could not report on the success of such techniques or of various others he pointed towards. His work served more as an illustration, as a clarion call, as I have described it, for the investigation of new methods. One of these new ways was being developed by Eleanor Wynn and Lucy Suchman. They were using anthropological techniques, which meant primarily ethnography, to study office procedure [72]. Their work reported how procedures are much more heterogeneous and complex than they first appear, and that the effective achievement of "due process" depended upon informal inter-action among office staff. Of crucial importance in their work was the claim that office activity has to be treated as a negotiated, "accomplished" phenomenon, where the agency of individual actors within the environment needs to be recognised and investigated in such a way as to specify those techniques—local, contingent, situated—which are used to "achieve" the work. Ultimately, Wynn and Suchman's work led to a recognition of the "sociality" that underscores work practice, a sociality that needs to be supported rather than undermined by tech-nology. Suchman's book, *Plans and Situated Action*, has come to have

---

[71] See Hirschheim (1985), especially pp. 259–70.

[72] See Suchman (1983) and Suchman & Wynn (1984). Their work derives from the tradition of studying organisational life from an anthropological perspective that goes right the way back to the 1920s. This tradition more of less submerged during the 1950s, only resurfacing in the late 1970s and 1980s. For a discussion see Schwartzman (1993).

a high profile in the research world, echoing and pushing harder on the arguments supporting social analysis first outlined by Hirschheim some two years before[73].

Meanwhile, in Scandinavia, *Participatory Design* was emerging. Here designers and users would work hand in hand to design, in a gradual and evolutionary way, systems that would benefit rather than displace the interests of users themselves[74]. There was an obvious political element to this procedure, reflecting to some extent the specific institutional and moral frameworks of Scandinavian society. Participatory Design has now broadened and what is meant by the term is now almost any design procedure that involves users[75].

Participatory design had its precursor in the *Socio-technical* approach developed years before by Mumford, Trist, Henshall and others. This was, and indeed still is, being carried out by the Tavistock Institute in London. According to this view, work (whatever type of work) is team-based. The introduction of new technology must incorporate ways of ensuring that this team working is preserved and enhanced. Behind this view were studies of English coal mining in the early 1950s which had shown how coal miners worked within informal social systems. Technologies that broke up the fabric of these systems undermined the moral order of coal mining, and this in turn led to reductions in productivity. Eventually this view emerged into the so-called ETHICS approach[76].

These were the most conspicuous of the developments around this time. Since then, numerous other approaches have been advocated[77]. The point was that academic and scholarly lines of research from a host of different disciplines were coalescing into a set of concerns focusing on the design, use and impact of systems in the workplace. These concerns were underlying the importance of the social organisation of work, and the need to better specify that in requirements capture. This in turn drew attention to the methods of social analysis.

At this point, however, it was not certain what methods would be

---

[73] See Suchman (1987).

[74] See, for instance, Ehn (1988).

[75] For a sample of papers on this topic, see Schuller & Namioka (1992).

[76] See, for instance, Mumford & Henshall (1979) and Trist (1981). For a review of the approach see Olerup (1989).

[77] For a recent collection of such approaches see Monk & Gilbert (1985).

appropriate: was it hermeneutics following Hirschheim[78], participatory design, the ETHICS approach or others I have not mentioned, such as action theory?[79] Ethnography was beginning to raise its head, but it took further argument, more articles, a series of projects and a development from outside of academic circles to help increase its profile further.

The claims of ethnography got a further boost from another area altogether: a new frame of mind began to appear on the part of users of systems themselves, and the corporations, both large and small, that paid for them. This view included placing more emphasis on the social nature of work, acknowledging the difficulties with "orthodox" methods of analysis and specification for systems, and a concern with what management theorists started calling *organisational culture*. It is to this change in perspective that I now turn.

Changes in the perspective of organisations

By the mid-1980s, most, if not all, organisations had some experience with computer systems and much of this was negative. This was not because the technology had failed to achieve anything (because in fact most systems did offer some benefits); it was that these achievements were not as great as had been expected. Vendors had, perhaps innocently (or perhaps not so innocently), exaggerated the promise of systems and, as a result, expectations had been developed which could never be realised[80]. At the same time, levels of investment were becoming so large that there was increasing organisational inertia: once systems had been introduced and irrespective of how bad they were, managers were loath to spend more on upgrades or replacement of them. The political and symbolic cost would be too high. In this way, organisations had burnt their fingers with technology, believing the salesmen and ending up with expensive, unsatisfactory kit that could be not replaced overnight. As a result, organisations and more

---

[78] This particular strand of work has been developed by Geoff Walsham, amongst others. In his *Interpreting Information Systems in Organisations* (Walsham, 1993), he proposes that the hermeneutic framework be evolved into "constitutive process theory".

[79] See Bodker (1989).

[80] See Salerno (1985).

specifically those responsible for IT-related decisions would be more circumspect in the future.

This circumspection did not just show itself in negativity and scepticism when vendors came knocking on the door. It also showed itself in positive ways. For example, some organisations responded to what they believed as the disappointments of the past by developing their own procedures for managing requirements capture, development and implementation. The emergence of so-called "end user" support structures within organisations reflected this: according to this view, organisations set up procedures whereby users would get more closely involved in the selection, implementation and development of technology[81]. This was a kind of Participatory Design[82].

However, end user processes did not always result in the improvements that organisations wanted. Organisations began to discover just how difficult it was to specify needs. Users are not always entirely certain of what they want. In any case, user practices are constantly changing, partly as a response to new technology and partly as a response to other developments. This could sometimes make some technology obsolete almost as soon it was implemented.

But beyond all this, organisations began to take more seriously what they viewed as their own "corporate" or "organisational culture". Although one can reasonably argue that organisations always have some kind of culture (after all, even the Hawthorne effect can be thought of as a cultural one and that occurred over 50 years ago!), its perceived importance has increased recently. Partly this is a response to some problems of user acceptability associated with new technology and partly also it is a response to new modalities of business analysis which purport to offer expertise on improving organisational culture.

As it happens, culture is a term that can get used in a rather flaccid way in relationship to organisations. It is as much an excuse for things

---

[81] See Brancheau & Brown (1993).

[82] Bonnie Nardi offers a somewhat deeper view and proposes a development of end user programming systems. Such systems would enable users to tailor and design the software for the applications they need. She argues that spreadsheets, various computer-aided design (CAD) systems, and statistical packages all offer a form of end user programming. The need is to expand the interactive functionalities to other applications. See Nardi (1993).

that cannot be explained (and a pretext for the high price of certain management consultants), as it is a term for some "thing" that shows itself in real ways in organisations[83]. But irrespective of its rather rough and ready usage, the term does point to consequential matters.

For instance, organisations began to recognise that the stresses and strains that arose when groups with different political interests tried to agree a specification was a manifestation of a kind of culture (fragmented, competitive, exclusive). They began to see that such things as user resistance are in part a function of broader patterns of resistance and conflict within the organisation.

There are of course many other facets to culture but, irrespective of what they might be, understanding cultural factors became something that was part and parcel of uncovering relevant matters in user requirements specification. What was once a problem of delineating some particular process (i.e. a process that a computer could support or automate), became instead a component of a larger array of concerns where cultural issues—meant in a rather broad, all encompassing sense—needed to be taken into account. These new concerns also required new methodologies.

Not all organisations turned this way, of course, and not all organisations had the same experience. But generally speaking, this was the case: organisational users were unsatisfied. For example, the excitement generated by the introduction of the first spreadsheet tools and the first personal computers turned into disconsolation when these machines were replaced by more powerful, networked workstations (i.e. as cost and hopes had been raised). As with earlier technological revolutions, great steps forward had been made, but ultimately the latest revolution looked like failing too.

The Fund's experience

The changes in perspective at the Fund can illustrate the experiences of organisational managers and users of organisational systems. Here there was an attempt to develop more effective, more subtle end user requirements capture processes, but these were not entirely successful. Here also there was a growing recognition that cultural factors impinged upon the use and role of systems.

The selection of desktop tools for economic analysis is illustrative of

---

[83] See, for example, Weick (1985).

difficulties with requirements capture. Without going into all the details, by the mid 1980s, the Fund recognised that its key users—its economists—needed to be in the requirements capture loop. Accordingly, the institution set up a committee of economists to determine what application would suit their computing needs. A time series tool, AREMOS, was selected. This application appeared to satisfy the complete list of the economists' collective needs for time-series processing, including data management, presentation and analysis. However, in practice AREMOS' success was uneven.

For example, data management practices varied (and still do as I shall show) depending upon the quality and consistency of data available from member countries. Economists dealing with countries with poor or incomplete data found AREMOS placed too great a burden on them: it required more or less full data sets and this they were unable to provide. As a result, they were unhappy about using the tool.

So, why did the committee choose such a tool? Let me cite just one reason reflecting the problems I have just mentioned. It might seem reasonable to assume that the Fund's economists consisted of a single group, a band of individuals unified by task and role. In a general sense, the Fund's economists do have a common role, but in practice their tasks vary quite widely. One criterion for this variance has to do with the data they have available for their work. Some economists are responsible for countries that generate complete data sets, whilst others are responsible for countries that produce hardly any at all. Economists will alter their work practices to suit. Most of the economists on the committee (for a variety of reasons we need not go into now) were ones with complete data sets, or at least were dealing with countries whose data could be worked up with a little bit of extra work. This group, although recognising that not every economist had the same data as they did, assumed and hoped that the introduction of AREMOS would encourage those economists with poor data sets to spend that extra time to improve their data.

But this was to hope for too much. It was simply impossible for every economist to do this, irrespective of their willingness or the time they had to do so. In effect, the committee underestimated the variance in the quality and scope of data at the Fund and wanted to use AREMOS as a device to mould the work of others to reflect more closely their own work. In this sense, their decision was as much political as it was based on reference to the actual details of the work of all other users. In being political it was therefore a reflection of the culture of the Fund[84].

Cultural factors were then showing their relevance in the user requirements process. But even once systems were introduced, culture was showing itself. Let me take another example from my field work. In a sense, this would appear to muddle up the actual order of events, because I want to claim that the Fund came to recognise that cultural factors impinged on technology before I undertook my own investigations. But the example I report now was one that many people within the Fund were all too familiar with. My observation of it confirmed the belief that they had developed before my research that their organisation had its own distinct and consequential culture.

The example has to do with the delivery of documents. When a network was introduced at the Fund, one of the justifications for doing so was the expectation that it would be used to send documents quickly and efficiently around the organisation. But in practice many documents continued to be delivered in person and by hand.

---

[84] Cultural factors such as this were not the only factors affecting AREMOS. Another factor had to do with the fact that the committee opted for a technology that supported a certain kind of structured work, but at the same time, another technology was being introduced to the Fund through the "back door" that supported more unstructured activities. The support it offered actually served to increase the extent and importance of these activities and thus served also to reduce the applicability of AREMOS. More specifically, AREMOS is good at extensive time series analysis. As it happens, this is labour-intensive and is over-burdensome for scenario and ad hoc types of data analysis. Such scenario and ad hoc investigations are useful in policy work but at that time (i.e. the early 1980s), there appeared to be a few tools that could effectively support it. Thus the committee was probably right to select a single application that supported at least some of the key analytical processes, in this case time series analysis. However, at the same time as the committee was making this decision, a new technology appeared which was more flexible and easier to use that AREMOS. This started working its way into the Fund. This tool, which would support scenario-based, as hoc analysis, was Lotus 1-2-3. It was being introduced by newly arrived economists. So successful was this application that it soon spread throughout the organisation, and ad hoc and scenario-based computational analysis came to have an increasingly important role in policy work. By the end of the 1980s, the Fund had to recognise this fact and made Lotus 1-2-3 a Fund standard along with AREMOS. Other spreadsheet tools are now in use in the Fund as well as Lotus.

To explain why this was so, let me focus on the process of getting staff reports reviewed. When an area department division finishes drafting an important document such as a staff report, it must be delivered to various functional departments. Although the Fund's network allowed automatic routing of such documents, on many occasions I observed that authors preferred to hand deliver documents, using hard copy rather than electronic forms. This was especially the case in relation to the most important reviewing department, the department of Policy Development and Review (PDR). There are a number of reasons for this which I would suggest are cultural. Let me focus on three[85].

First, discussion can *add value* to the document at the point of delivery. There are many things that may be discussed such as how much time the review is likely to take, the issues that are unusual in the particular report, the general context of the document and so on.

Second, authors prefer to hand deliver documents to PDR in order to reflect the importance of the documents in question. As one deputy chief put it, "delivering papers to PDR is too important to leave to email". This can also be taken to be a comment on the importance of the relationship of PDR with the divisions: hand delivery to PDR serves as a demonstration of the ritual and symbolic importance of relations between an area department division and PDR.

Third, and related to the above, hand delivery enables divisional staff to personalise their relations with PDR. This may be important when, organisationally speaking, PDR may be in a potentially antagonistic position. By delivering a document, divisional staff are helping to smooth and oil that relationship, not so much to bypass the concerns of PDR, as to make elicitation of those concerns something that can be done more easily. In other words, hand delivery humanises and personalises these processes.

This example is based on observation of current practice at the Fund (i.e in the 1990s). But my point is that similar practices were showing themselves in the late 1980s, and this led the Fund—like many other organisations—to recognise the importance of cultural factors on systems. Indeed, it was precisely this concern that led the Fund to be receptive to the research reported here—so receptive that it partly funded that research. For, although the Fund was keen to support

---

[85] For fuller discussion of this in relation to workflow technology, see Sellen & Harper (1996).

what it viewed as essentially "pure" research, it also recognised that the evidence generated by such enquiries could help it better understand the complex of issues that surround the use of technology and associated work practices.

The Fund was not alone in coming to this realisation. Many other organisations began to recognise that studies of the *social organisation* of their work would provide them with important information they could use in their IT-related decision-making. These organisations included computer manufacturers, financial institutions, communications businesses, civil aviation authorities, and others. The technique that these organisations came to have an interest in was ethnography.

What is ethnography?

Though these corporations turned to ethnography, just what it involves and just what it is, was not then (nor is it now) entirely clear. As I said at the beginning of the chapter, ethnography is one of those catch-all words whose meaning is extremely general and vague. So varied is the interpretation that can be given to it, that one of the organisations who took up ethnography has claimed to have invented it—thereby ignoring decades of research in anthropology and sociology[86].

Their arrogance may be excused by the fact that if they were to look at the sociological and anthropological canon of ethnographic work (i.e. not ethnography under the guise of IT research, of which I will say something in a moment), they are unlikely to come away with an exact sense of how it is done. Worse, they may not even learn what is systematic about what "it" comes up with. Just to take what comes to mind from the long and rich history of ethnography (a list of personal favourites if you like), one finds Goffman's studies of how inmates in an asylum deal with their predicament through personal and social habits[87]; Wieder's examination of the ways in which ex-cons and staff in a halfway house instruct each other as to what is and is not acceptable conduct[88]; Skolnick's (to my mind classic) study of the way police officers are compromised by tensions between "due process"

---

[86] Though for obvious reasons I cannot identify this organisation.

[87] See Goffman (1959).

[88] See Wieder (1974).

and what they perceive as "moral justice" in their dealings with criminals[89]; and Blau's study of the changes brought about by new productivity measures in public welfare agencies[90]. The list of contemporary studies could include (though nothing more than the mere fact that one recollects them easily is implied about their quality): Lynch's studies of biochemistry laboratories[91]; on the same theme, Latour and Woolgar's work[92]; Anderson, Hughes and Sharrock's account of a small-time fast food retailer[93]; Hockey's participant observation of the parochial world of squaddies[94]; and this is to leave aside the anthropological literature.

Under the term ethnography one will find, then, great diversity of enquiries. Moreover, what makes so many of these studies so interesting to read is the way they evoke the situation in question, their own reference to previous ethnographies, the interweaving of argument and description: this seems so diverse, broad and various as to defy formulation[95]. Ethnographic tools, techniques and presentational formats would appear, therefore, something of a collage, a mish-mash of things. Consequently it is difficult to know quite what to make of claims that ethnography can help in "requirements capture" or "domain specification" in system design (two amongst the various possibilities), for the simple fact that it is difficult to know what is meant by the term "ethnography".

There are some books that report on some of the mechanics of ethnography. These are at best rather simple, advising the use of tape recorders, daily note-keeping, and recommending the sharing of draft descriptions with those studied[96]. More than anything else, they are encouragements for those solitary individuals, post-graduate students, who are obliged to commence their career with the injunction from

---

[89] See Skolnick (1966).

[90] See Blau (1955).

[91] See Lynch, (1982, 1985a, 1985b, 1988).

[92] See Latour & Woolgar (1986) and also Latour (1987, 1988).

[93] See Anderson et al. (1989).

[94] See Hockey (1986).

[95] See Atkinson (1990). For a review of this see Harper (1991a). See also Hammersly & Atkinson (1983).

[96] See, for instance, Hammersley & Atkinson (1983). My personal favourite, though, which is getting old, is Lofland (1971).

their supervisor, "go do an ethnography". Most, if not all, will have had no training, no guidance, and certainly no experience in field work. Consequently they are full of doubt when they undertake their research, unsure of what to do at each stage, and unconvinced that they are finding anything interesting.

Some of the senior players in the ethnographic field offer another set of encouragements by writing frank exposés of the serendipitous nature of their own research. Van Maanen's charming *Tales of the Field* is of this kind[97]. But these books serve only to add to the problem. For what the novice discovers is that senior researchers got access to a setting purely by chance, had no systematic plans for exploring that setting, and found interesting materials by "bumping into them". What hope then for the post-graduate student, the novice, except trust in Fate?[98]

Within current IT research and in CSCW (where most of the ethno-graphically informed research has appeared) one will find no solace. Here one finds three basic strands of commentary on ethnography. One, a set of papers that simply uses the term ethnography to label their study of some workplace by close observation. The actual methods used during this close observation are typically left unspecified. Each particular "CSCW ethnographer" apparently chooses for himself or herself. If they do report on their choices, they give only the most superficial rendering of what was done.

A second strand focuses on what one might call the analytic or theoretical programmes that ethnographic data may be used to inform. Unfortunately, most are rather arcane, and are of interest only to old dogs from the ethnographic traditions in sociology and anthropology and their private debates[99]. One key element of these debates has to do with the nature of ethnographic reportage as text. This harks back to the obsession that is current in sociology[100]. Other concerns include

---

[97] See Van Maanen (1988).

[98] This is not to say that this curious position has been unremarked within sociology. The contrast between the cookbook recipes offered to students in many methods books, and the varied sets of practical and analytical skills those students would actually need to use if they were to do any field work, is often made. One of the more intelligent discussions of this can be found in Bryman (1988).

[99] Myself included. See Button & Harper (1996).

[100] The book that is most often cited in relation to this debate is Clifford & Marcus (1986). A more recent collection is presented by Van Maanen (1995).

such things as how "cooperative work" can be conceived from a sociological perspective[101]; various sociological conceptions of 'organisation'[102]; sociological interpretations of negotiation[103] and sociological views of conversational interaction[104]. As it happens, this latter has produced some of the more interesting and genuine attempts to bridge between fine-grained analysis and technical design in the work of Heath and Luff, amongst others[105].

The work of these last authors notwithstanding, most of these are devoid of any concern with how to map out design choice. In the *Limits of Ethnography*, Shapiro remarks that these debates have more to do with conflicts within sociology and anthropology, and very little to do with a purposive ethnography for CSCW[106]. He recommends something of a hybrid form of ethnography, one which is specific to CSCW and IT research more generally. I shall come back to this.

As to the third set, these remark on the apparent unwillingness of most ethnographers in the CSCW field to make any serious attempt to specify design choices[107]. The concern of these papers is not with the actual work that gets done in the field, with but the motivations behind that research. Their analysis of these motivations has provoked some resentment from the sociological and anthropological voyagers in CSCW, but that analysis is, broadly speaking, correct: many of the ethnographers in CSCW have a tacit agenda that is opposed to technology in general and technologically driven change in particular. Irrespective of whether ethnography as a general modality of field work needs to carry these oppositions is a moot point[108]. In practice, this is what most ethnography in CSCW consists of and complaints about it not generating the right materials for design are then, in my view, spot on.

So in short, those who want to undertake ethnography for IT design

---

[101] For a review see Bannon & Schmidt (1992), especially pp. 12–18.

[102] See Jirotka et al. (1992).

[103] See Bannon & Schmidt (1992).

[104] See Luff et al. (1990).

[105] These researchers are prolific. Amongst their more interesting papers are Heath & Luff (1991a, 1991b).

[106] See Shapiro (1994).

[107] See Plowman et al. (1995) and also Grudin & Grinter (1995).

[108] Anderson (1997).

or CSCW in particular will not find any guidance. Of course, they may presume that what others have been doing involves some kind of systematicity. Presumably it is not a case of "anything goes"[109]. But what is it that does get done?

I want to answer that question. I am not interested in discussing the theoretical and ontological assumptions that underscore an ethnographic piece of research. I have discussed them sufficiently in the previous chapter. My concern here is what is the organisation of ethnography that is motivated by IT type research issues. I think there are two concerns one needs to consider. One has to do with the specific programmes of work that are undertaken (i.e. the things done in the field). This requires some more discussion and it is here that I will outline my own *field work programme*. And the second has to do with the location of that programme within the broader process of design and development. Here I am thinking of the categorisation that the Lancastrians[110] mapped out in their *Ethnography in Systems Design*. Let me deal with each in turn.

Field work programmes

So what is an appropriate programme for the kind of ethnography I am pointing toward? The absence of any discussion of such programmes is one of the lacunas of much reported ethnography in IT research. I have been undertaking ethnographic studies within this area for many years now and have found myself in the most unlikely places. I have done good jobs and bad jobs—some of these ethnographies have produced good materials and others have not. But I am now convinced that to be successful in the field requires a systematic, organised approach. This is all the more important, I believe, when it comes to delivering materials for IT research. For though it may be reasonable to argue that ethnographers who are in the straight sociology or anthropology trades do not need to bother with such organisation, and like so many others before, can just wait and see what they bump into (if anything at

---

[109] See Feyerabend (1975).

[110] I use the term Lancastrian since there have been quite a number of different researchers working in CSCW related projects at Lancaster. Key researchers include J. Hughes, R. Bentley, D. Randall, M. Rouncefield, M. O'Brien and D. Shapiro.

all), such an insousciant manner is inappropriate in IT research where the interests of too many people turn on the results[111].

My own programme of work is in many ways simple. It has three main components. The first of these has to do with following the career of information (and its various modalities) through an organisation. A document career is a subset or a manifestation of this. This generates the basic materials for the ethnography, an overview of the organisational processes and a basis for the determination of key sub-processes.

A second component has to do with going through "ritual inductions". I say ritual because these events do not, in themselves, necessarily guarantee that what the ethnographer understands is the truth of the matter, so much as that they symbolically display an experience that members of the setting believe everyone needs to go through if they are to "know what that workplace is about". In each setting what these rituals are varies, but they can normally be determined by evidence gained from the career examination.

The third component has to do with the motivation behind interviews and, related to that, the observations that are undertaken. By and large ethnographic interviews are reported to be semi-structured or informal. But a well organised ethnographer with IT concerns has very particular purposes when undertaking interviews. These have to do with getting to the actual, practical organisation of the things people do as against such things as what they think the ethnographer might be interested in, what they ought to be doing, or even the things they would like to do. Observations are also important to see these actualities. Although it is often important to learn about what people would like to do in their work, the bottom line, in my view, is to get to the practical realities which confront individuals in organisational life. This is what motivates the IT-cum-sociological–anthropological ethnographer.

I want to illustrate these different components with reference to three settings I have studied: air traffic control, hospitals and the Fund itself. These are sufficiently different for the general applicability of the programme to be demonstrated and to allow me to explicate the relevant details fully.

---

[111] Though this particular policy can sometimes pay dividends, my point is that one cannot rely on it. Some commentators think that it is the essential characteristic of ethnography to come up with surprises. See, for example, Nardi (1993), especially pp. 6–9.

Information careers

The term "information career" may sound as if it comes from the corporate world: seemingly pointing towards something, but at the same time vague and a little pretentious. Certainly my own corporation likes to use the term, but the meaning Xerox gives to it is quite unlike my own. When I use the term, all I am pointing towards is the fact that information is marshalled, is worked up, reviewed, circulated, used, stored and then forgotten about. Information within organisations has, if you like, a birth, a life and a death. Further, during its life, information will exist in various modalities. The most obvious is when it gets presented in documents. But sometimes the information can be in a database, and at other times it can be latched to some artefact (i.e. information may exist in the form of marks on an object going through a production line). But whatever its form, one way an ethnographer can get around an organisation is by following the career of the key information in that organisation.

To illustrate with the Fund: here information is gathered about member countries, worked up, documented in staff reports, and then "used" by the Executive Board. In broad outline, this is the information career, and this is what I oriented toward during my field work programme.

Before I say anything about that I should make clear that I had to discover what this general career looked like before I started the bulk of my field work. I did so by first reading as much material as possible on the organisation and, second, by asking those I had made my original presentation to what were the most important information processes and what were the key modalities of that information.

On the basis of this, I was able to organise the bulk of my field work in such a way as to ensure that I would look at the activities involved in the information career from beginning to end. This meant I interviewed desk officers and chiefs who gather the information used in staff reports and ultimately are the authors of those reports; secretarial and research assistant staff who help in the composition of staff reports; and participants in the review of those reports, ranging from the most junior economists to the front office chiefs and senior managers. I interviewed Assistants to Executive Board Directors who use those reports; the clerical staff who issue and release staff reports once they have been "cleared"; those who copy and print staff reports;

translators; and finally archivists. In all, 138 personnel, including 90 economists were interviewed.

The point of the programme of work was to:

1. map out the key processes of the organisation;
2. understand the diversities of work within the organisation;
3. understand how different sets of persons depend upon one another;
4. determine what were viewed as the salient junctures in the (information) career.

Now, the fact that the Fund is, in an obvious way, document-centred, made it relatively easy for the ethnographer (i.e. myself) to discover the key aspects of the information career. For, in a sense, the career of a Fund *staff report* was a manifest proxy for—if not the very embodiment of—the career of information within the Fund. It was for this reason that my programme of enquiry involved following a hypothetical staff report around the organisation. Accordingly, my task was to interview all those parties involved in the career of staff reports. But in this chapter I am talking about information careers rather than the careers of documents because it has more general applicability. Some organisations are not so clearly document-centred as the Fund. My view is that reference to the career of information (irrespective of whether that career be manifest in documents or other artefacts) is a technique through which nearly all organisations can be mapped out.

Other settings

I can justify this assertion by remarking briefly on the use of the technique in air traffic control (ATC) settings and hospitals. As I say, these settings are in themselves quite distinct, and once added to the Fund make for a bundle of workplaces that are in many ways extremely different. But nonetheless, I believe I was able to map out the key features of these organisations and organise my study of them by use of the same device: following the information career.

When I entered the operations room at London Air Traffic Control Centre, I had very little idea of the organisation of controlling work, and though I knew them to be important, I had little sense of how *flight progress strips* played an important part in the work. I had a vague idea of what went on, but that was largely superficial. To map out the organisation of the work, I traced through the career of the information that seemed to be central to their activities, as I understood them. This information related to flight progress data.

In the first instance, this information has its source in the flight plans prepared by pilots before they enter the airways. Pilots are obliged to send this information to the ATC authorities and these authorities enter it in their own flight progress data computers. Here additional data are added, including weather information and radar tracking data. These are combined to generate estimated times of arrivals for aircraft at various key points in the airways. These in turn are used to print data on flight progress strips and these are the key tools that the various individuals working at the control suites within the operations room use when they actually control aircraft.

Of most importance at the flight progress strip stage is how information on these strips is "worked up" in such a way as to ensure that what is presented is a highly accurate and cogent set of information about the dynamics of air movements. This information is only accurate for a specific and quite short period of time—usually about 5–10 minutes. This is, of course, the rub of the matter for the much celebrated ATC Project at Lancaster University[112].

Once this intensive period of interest has passed, the strip gradually works its way on to another stage in its career. In so doing, the modality of that information changes from being paper-based (on the flight strips) into being purely electronic. For the information ultimately enters another giant database, this time to be used for the charging of airlines.

Before saying more about the ATC setting I want to comment briefly on how a study of anaesthetists at an open heart surgery hospital was organised. The purpose of the study was to determine what role electronic document systems could play in their work[113]. Of importance was to determine the balance between those documents that would be

---

[112] It is perhaps worth noting that this reseach followed on from one I had been involved with previously. This prior research had mapped out the processes of ATC work as a whole. The later project focused in more detail on the interface and required the ethnographer, David Randall, to make closer observation of controlling work at the radar screens. Key research publications on this first project are: Hughes et al. (1988); Harper et al. (1989a, 1989b, 1997). As regards the second project, a number of the papers dicussing ethnography have already been cited. But see also Shapiro et al. (1991).

[113] See Harper et al. (1997).

best suited for paper media and those that would benefit from existing in digital, electronic form. To understand this, my colleagues and I organised the field work to follow the key information used in that work. This information related to the patient and was embodied in the pre-operative risk assessment form or PRA.

Accordingly we followed a hypothetical PRA around the organisation and observed what activities are undertaken at each stage in its career. Anaesthetists start the information career by going through a patient's file at the ward reception and using that to create a PRA. They then take this draft PRA to the patient's bedside and undertake a pre-operative interview. Notes from this are added to the PRA which is then used in the anaesthetic room on the following day. The patient is brought here prior to the operation. As its name suggests, it is here that the anaesthetic is administered. We then observed what anaesthetists do in the operating theatre and, finally, traced how the PRAs were used post-operatively. As part of this process, we interviewed all those involved, namely, the ward sisters who prepared the patients' notes, the trainee anaesthetists, the registrars and consultants who constructed and used the PRAs, and the secretaries and administrators who used the PRAs post-operatively.

Comment

I do not want to say too much about the results of the research either at the hospital or in ATC. What I do want to do is make some further remarks on what I have suggested are the basic purposes of such programmes of work and, in particular, on how important it is to map out the key processes within an organisation and how this in turn enables one to recognise the salient junctures in that process. With this, one not only gains an overview, but one can also make effective comparisons.

Taking ATC as an example, I was able to use the information career to compare civilian and military ATC. I was interested in what were the important junctures in the work, and the key stages in each domain. As it happened, both had more or less identical overall processes (i.e. the same information career), but what was crucial, what was important within each career (what was a "problem" if you will), was different in each.

In simple terms, in civilian ATC the important stage occurs when the controllers are using the strips. The activities here are complex and subtle, and this reflects the overall organisation of the airways and the relationship between pilots and controllers. In a phrase, because the civilian airspace system is flexible, the controlling is complex. In contrast, in military control the juncture in the information career when controllers actually use strips is one that causes few problems. Controlling in military operations is, to put it bluntly, rather facile. Controllers rarely have any difficulties undertaking this part of their work; it is relaxed and unproblematic. This is because of the character of the relationship between the pilots and the controllers and the different flight procedures in operation. Military controllers have to bring military pilots together, and it is the pilots who solve all collision difficulties.

However, military control does have its problems, but these occur at another juncture. This juncture is when the rostering of staff occurs. For, in military operations, there can be very little prediction of what the workload will be: air exercises will be undertaken at short notice, reflecting such things as the weather and the need for the practice of emergency operations. As a result, it is difficult to determine how many staff should be on duty at any one time. Often military control finds it has too many staff idle; a few hours later it may have too few staff on duty. Their problem within the career of information is being able to predict what work will arrive and when.

So reference to the information career can enable one to map out fundamental differences in the organisation of two (or more) work-places. Further, it enables one to determine matters that are relevant to any specific locus of work within that career. If one wants to design systems to support work, one needs to bear in mind these factors. For instance, an interface for the use of electronic flight progress strips in civilian ATC needs to be designed in recognition of the fact that the relationship between the controller and the pilots and the patterns of airspace procedure they are part of is extremely important. It is not solely a matter of an interface between an individual and data base. Rather, that interface is located within a broader process[114].

Similarly with anaesthetists, observation of the career of information in their work led to the discovery that although one might imagine that the main part of their work was undertaken in the operating theatre, in fact what was crucial was getting data on to

---

[114] See Harper & Sellen (1995).

the PRAs in the pre-operative interviews and from the ward room, and being able to use that information in the anaesthetic room. Thereafter their work was mainly to observe what happens to a patient, making notes, but effectively taking a back seat. To some extent, what was most salient for an anaesthetist, then, was the information-gathering stage, not necessarily the drama that unfolds when an incision is made into a patient's chest.

Ritual inductions

One of the problems ethnographers often have to deal with is how to be accepted by those studied. This is sometimes called the problem of *rapport*. Unfortunately the problems involved are all too frequently exaggerated and claims that the ethnographer has to "go native" are best taken with a pinch of salt. But this is not to deny the fact that there are problems. From the IT research point of view, the concern is not so much to ensure that the ethnographer is "one of them" as to ensure that his or her views are treated with respect by those observed. By respect I mean that the ethnographic analysis is treated as cogent, accurate and worth taking heed of. In short, that it is sufficient to base design decisions on[115]. Here the issue is whether the ethnographer is entitled to have a view which those studies ought to accept, or whether that view will be rejected out of hand. The question is not just to do with how thorough an ethnographer has been in his or her programme of work (how many individuals they have interviewed and the extent of the observation of the information career and so on). The issue is rather consideration of what activities an ethnographer has undertaken in order to determine whether his or her views are to be treated as from the "inside" rather than the "outside" of work. This is not an empirical question but a *moral* one.

Let me illustrate. In Chapter 8, I will explain that many members of the Fund said to me "Look, to understand this place you have to go on a mission". Although I was always keen to go on one (as part of my field work programme), just why *having* to go on one, what it was about *being there* that would transform my outlook and identity was

---

[115] Gaining the respect of those studied can be very difficult when an ethnographer has been "tainted by technology". See Harper (1996a).

unclear. Nonetheless, once it had been agreed I would go on one (and of course once I had been on one), the treatment I received from those I interviewed altered. Interviewees were much more forthcoming; people were more frank and offered me materials that hitherto had remained closed.

Why was this? One phrase comes to mind here. When I told one of the front office staff I was interviewing that I was about to go on an Article IV mission he suddenly paused and said, "Oh, well you are going to really understand this place then! You are doing it properly. Well, let's get down to business!" At first I was slightly insulted by this. Was he implying that if I had not arranged to go on a mission I would not have been undertaking a serious study? Once I had got over the pique, I realised what he was alluding to. He was pointing towards the fact that to understand the experience of life at the Fund one needs to understand what goes on on a mission. Although this can be described, there is no equal to being there. For it is in this way the observer can *suffer* along with everyone else on the mission. They too can see how hard everyone works, how tempers get frayed, how difficult it sometimes is to make the figures work. Going on a mission is, if you like, the most important stage of the initiation ceremony transforming an outsider to an insider. In going on a mission, knowledge would not necessarily be altered, but the moral identity of the observer would.

Sometimes these transformations do alter the materials that are made available (as at the Fund), and sometimes they do not. Further, what the transformation might be in any particular setting will vary. In some places these rituals are rather ordinary, everyday events. In other settings, they are considerably more dramatic.

If observing discussions between a Fund mission chief and a Minister of Finance is obviously a privileged "insider" thing to do, in other workplaces just turning up can be sufficient. Take the case of ATC, for example. The fact that I was willing to spend several weeks—indeed months—watching controllers at work was key to getting my analysis taken seriously by those controllers. If truth be known, I reached a threshold of understanding within weeks of starting my study, but further stay was needed to pay respect to the operations room staff. I also had to get my "hands dirty". In this case, this did not mean actually controlling aircraft but turning up when no one else wanted to: namely, for the night shift on Saturdays. The fact that I turned up for several Saturdays in a row became proof that I "really wanted to know".[116]

In the case of the anaesthetists, the rituals were more difficult to specify. It was certainly not in the watching of an operation. (For one thing, in the hospital in question there were so many operations that it was like a production line. An operation was thus hardly a special event. For another, there were too many strangers observing operations to make it a privilege to be there.) Rather, it came through recognising what one might loosely describe as industrial relations. One facet of this was the considerable bitterness felt by trainees about consultant anaesthetists. One did not have to take sides here since the consultants recognised and accepted the grounds for the bitterness (though most did little about it)[117]. Another had to do with the animosity between anaesthetists and other clinical professionals, particularly surgeons. By commenting on these topics and discussing them in our draft analyses, we came to be treated as viewing anaesthetic work from "within".

Other inductions take even more simple forms. Office life is obviously something that IT researchers look at a great deal. Much of office administration is uneventful and, perhaps more importantly, one often has difficulty getting those studied to talk about their work. "You don't really want to know" they say. So how does the ethnographer get an insider's view? One way is to pick up on the industrial relations circumstances in the office in much the same way as I have mentioned we did in hospital life. But another more effective way is simply to ask to do some of the work in question. It is only then that one gets treated as genuinely interested in that work. It is then that

---

[116] It also led me to discover that UFOs are rather regular occurences in the sky at night. This had nothing to do with the research but was very interesting. To describe the events: all the controllers would see (if "see" is the right word) is what the pilots described over the headphones. For the radar processing systems systematically removed all UFOs from the radar screens on the grounds that an unidentified flying object is of no interest to a controller. Sometimes these UFOs would cause a great deal of commotion, with pilots shouting at each other and calling excitedly at the wonders in the night sky. The controllers would sit around the radars and listen to the radio talk, gazing at the purple blips on the screens that told them nothing of what was really going on.

[117] There is no news in this. Many studies of hospital life have noted the same. But to illustrate from our own research, trainees often described the consultants as "braindead" and the consultants describe the trainees as "cheap labour for the dirty work".

those who ordinarily undertake it will start explaining what one needs to know to do it. From their perspective, their work is still boring and unremarkable, but "since you really want to know", they will share the details of how it is done. Then they will treat you as an "insider".

Sometimes the ethnographer simply has to wait. In police work, for example, which I have not mentioned so far but which I have studied extensively[118], the induction does not occur when the ethnographer turns up for night duty, nor when he or she helps break up a pub brawl. The transformation comes about when the ethnographer is taken to a *domestic dispute*. The ethnographer will only be taken to such events once the police officers trust in the ethnographer's ability not to make premature judgements about who is or is not at fault. These matters are nearly always very difficult to determine in "a domestic", and it is often very divisive to try to ascertain. What the police officers need to do, and require the ethnographer to do, is to grieve with the victims over the damage they have done to their bodies and the mess they have made of their lives.

Undertaking interviews and observing work

The last component of the programme relates to the motivations behind the interviews and observation of work. Ethnographic interviews are typically described as informal and open-ended. One mistake is to think that anything at all is of interest to the interviewer. As Anderson notes, for the sociological and anthropological ethnographer there certainly is a baggage of concerns that they carry with them and this lies implicit in the questions they ask[119]. In IT research it seems to me that one still needs such baggage but they will not be exactly the same. I have discussed my own specific concerns during my research at the Fund in the previous chapter. But it is perhaps worth giving some more time to explain how they showed themselves in the interviews I undertook.

One may begin to unpack what is distinct to the approach I used by considering what one of the most eloquent exponents of sociological and anthropological ethnography has to say on the subject. The individual I have in mind is Clifford Geertz. He commenced his *The Interpretation of Cultures* with the following definition of sociological

---

[118] See Harper (1991b).

[119] See Anderson (1994a).

inquiry[120]. "Believing, with Max Weber, that man is an animal suspended in webs of significance he himself has spun, I take culture to be those webs, and the analysis of it to be therefore not an experimental science in search of law but an interpretative one in search of meaning" (1973: 5). The subsequent essays in that book deal with sacred symbols, death by Suttee, and perhaps most famously, Balinese cockfighting. These are aspects of human action that it seems quite reasonable to claim can only be analysed through reference to such things as religious systems and moral conduct, patterns of social status and more. Quite obviously what Geertz describes is not a world of silent orbs and eddying bodies (i.e. one without meaning), but a world of complex symbols, of religious faith, arcane rituals and, moreover, to Western eyes at least, peculiar characters. In other settings, nearer to home than the Far East or the Atlas Mountains, it may be claimed that there are no exotic ways of seeing, no shocking and inexplicable rituals like Suttee. Therefore, what is the level of meaning one is after? What would one want to describe?

Consider office work. Does one need to delve into the inner recesses of an office worker's mind to understand what he or she is about? Does one have to link their working routines to deeply held beliefs about the relationship between, say, the stars above and the Managing Director below? Perhaps in some cases, but not as a whole. Similarly, one can ask about my concerns here: the activities of individuals at the Fund. Are there complex meanings to the things that staff of this organisation do? Are the Fund's staff like clowns to a Martian—living in a world whose meanings are nigh-on inexplicable?

The answer is no. Office work is much more mundane than the things that Geertz writes about in his studies of Indonesia and elsewhere. This does not mean that Geertz is wrong or that his argument is irrelevant. It means that it becomes difficult to see the parallels between what he offers as *thick description* and what one might seek in interviews of the Fund's staff. So what, then, was I after when I interviewed the economists, the chiefs, the staff assistants and the administrators?

Let me answer this question at first indirectly. Let me describe some of the things that I was not interested in during these interviews, or rather treated as interesting background information.

At the beginning of each day, there are gatherings of senior econo-

---

[120] See Geertz (1973).

mists at the Fund, often but not always divided according to area department, in the canteen. These "breakfast clubs", as they are known, are informal forums for the exchange of gossip and intrigue, and for the sharing and debating of current Fund "views". But membership of them is also a symbol of status: newcomers rarely venture into them; individuals can only join when invited. Those who do not participate, outsiders as it were, talk about these clubs as the cliques that "really control" such things as promotion and informal measures of status within the Fund. It is also believed that this control has to some extent abated in recent years as the Fund has increased in size, reducing the knowledge individual members have of the organisation as a whole. Prior to these changes, when everyone knew everyone else, "in the old days", these clubs are said to have been an important mechanism whereby information about candidates for promotion was exchanged. Here, careers were made or broken[121].

Not only are there these clubs in the Fund but there are broader divides that are often spoken about as setting one part of the institution against another. Here I am thinking of how the area and functional departments are said to often engage in battles with one another over budgets, staffing and access to data over the computer network. When they are not busy fighting these internal battles, they are often at loggerheads with the executive staff—the Managing Director and his Deputies. All these disputes are often characterised in medieval terms: the area and functional departments are fiefdoms, their directors being medieval barons and the chiefs feudal lords. The rights and privileges of these fiefdoms are fiercely defended against the intrusions of one another and particularly the advances of the centralising monarch, the Managing Director, and his coterie of staff in the Managing Director's office and its sheriffs, the Deputy Managing Director's, or the DMD's[122].

Those I interviewed would happily talk about breakfast clubs and the conflict between the barons in the area departments. For these are the things of which gossip and work-chat is made. These are the topics that staff of the Fund use to spice up their coffee breaks. And there is some truth in these conversations. But the concern that drove my interviews was focused on something else, something more detailed and more

---

[121] Those who are interested in the role of informal groupings in organisations should see the now aged but nonetheless fascinating Dalton (1950).

[122] This view would appear to be current in many organisations. See Davenport et al. (1992).

mundane. What I was after, and indeed what I think IT motivated ethnography should be after, are the details of the work that individuals do, the particularities through which the various processes that need to be done get undertaken.

The purpose here is not to elicit "juicy examples" (though sometimes these can be very useful in illustrating the character of the work[123]). The question is to get to the organisation of the work at a level that reflects the practical concerns of the individuals who undertake it. It is the practicalities that are at issue here, not the gloss that is built on top of the practicalities. In this case, the details I was after had to do with the relationship Fund staff had to the documents they had at hand. That relationship would reflect such things as whether the documents in question were delivered to them for review or were objects that they were trying to constitute (write, compose) themselves. There were of course other forms of relationships to documents.

Unfortunately it is not always easy to get those interviewed to talk about these details. Often interviewees do not think that it is these kinds of details that the ethnographer is interested in. As I remarked a moment ago, some individuals cannot believe that the ethnographer really wants to know. Sometimes one has to go through certain routines or tricks to get the interviewees to believe in that interest. But more often it is little more than directing the interview.

This is well illustrated in the work of Eleanor Wynn. Although her voice seems to have disappeared from the academic community recently, the example I take from one of the papers she co-authored with Lucy Suchman and presented below is one of the best illustrations of how to get interviewees to talk about the matters of concern[124]. The example consists of a transcript of an interview Wynn undertook. I will break up the transcript to highlight some issues. Here is the first section, commencing with the claim by the "user" that there is not much to her work:

E (interviewer): Did you describe your job to me already? Have we gotten that far?

G (user): I'm in the Collections department. I'm the Lead Collector. You've met Jerry and Christine? OK, they're in my group.

There's not much to say about it . . . We just collect past-due balances, and we do a lot of things at—you do a lot of customer care, you do a lot of

---

[123] Such examples can be found in Randall et al. (1995).

[124] See Suchman & Wynn (1984).

check refunds, and you're cleaning their accounts, and a lot of it is not even delinquent accounts, but *problem* accounts, they have the money . . . and it's just not the fact that you convince the customer that they *owe* the money, number one, which, you know, is a big step right there, but then to get it through their system, you have to understand what they have to do to get a check cut, and you have to understand their system a little bit. You have to be able to . . . know how to set a fire under somebody to get that moving, if it needs to be prioritized. And that, at times—people don't understand how hard that can be.

The key to the interview is to pursue the pointers that are nearly always made in the first few remarks. Wynn shows us what to do:

E: What is involved in that, "setting a fire under somebody"?

G: Well, see, I have to—you begin to immediately move it upward, up through the management, okay? You start with a clerk, okay? They definitely cannot solve the problem. It's out of their hands. Okay, you ask whose hands is it in? Who can make the decision—the buyer.

Okay, you call the buyer, the buyer says, "Um, the reason why I'm not paying this is, I said I would pay *twenty* dollars and seventy-*three* cents for a carton, not twenty-*four* dollars and seventy-*two* cents, which you bill me on this five thousand dollar shipment of paper." So then you say, "That's all I need to know, let me get back with you." You get back, you go through your billing system, you try to find out, you know . . .

In the meantime, let's suppose time is running out and you do not have time to get a billing adjustment through. So you got to sit there and think, *How can I get this person to pay this invoice?* It's wrong, they got the wrong PO, they billed them wrong, Accounts Payable doesn't want to do nothing with it. So you call them back up and say, "I'm not asking you to pay something that is not due. What I want you to do is to pay *according to your PO*. Pay that invoice short, okay?" Then he says, "I will not pay the invoice short because I've had too many problems with that. Unless I get a typed invoice from you, specifically."

So you sit there and think, I can't go through the billing system, it's too late. I can type them an invoice, set the system going through the billing system at the same time, co-ordinate that so when he pays the check short, there will be a balance on the account. When the credit issues through I'll have the billing department hold that credit, deliver that credit to me, not deliver it to the customer 'cuz the customer will wonder *Why am I getting the credit* if they think they're already gonna receive a bill, right? Then I would just clean up their account later. But in the meantime . . .

E: So you kind of short circuit it?

G: Yeah. So in the meantime I have got to type them an invoice telling them that this is an invoice for the amount of supplies, send that out there, send copies to everybody, prepare a billing adjustment, send that on its way and get the appropriate signatures, call up the buyer, call up the sales rep, tell them to meet together, tell him to present the invoice to him. Then he will release it to Accounts Payable.

Once Accounts Payable gets it, then you get a-hold and she'll say, "I have your invoice here, but it cannot be cut for two weeks." Your cut-off is one week. Okay. You say, "May I speak to your supervisor please," in a nice way because you don't want to offend them, to think, *May I speak to your supervisor please.* You know, you don't want to say, make em feel like, *because you are so incompetent*, you know. What you want to say is, Well fine, thank you, I understand that's your job, you know. Just, you have a job to do like I do, I just want to speak to your supervisor so that maybe we can work out something, that I need that check a little bit early, if we can work out *some* way in your system working with our system so that we can get this out early. So they transfer you to their supervisor and she comes on and says, "That's it, I cannot do it. I can get the check out, but maybe two hours later than you need it." So you're getting closer, okay?

E (laughing): Yeah!

G: So then you go to Jennie: you tell my manager to call this manager, and you tell her what the situation is. She calls, maybe she can't get them. So then *she* goes to Chuck, which is our Controller here. And when you get a call from the Controller of XYZ Corporation, you know it's gone up quite a bit. And then *he* will call the supervisor there and tell her, "If you can't get that check out to me by that date will you please let me know so that I can call somebody who can get it out. Either if I have to talk to your controller, or whoever." And it's amazing how many times that—you don't have that all the time, but you have situations where you're working with about five or six people, and you're co-ordinating—just to get a check cut.

Now this complex—one might also be tempted to suggest long-winded procedure—may appear to be just the kind of thing that one would want to tidy up with technology. That would miss the point I am wanting to make, however. I am not interested in this particular process, so much as wanting to illustrate the level of detail that it is necessary to uncover in an interview. Perhaps this process should have been automated in some way. (Wynn and Suchman are rather quiet on this point too.) What I am drawing attention to is that the ethnographer needs to investigate all the oddities, the strange cul-de-sac, the apparently arbitrary social processes and ritualised organisational protocols that embody the work in question. They need to understand what it means to "light a fire", as the subject described her work.

Let me illustrate this with the concerns I raised in my interviews with the Fund's desk officers. At a superficial level the desk officers are responsible for maintaining information about a particular country. But what does this mean? What do they do on a day to day basis? How does this work show itself in the documents they produce?

I was particularly interested in what they found it *economic* to do rather than what they thought it might be ideal to do. I was not motivated by a concern to ironicise their work, to find evidence to show that the desk officers were failing in their task. I was primarily interested in prising open what it is they do in practice—the mundane organisation of their work. What I found was that for many desk officers, the collection and management of information was undertaken on a demand-driven basis. These demands were related to the documents they were asked to produce as part of their routine cycle of work (the mission-related documents and the Fund's *World Economic Outlook* for example) or on a more ad hoc basis (for instance a brief for when a Deputy Managing Director hosted a visit from the President of the country the desk officer was responsible for).

One consequence of this is that desk officers' data management tends to be demand-driven. In this sense their work consists of a matrix of competing concerns, prioritised on a day by day, and task by task basis[125]. What I needed to understand was how the nature of the documents they produced—most importantly the mission related—imposed certain characteristics on their data management practices. For it was the documents they worked towards that drove the structure of their data management activities rather than say, some idealised view of a generally applicable data management process.

This level of analysis—getting to the mundane details as some sociologists like to describe it (namely, ethnomethodologists)—should be the basic fabric of material that is gathered, but does not limit what the ethnographer can create in the deriving analysis of work practice. For my case is that one should start with this level, since this provides an empirical foundation. One can then add to that foundation a whole host of elaborations that may, in one way or another, move on from and develop matters first pointed out in the details.

Thus a text which deals with what would appear to be similar

---

[125] For a discussion of this in office work generally see Gasser (1986).

institutional processes as one finds at the Fund (i.e. essentially to do with economic policy analysis) but at a much more abstract level, namely Heclo and Wildavsky's *Private Government and Public Money*, is not that divorced from what is possible on the basis of my programme of enquiries. In that book, Heclo and Wildavsky analyse the tensions that arise between civil servants who remain in their departments for many years and the politically appointed directors of these departments who will only "survive" a short period, perhaps months, rarely years[126]. As far as one can tell from the appendix on methods in that text, it does not look as if Heclo and Wildavsky did focus on the level of detail I commend, but it does seem that one can get to their more abstract level of analysis from starting there. Moreover, I would argue that it is in the way in which the mundane details of daily work are dealt with that one finds the manifestation of the broader patterns of dependence and trust on which Heclo and Wildavsky focus[127].

This leads me back to the issue of culture in the workplace. A short time ago I said that I was not too interested in breakfast clubs or the notion that the Fund is made up of baronies. Even so, I am interested in culture at the Fund, but in another sense. For I would argue that just as Heclo and Wildavsky uncover the salient features of relationships between political appointees and civil servants (and this they call the culture of government), so too is my analysis about important elements of culture within the Fund. Here though, the focus is on such things as a culture that recognises and reflects the time pressures that desk officers find themselves working within; that treats policy analysis as a particular mode of activity with associated criteria of objectivity and assessment. It is an approach that recognises and tries to explain how that activity is also based in very large part on text and textual commentaries as embodied in such things as briefing papers and staff reports. From this view, Fund culture turns around essentially *literary* tasks (i.e. writing and reading). I will have a great deal more to say later on these matters in the book, especially once I have described the mission process in more detail.

But irrespective of what one comes to define as the culture of a workplace, the ethnographer should start with the details. It is in reference to these that that culture can be mapped out. Although

---

[126] See Heclo & Wildavsky (1974) and also Heclo (1977). For a more recent study of policy making, see Thain & Wright (1996).

[127] This is a point I shall develop in Chapter 8. See Button & Sharrock (1993).

members of an organisation may well volunteer aspects of what they believe is their organisational culture from the first moment an interview is undertaken, the ethnographer should put their remarks on hold until he or she has understood the essential details of the work. It is only in this way that ethnographers can ensure the empirical adequacy of their analysis.

Interviews are only a part of the techniques used to learn about the work in question. Another is to observe the work and even to undertake it if possible. *Participant observation* is sometimes treated as the sine qua non of good ethnography. This is errant nonsense. In some settings it is certainly easy to observe, but downright impossible to participate. In ATC one can while away hours watching the work, but it would be extremely unwise actually to undertake that work (even if one were allowed to). One needs to observe and sometimes to supplement that with participation, if it is appropriate. It is certainly not essential.

Even so, in some workplaces it is difficult to know what to observe. In police organisations, for example, certain of the middle managers (namely Inspectors) have quite literally nothing to do: they cannot patrol the streets since they are too senior, but the organisation does not require them to do any administration. They find themselves in the symbolic middle: neither Bobbies (an English term) fighting crime nor senior staff determining strategy.

But other activities which might seem at first glance intangible are especially good to observe. Meetings are a case in point. At the Fund, meetings during which a mission team prepared a briefing paper were particularly informative (in ways I shall describe), as were meetings between the member authorities and the team itself. As regards the latter, here there were intricate rituals of negotiation and discussion, elaborate patterns of deference and status that one expects to find in all high level meetings (though one cannot predict beforehand what their forms will take). Meetings between the mission members both before and during the mission were worth observing because it was during these that the key concerns of the team were discussed, worked over and refined. It was here that the ambiguities were clarified and the rationale of the mission reiterated.

Ethnography within a process

My last concern in this chapter is the location of ethnographic enquiries within a larger process. At the outset I mentioned one paper that attempts to list the various roles ethnography can have. This was Hughes et al.'s "Moving out of the control room: Ethnography in systems design"[128]. Here the suggestion is made that there are at least four ways in which ethnography can connect to design.

The first involves undertaking an ethnography concurrent with design. This was the process used in the Lancaster ATC project. The ethnographer would visit the work site and then report back findings to the design team. The team would then develop new, more detailed, questions and the ethnographer would return to the site to find answers[129]. The second process is one where the ethnography is undertaken quickly and roughly. Hughes and colleagues use a pejorative term here to distinguish between the "proper length" that they assume to be required for ethnographic studies and the short time periods sometimes available in design processes. I think the problem is exaggerated since a well organised ethnography can uncover a great deal in a very short time, depending upon the setting. Their own comments derive from a study that involved only a few hours of observation and the quality of that work seems to undermine their own complaint about it being "quick and dirty"[130]. The third is using ethnography to evaluate systems. Ethnography can be particularly effective here since it can deal with issues and complexities that impinge on system use that more formal evaluation techniques simply cannot deal with[131]. The fourth involves using ethnography to re-examine previous studies of the workplace in question[132].

The ethnography reported in this book consisted of two parts, each within a distinct process. The first fitted into none of these categories being more the result of serendipity than anything else. As I explained earlier, by the late 1980s and early 1990s, the Fund, like many organisations, had come to the realisation that it needed better understanding its own work practices and its own culture if it was to make more effective use of the investment it made in technology. At the same time, the laboratory I work for was seeking to undertake an ethnographic case study of technology in contemporary organisational life. Our interests then coincided.

---

[128] See Hughes et al. (1994).

[129] See Hughes et al. (1993b).

[130] See Rouncefield et al. (1994).

[131] See Randall et al. (1996).

[132] See Hughes et al. (1993b).

However, the Fund was sufficiently motivated by the results from the first study to help finance a further one during which a more focused examination of authoring work within the area departments was undertaken. A concern here was to determine the likely role and benefits (or otherwise) of new document editors, especially of a structuring kind (e.g. SGML (standard generalised mark-up language) editors and the associated structured document databases)[133]. In this respect, the first study of the Fund and its leading to a second, more detailed one, was similar to the procedure used in the ATC project at Lancaster. At first it was a "pure" ethnography, and then a second, subsequent study examining a predetermined area of work practice and technology took place. The combined research from both Fund studies is also expected to be revisited in a few years' time thus making the ethnographic analysis a benchmark for the future—a role that has not been mentioned in the literature before.

The four different processes in which ethnography can play a part in design are not likely to be the only ones, as the idea of benchmarking suggests. I do not think it appropriate to remark on what those other processes might be since it is more important at this juncture to discuss the relationship between a text such as this and design. As it happens, some of the work I have undertaken with the Fund does fit into the various categories Hughes describes. But clearly this particular book is about something else. This leads me back to my opening gambit: that I hope to offer some guidance as to how to move towards the future by describing the present. In this sense, this text has a different relationship to design than the ethnographic studies reported by Hughes and his colleagues.

What that relationship is begs a number of questions that need to be noted—though not necessarily answered—before I can move on to the empirical investigations that follow. Amongst these is the discursive nature of ethnographic reportage. It has been a tradition, one might say almost a necessity, for ethnographic findings to be presented at considerable length. A book is the typical product. Within sociology and social anthropology such length is not viewed as a problem—indeed

---

[133] This research also involved A.J. Sellen, M. Eldridge and W. Newman, all of Rank Xerox Research Centre (RXRC), Cambridge, UK. This project also involved the investigation of interdisciplinary techniques for the analysis and description of work processes. Published papers on this part of the project include: Harper & Newman (1996); Newman et al. (1996); and Sellen & Harper (1996).

quite the opposite. It is seen as essential to preserve the thoroughness required. But how is this discursiveness of benefit for the purpose I have set myself?

Let me point towards another issue: that a book-based ethnographic reportage is likely to cover a far broader range of issues than designers will necessarily need. Of course in part this may well be one of the very benefits of ethnography. But often designers may need to know about only one part of a social setting, albeit that an understanding of the broader context of that setting will also be useful. Is the analysis I offer here too general to derive any specific recommendations?

A third problem might have to do with the thoroughness of the ethnography. How can the designer be sure that I cover all the relevant details? After all, many details may not have been perceived as important when the field work was done or may have "slipped through" during the writing up process. How can this be checked? One cannot replicate ethnography in the same way that one can repeat, for instance, a laboratory experiment. To answer this and the preceding questions leads me on to the conclusion of this chapter.

Conclusion

Let me answer these questions in the following way. My hope is that though this text may be somewhat longer than designers may be used to, it offers them an analysis of the relationship between documents and organisational action. As I said in the introductory chapter, I believe this can be a resource for design thinking. As regards the text's discursiveness, I hope that this is justified to the extent that I am able to convey the complex interweave of issues that need to be thought about. One of the problems that Kling and other researchers drew attention to in the early 1980s was the excessive simplicity of descriptions of work practice. And this leads me on to the related and last issue, the one of thoroughness.

For though I will be (and have been thus far) discursive this does not meant that I will be able to cover every aspect of Fund work practice. There are a number of reasons for this. First of all, there is the question of the representativeness of the materials I uncovered. Often this is viewed as a problem unique or peculiar to the analyst (be they ethnographic or any other sort of "analyst") and not one for those studied.

This is a mistake. Members of organisations are all too aware of similar problems.

So it was at the Fund. They know for themselves that there are differences in missions according to such things as the expertise of the country in question, according to the amount of macroeconomic data available and differences to do with the kinds of problems the member authorities have to deal with. There is also the fundamental difference between a routine surveillance mission and a negotiating mission. Fund staff have to orient to these differences and yet ensure that member countries get equal treatment. With this in mind, the same staff were at pains to point out that a study which confined itself to only one mission—as mine did—would be limited. I believe that they were right. From this view, study of more Fund missions would need to be undertaken to create a *thorough ethnographic record.*

Nonetheless, I think that my analysis of just one case does provide substantive insight into Fund work practice to stand alone. Feedback from Fund staff would appear to confirm this. Whether those outside the Fund—readers of this book, for example—feel the same is not yet clear.

It is perhaps worth noting why I studied only one mission. The reason was this: if a Fund mission lasts for only two or three weeks, my ethnographic mission to Washington lasted many months. It took that long to understand the main principles of the institution and to observe a single Article IV mission. To undertake a study of another mission would have prolonged my own travelling and to be blunt, after so many months, I had had enough.

There was another side to this desire to call an end to my work. And this related to the fact that the mission team I observed had had enough of me by the time we returned to Washington. Not in the sense that they found my presence irritating. As it happened the chief— the boss as he was called—remarked that "(your) cheerful countenance had helped keep everyone's spirits up". But nonetheless, he and his team felt that they had done their fair share of providing access to Fund activities. As a result he did not allow me to observe the work of constructing the Arcadian staff report. I think that the Arcadian mission chief (and the mission team) were being perfectly reasonable in refusing further access. One of the other things that is so lacking in ethnographic reportage is full acknowledgement of the burden the ethnographer imposes. In this case, as I say, after two weeks (on mission) the chief and his team had had enough of me.

Still, there was one important consequence of this: I could not observe in detail the process of constituting the particular staff report. Instead my resource for understanding the post-mission process was an amalgam of materials deriving from interviews with members of other missions. (As it happens, many of these discussions did lead to aspects of the Arcadian staff report.)

Finally, the process of constructing this book has meant that a lot of materials have been left aside. Earlier on I remarked that one of the outcomes of doing an information career analysis is that that it enables one to recognise the salient junctures within an organisation. Thereby one can discover where "the action" occurs; thereby one can find out what an organisation is "all about". Within the Fund—as should be clear—this juncture is the mission process. But in coming to focus on that I have had to compromise my analyses of other elements of the Fund's activities. An additional factor here has been the need to present a text that has a sufficient narrative structure to hold the reader. As Clifford and Marcus note, the construction of ethnographic stories can sometimes lead to certain issues slipping from view[134]. I am sure that this has happened to some extent here.

In these ways then my ethnography suffers from the problems and advantages of all ethnography. But that said, I hope that what I provide is illustrative of how ethnography can be a resource. My view is that ethnographic analysis (represented in this case by a book but it could take many other forms such as short papers and reports, presentations, workshops, scenario-based design analyses and so on) can be linked to design considerations. One way it can do so is by a systematic investigation of the organisation at large. The concept of an information career is meant to be helpful in this. There are doubtless other ways in which the ethnographic technique can be refined. But disregarding what they may be, what I offer is what one might call a hybrid ethnography—one that maps out the present to help navigation of the future.

---

[134] See Clifford & Marcus (1986)

CHAPTER 4
A sketch of the Fund

The Fund is one of those institutions whose name is often heard and whose role, largely invisible to the general public, is often described as fundamental to the international financial system. Certainly, the Fund does have a very important role to play in international monetary affairs, but all too often that role remains obscure, clouded not so much in mystique but in dubious assertions about its hidden motives or supposed political agenda. The Fund is, for some, an icon of the West's exploitation of the underdeveloped world; for others, it is a symbol of a now dated Keynesian vision of economic order; for yet others, it is an institution that forces monetarist policies on unwilling governments; finally, for others, it is an institution that props up inefficient regimes[135]. In short, there are almost as many versions of what the Fund does as there are people who have heard of it[136].

These muddled perceptions are not helped by the fact that what the Fund does is constantly changing or, as the Fund would like to have it, constantly evolving. For, since it first opened its doors in 1946, it has

---

[135] For a concise review of some of the issues that cause contention about the Fund's role, see *The Economist*, 12 October, 1991. These debates are often more to do with the general context of the Fund's activity, rather than the particular manner or praxis of its activities. Thus, the Fund is often cited in discussions of development. Here, such things as structural adjustment programmes are the subject of fierce critique. But the exact nature of any Fund structural adjustment programme has rarely been examined directly, and instead such programmes have been bundled up with analyses of the World Bank's activities. Though they are conjoined, it needs to be clear that the Fund's concerns and the Bank's are distinct. One particular difference relates to the Fund's concerns with macroeconomic decision-making rather than with specific development projects. As the anthropologists Gardner and Lewis note, outside of the economic paradigm itself, there is very little examination of what macroeconomics consists of as a social practice (Gardner & Lewis, 1996, pp. ix). For discussion of the IMF from within the economics "paradigm", see Bandow & Vasques (1992).

[136] The Fund is not unique in being an institution about which little is understood. Many of the institutions in the world of international monetary exchange and finance are obscure to the general public. Two texts which go some way toward bringing light into this area are Block (1977) and Solomon (1995).

gradually but continually changed its role. Sometimes this has been
due to changes in international circumstances and sometimes this has
been because of its own initiatives. I will not describe this evolution in
detail, suffice to say that the most important thing I want to convey in
this chapter is that the Fund has become a *surveillance institution*. I
take this term from Manuel Guitián[137]. He uses it because the Fund is
an organisation that gathers and analyses information about its members to ensure that they abide by its code of conduct. This surveillance
is not only of those members who are currently using Fund resources
but of all its membership, since the Fund takes the view that the
internal monetary policies of each and every country have implications
at an international level.

The Fund's surveillance role necessarily has implications for the
organisation of the institution, for the practices of its staff, and for
the documents produced. The information production work and the
staff reports which derive from it are the main staple of the Fund's
economists. Moreover, ensuring the adequacy of the information contained in staff reports requires elaborate processes of review, and these
are a key characteristic of the Fund's organisational structure, as well
as being bound up with its culture.

Overview of the chapter

To explain how the Fund has come to be a surveillance institution and
what that means, I shall organise my discussion in the following way. I
shall describe the founding of the Fund at the Bretton Woods conference and then say something about the code of conduct the Fund
obliges its members to abide by. I shall then provide a quick history
of the institution and its role in terms of phases. I shall draw attention
to five phases.

1. The period from the founding of the Fund in 1946 through to 1966.
2. The period between 1966 and 1971 when international liquidity
   problems began to show themselves.
3. The period from 1972 to 1978 when the US dollar was taken off
   gold convertibility and when the second amendment to the Fund's

---

[137] See Guitián (undated) and Guitián (1992).

Articles was made. Here I will also sketch out the form of Fund lending at this time.

4. The period from 1978 to 1982 which saw the worst recession since before the war.
5. The period from 1985 until the present.

I shall then outline how the current pattern of Fund activity is reflected in its Articles. I then describe the current organisational structure of the Fund before concluding with some remarks on my concern with the Fund's documents[138].

Bretton Woods

The Fund's duties were set out at a conference attended by represent-atives of Britain, the USA and their war-time allies, at Bretton Woods, a village in New Hampshire, in July 1944. The goal of the participants at Bretton Woods was to build a new economic order from scratch. They believed it was not enough to restore the economic system of the 1930s. Many thought that that system had not been a success. In particular, with the onset of recession at the beginning of that decade, monetary relations between the main economies had broken down. Some countries let their currencies float; others, with little conviction, pegged their currencies to gold or to other currencies. There were outbreaks of "competitive devaluation". To protect their reserves, governments introduced new restrictions on the use of foreign currency (exchange controls) and raised tariff barriers against imports. World trade slumped and thanks to these new policies it was extremely slow to recover.

Participants at Bretton Woods believed that this scenario, these beggar-thy-neighbour policies, had to be avoided in the future. What was needed was a set of institutions that would govern the global economy. These institutions would need to be designed to promote

---

[138] What should be made clear at the outset is what follows is a sketch, and is certainly not to be confused with a proper, detailed history of the Fund's purposes and role. Moreover, the materials I have drawn on derive mainly from a number of articles and pamphlets produced by the Fund itself, and the work of its own historian, M.G. de Vries. I have not attempted to review the general literature on the Fund, nor attempted to assess its role and future. The texts I draw on are primarily de Vries (1986) and Driscoll (1992).

international trade. There were to be three: namely, the International
Monetary Fund, the International Bank for Reconstruction and Development (IBRD) or the World Bank, and the International Trade Organisation (ITO). The US Congress refused to go along with the idea of
a trade organisation and this was abandoned in 1950. A treaty-cum-
organisation with weaker powers, the General Agreement on Tariffs
and Trade (GATT), was left to take the ITO's place. The remaining
two institutions, the World Bank and the Fund, were thus given the
responsibility of being the twin pillars of a post-war economic order.

Defined in the broadest terms, the responsibilities of these two
organisations have remained the same since that time. The World
Bank was to be a publicly owned financial intermediary—a bank, in
fact. For the most part it would borrow on commercial terms by selling
bonds. Then it would lend the proceeds to finance investments in
countries in need. The Fund would not be a bank, but a club. Member
countries would pay a subscription and agree to abide by a mutually
advantageous code of economic conduct. Sometimes, if necessary to
uphold this code of economic conduct, the club would let members
borrow briefly and on certain conditions from its pool of subscriptions.
The World Bank's task would be to promote development; the Fund's
to maintain order in the international monetary system.

The code of conduct

The new international order would be based on a code of conduct. This
code related to a global regime of fixed but adjustable exchange rates.
Parities would be fixed in terms of gold. These values could be altered,
but only if the Fund certified that this was needed to correct a "fundamental disequilibrium". Broadly, the thinking behind this was as
follows.

It was assumed that countries would run external deficits from time
to time. The international monetary system should allow such deficits
to be smoothly financed: countries should be able to borrow easily
when in deficit and lend when in surplus. A chronic, or *fundamental*
deficit should not be financed indefinitely, however. It would have to
be reduced either:

• by "adjusting" (i.e. cutting domestic demand, typically through
  lower public spending or higher taxes);

- by devaluing the currency (with the hope of reducing imports and improving exports);
- or by resorting to trade and other restrictions (protectionism).

The participants at Bretton Woods believed that adjustment would need to be part of any remedy. They believed that the second method, devaluation, could help to make the need for adjustment less severe—though the 1930s showed that governments could not be allowed to devalue whenever they liked. They believed that the third course, protectionism, was to be avoided at any cost.

With these concerns in mind, the participants of the Bretton Woods conference proposed that the Fund would supervise international exchange rates. Whenever a member country wanted to devalue it would have to agree this with the Fund. That is to say, they proposed that the Fund's main job would be to *monitor* the economic policies of its members so that it would say "yes" or "no" to requests for parity changes.

In addition to this supervisory role, the IMF was to be endowed with a supply of gold and currencies—the subscriptions of the 40 or so countries that were the original members (these resources would increase as more countries joined the club). If necessary, these resources could be lent to members with deficits in order to supplement the countries' own reserves. As with parity changes, the IMF would have a duty to see that a deficit country intending to draw on its position with the Fund was behaving responsibly.

Furthermore, the Bretton Woods conference also insisted that troublesome external imbalances called for adjustment on both sides. Countries that were persistently in surplus needed to behave responsibly, too; the burden of adjustment should not fall entirely on the deficit countries. If it did, that would impart a deflationary bias to the world economy as a whole: the deficit countries would cut demand while the surplus countries failed to stimulate it. In other words, the obligations of membership were to apply equally to all, whoever they may be, rich or poor, powerful or weak.

Phase 1: 1946–1966

The system that resulted was called the *par rate* system. Under this system, currencies of the member countries were pegged to within 1%

of the value of the US dollar, which itself was pegged to the value of gold. Any change in the par value of a currency could only be implemented with the agreement of the Fund. This agreement would be made if such a change was perceived to be to the benefit of all, and not just that country in particular.

The success of the Fund during this initial period of its existence from 1946 to 1966 was varied, however. There was a gradual integration of the world's economies but this did not coincide with the emergence of an international monetary system as had been envisaged at Bretton Woods. The massive economic disarray at the end of the war meant that many economies could not in any simple way progress towards a stabilised exchange system and, moreover, some of the major economies took unilateral action as regards their exchange policies in defiance of the Fund. Thereby some of these countries found themselves ineligible for financial assistance from the Fund, at least for short periods of time. In addition, and as part of protecting their fragile economies, many countries maintained a complex set of trade and exchange restrictions and the Fund was unable to simplify and remove all of these.

Still, considerable progress was made: the quota system, whereby members of the Fund would be entitled to access resources in relation to how much they had deposited at the Fund, formed itself, and, after 1951, the Fund began to spread its surveillance activities not only to those countries using Fund resources but to all the membership. This latter development caused considerable controversy at first, since some believed that members should be able to take funds as a matter of entitlement, while others believed that there should be some control over this. The tension here, between the Fund and users of its resources, has developed and altered over the years as the nature of surveillance or conditionality has altered. This has now become an unavoidable feature of the Fund as a surveillance institution[139].

Phase 2: 1966–1971

By the mid-1960s strains began to appear in the system. These related to limits on the amount of liquidity in the system, excessive use of the

---

[139] See Guitián (1992).

US dollar and, related to these issues, increasing problems in maintaining stability in the par rate system. In detail the problems were as follows.

First, the growth in the world's demand for capital was not equalled by increases in the production of gold. At the same time, the USA ran a large external deficit and central banks in the rest of the world filled up with US dollars. There became a *de facto* US dollar standard. But it became clear that if the central banks chose to swap these dollars for gold, the system would be in trouble. The USA might be unable to honour its obligation: it certainly did not have enough gold, nor was there enough gold in the world at large. Thus there was a problem in liquidity. This could affect the ultimate stability of the system. The Fund began to deal with the problem in the following way.

It started talks on reforming the international reserve system. The aim was to bring global reserves under tighter central management and so avoid a future shortage of liquidity. The method was to create a new reserve asset: the *special drawing right* (SDR). Fund members were issued SDRs in proportion to their subscriptions (known as "quotas") to the Fund. Subscriptions, in turn, were linked (crudely speaking) to a country's overall economic importance in the world. The First Amendment incorporated SDRs in the Fund's Articles and as of 1969 allowed the Fund to supplant international liquidity with, in effect, its own money. But these developments proved insufficient.

For there was a fundamental problem with the system. It was this: a fixed exchange-rate system imposes a requirement on governments to co-ordinate their monetary policies. If one country has a persistently higher inflation rate than the others, its exports will become uncompetitive, its consumers will binge on cheap imports and it will move into external deficit. In other words, governments needed to control inflation through their monetary policies and these policies needed to be, in part, co-ordinated with those of their major trading partners. Not all governments were successful or willing to do this. Under the pre-1914 gold standard, this did not matter. Deficit countries saw their reserves of gold fall. This caused a contraction of the money supply which in turn reduced inflation. Gradually inflation rates across countries would converge. Under the par value system, however, this mechanism was missing. Lack of co-ordination of monetary policies and, in particular, the implementation of inappropriate policies by any individual member, resulted in the countries in question facing runs on their currency when there was perceived to be an imbalance between their internal monetary policies and external exchange rates. This happened most notably to the pound sterling in November 1967.

As a result, the system became increasingly unstable. Ultimately it collapsed. This occurred in 1971 when for a variety of reasons the USA relaxed its monetary policy. This resulted in a run on the US dollar. This in turn forced US officials to suspend the convertibility of dollars into gold, forcing other countries to *float* their currencies (i.e. allow the relative value of currencies to go freely up and down).

Phase 3: 1971–1978

Attempts to reconstruct the system followed but came to nothing. In 1974, a meeting of the Committee of Twenty, set up in 1972 with the purpose of coming up with reforms for a new system, decided to let the system evolve itself. In doing so, the members were also recognising the fact that the Fund's role was becoming increasingly unclear. If the system that it was intended to supervise no longer existed, what was the Fund to do? As one economist, Robert Aliber, put it:

Within a few years all that remained of the IMF system was the IMF—a pool of currencies modest in size and largely irrelevant in function, given the rapid growth in international reserves, and 1800 highly paid international civil servants, to police a set of rules that no longer existed. (Quoted in *The Economist*, 12 October, 1991, p. 6)

This rather blunt statement ignored two things, however: first, the increasing role of the Fund as a lender, and second, the shock on the international economic system resulting from the oil crisis of 1972–3. This resulted in even more loans. In other words, the Fund's role was changing, and it was doing so in a way that was making the Fund even more important, not less.

To understand this change, one needs to know a little about the nature of borrowing from the Fund. The amounts a country could borrow were, and still are, related to its quota. Members have virtually unimpeded access to the so-called "reserve" that is kept on deposit with the Fund. After that reserve is exhausted, if the Fund agrees, the member can borrow four further "credit tranches" each equivalent to 25% of its quota. The first tranche is easily obtained. The other three, the "upper credit tranches", bring much closer security down on the borrower.

Access to funds almost always requires a "stand-by" or similar arrangement. A stand-by is the Fund's name for its agreement that a member can borrow hard currencies—or in Fund jargon, can "purchase" them—should the need arise. Stand-bys are intended to "provide short-term balance-of-payments assistance for deficits of a temporary or cyclical nature". Originally, a stand-by was just that: a line of credit ready to be drawn. Later, most such arrangements provided the permission and a tranche of cash simultaneously. The loan has to be repaid ("repurchased") in three to five years. During the 1950s, the Fund concluded 43 stand-by arrangements, altogether worth $4 billion. In the 1960s, the pace of lending increased: the Fund arranged 188 stand-bys, worth $12 billion.

Gradually, the Fund's methods of lending also broadened. In 1963 it opened a new window: the "compensatory financing facility". This let a member borrow to make up for sudden shortfalls in export earnings (caused, for instance, by a fall in price). Later in the 1960s it created a "buffer-stock financing facility". These all reflected the changing and growing needs of the membership.

The period between 1972 and 1978 saw an even greater need for the Fund's operations as a lender. This was a result of the immediate shock of the massive price rises in oil which affected previously stable economies dramatically. It forced many of them from a balance of payments equilibrium into deficit almost overnight. It also caused chronic and long-term problems for many of the developing countries. As a response to this, the Fund set up two new oil facilities. What was significant about these was that they involved borrowings from members. Thereby the Fund became in effect a clearing house, borrowing from some members to lend to others.

These and other changes were reflected in the Second Amendment to the Fund's Articles in April 1978. This extended the Fund's powers as a surveillance institution, given that it was now more involved in loan operations than ever before and much less involved in maintaining a regulatory framework. It also gave legal sanction to floating exchange rates.

Phase 4: 1978–1985

The evolution and increase in the Fund's role as a lender continued into the next decade, most especially as a result of a number of problems showing themselves in the world economy at the beginning of the 1980s. These were related to the second round of oil price increases and the strong efforts of the industrial countries to keep inflation down, which, combined with cyclical effects, produced the worst recession since the 1930s. Concurrent with these factors were deepening difficulties in international debt, some of which became critical and led to the so-called world debt crisis.

This crisis was effectively an outcome of the floating exchange rate system, combined with the other shocks to the economic system such as stagflation and recession. To explain, when the big economies had moved to floating exchange rates, the international capital market had grown hugely. The long preoccupation with reserves and international liquidity had therefore faded away. Countries could borrow reserves from the markets as and when they chose. As a result, the very notion of balance-of-payments disequilibrium began to look empty. If deficit countries chose not to reduce demand at home, then, provided they were creditworthy, they could finance their deficits on the capital market. Failing that, they could let their currencies depreciate. The problem, of course, was if they lost their creditworthiness. For then they would not be able to finance themselves from the international capital markets—money would simply steer away from them.

As it turned out, for a number of years the problem of creditworthiness did not show itself. Many developing countries took advantage of the international capital markets and the low interest rate to invest heavily. When recession hit at the end of the 1970s, combined with stagflation, the trouble started.

More specifically, the interest burden on the debts increased while the revenues for the developing economies (through exports) declined. Gradually, it became increasingly difficult for these countries to service their debts. As this became clear, so the capital markets responded by withdrawing funds from the currencies of these countries, forcing devaluation, and hence further reductions in income. This in turn resulted in even more difficulties for the countries in question who found it increasingly difficult to service their international debt. A nadir was reached in August 1982, when Mexico closed its foreign

exchange markets and announced it would have difficulties in paying
its international debts. This had potentially catastrophic consequences.
This could have led to the complete collapse of the international
banking system.

The Fund responded with a plan, proposed originally by Mr Baker of
the US Treasury, whereby the Fund would arrange a package of
assistance for countries in severe debt crisis. This would involve not
just the Fund but also commercial banks and others involved in a
country's debt. In essence, these packages provided medium-term
support to allow countries to achieve structural changes without the
crippling burden of debt servicing. In simple terms, the Fund began to
use its resources to help countries repay their commercial debt
(although this did not mean that the Fund repaid their debt directly).

At the same time, the Fund became increasingly convinced that the
problems with balance of payments required medium-term, structural
adjustments. These adjustments were difficult to make for a whole host
of reasons, not least because of the internal political repercussions for
the country in question. To help member countries pursue these structural changes, the Fund further expanded its role, helping members to
design and implement adjustment programmes. The Fund also took a
greater interest in the international repercussions of internal monetary
policies, and this resulted in it deepening and extending its relations
with member authorities.

Phase 5: 1985 onwards

By 1986 the debt crisis had been more or less resolved. The Fund
continued to develop its structural adjustment programmes and further
refined its procedures for gathering information about its members.
These related to the effective control over disbursement and use of
Fund resources.

In this period, it was political changes rather than economic changes
that were most notable. In particular, the collapse of the former Soviet
Union led to a whole host of new countries applying for membership,
all with previously unheard of problems. These included the need to
change from a centralised economy to a market-driven one. Furthermore, these countries not only needed finance for these changes but
they also needed a great deal of expertise and training. As a response to
this, there was a massive increase in the resources available to the Fund

(up to 150 billion SDRs) and a very large increase in the Fund's staff. There was also a large increase in the amount of technical assistance the Fund provided, both in terms of missions expressly for that purpose, and in terms of training and education. An institute was set up in Vienna for training individuals from the former Soviet Union and from Eastern Bloc countries.

The Fund's Articles

All of this development and evolution has been bound up with the premises and purposes outlined in the original *Articles of Agreement* and in the various amendments to these over the decades since. These articles set out a framework whereby this surveillance and how it results in participation in decision-making is not occasional or as need demands, but is systematic and regular.

More specifically, members are obliged to provide the Fund with a range of economic information. Section 5(a) of Article VIII, for example, lists the minimal level of information members have to provide. Since this is pertinent for further discussion, it is worth quoting in full.

(a) The Fund may require members to furnish it with such information as it deems necessary for its activities, including, as the minimum necessary for the effective discharge of the Fund's duties, national data on the following matters:
    (i) official holdings at home and abroad of (1) gold, (2) foreign exchange;
   (ii) holdings at home and abroad of banking and financial agencies other than official agencies, of (1) gold, (2) foreign exchange;
  (iii) production of gold;
  (iv) gold exports and imports according to countries of destination and origin;
   (v) total exports and imports of merchandise, in terms of local currency values, according to countries of destination and origin;
  (vi) international balance of payments, including (1) trade in goods and services, (2) gold transactions, (3) known capital transactions, and (4) other items;
 (vii) international investment position, i.e., investments within the territories of the member owned abroad and investments abroad owned

by persons in its territories so far as it is possible to furnish this
information;
(viii) national income;
 (ix) price indices, i.e., indices of commodity prices in wholesale and
      retail markets and of export and import prices;
  (x) buying and selling rates for foreign currency;
 (xi) exchange controls, i.e. a comprehensive statement of exchange
      controls in effect at the time of assuming membership in the
      Fund and details of subsequent changes as they occur; and
(xii) where official clearing arrangements exist, details of amounts
      awaiting clearance in respect of commercial and financial transac-
      tions, and of the length of time during which such arrears have been
      outstanding.

With the evolution of the Fund's role some of these concerns have
reduced in importance. For example, gold deposits and volumes of
gold exports are now no longer as important as they were in 1946.
Nonetheless, this is quite an extensive and detailed list: members are
obliged to provide the Fund with a great deal of information about
themselves. However, the authors of the Articles have attempted to be
realistic about whether all members would be able to provide this data.
Section (b) of the same article states:

(b) In requesting information the Fund shall take into consideration the
    varying ability of members to furnish the data requested. Members shall
    be under no obligation to furnish information in such detail that the affairs
    of individuals or corporations are disclosed. Members undertake however,
    to furnish the desired information in as detailed and accurate manner as is
    practical and, so far as is possible, to avoid mere estimates.

It is worth noting also that the Fund does not just collect this data for
its own purposes. Section (c) of the same Article states that:

(c) The Fund may arrange to obtain further information by agreement with
    members. It shall act as a centre for the collection and exchange of
    information on monetary and financial problems, thus facilitating the
    preparation of studies designed to assist the members in developing
    policies which further the purposes of the Fund.

These clauses necessarily have implications for the work of the Fund.
Gathering data—irrespective of members' ability to furnish it—is a

major logistical problem; collating that information for the use of
members as a whole is another.

But my concern in this chapter is to underline how the Fund is not
just gathering and distributing information. As should be clear, it has
evolved from being an institution that monitors its members into one
that has a surveillance role. Article IV, Sections 3(a) and (b) are
pertinent here:

(a) The Fund shall oversee the international monetary system in order to
    ensure its effective operation, and shall oversee the compliance of each
    member with its obligations . . .;
(b) In order to fulfil its functions under (a) above, the Fund shall exercise firm
    surveillance over the exchange rate of members, and shall adopt specific
    principles for the guidance of all members with respect to those policies.
    Each member shall provide the Fund with the information necessary for
    such surveillance and, when requested by the Fund, shall consult with it
    on the member's exchange rate policies. The principles adopted by the
    Fund shall be consistent with cooperative arrangements by which mem-
    bers maintain the value of their currencies in relation to the value of the
    currency or currencies of other member, as well as with other exchange
    arrangements of a member's choice consistent with the purposes of the
    Fund. . . . These principles shall respect the domestic, social and political
    policies of members, and in applying these principles the Fund shall pay
    due regard to the circumstances of members.

What this means in practice reflects the changes I have described. Of
particular importance is how during the late 1970s and 1980s there
came to be a recognition of the close interconnection between internal
monetary policy and external financial flows. This, combined with
better understanding of the structural changes required to manage
stability in the realm of balance of payments, has resulted in the
Fund exercising considerably more influence than was originally
anticipated in 1944. In particular, the surveillance now also means
participation in the policy decision-making of members. This decision-
making is not just related to the external monetary affairs of members,
but includes both those affairs and the internal monetary policies that
affect them.

This surveillance and participation will, as a matter of course, lead to
some tension between members and the Fund. It is this tension, probably more than anything else, that results in the institution being in the

news headlines as often as it is. Its other activities, its data gathering and production, for example, very rarely make the news.

Irrespective of that, the important point here is that the evolution of what the Fund does and its embodiment in the Articles provides a framework through which the Fund's staff operate. This creates an interpretative schema through which the Fund sees the world. I am not saying anything dramatic here; all I am noting is that these concerns provide the framework through which what is of concern gets distinguished from what is not[140].

In later chapters I will attempt to explain what this means in practice and to uncover how this interpretative schema is used. I will illustrate this with reference to how Fund staff view one of its members, namely a country I will call "Arcadia". I hope to use that example to illustrate some of the generally applicable social organisational characteristics of this interpretative schema. Before I do so, however, there is one last stage of this sketch of the Fund that needs completing and that has to do with its current internal structure.

The current structure of the Fund

The top link of command of the Fund is the *Board of Governors*, there being one Governor from each member country, and an equal number of alternates. As the Governors and their alternates are typically ministers of finance or heads of central banks, they speak authoritatively for their governments. An *Interim Committee* gives them advice on the functioning of the international monetary system, and a *Development Committee* advises them on the special needs of poor countries. Since Governors and their alternates are fully occupied in their own capitals, they gather only on the occasion of annual meetings to deal formally and as a group with Fund matters.

---

[140] It is worth noting at this point that there is now some considerable literature on the perspectives of those organisations that, like the Fund, have a role in development. According to many of these commentators, these interpretative schemata create perspectives which are as significant for what they leave out as for what they bring in. Amongst the concerns of anthropological–ethnographic researchers in the area of multinational agencies and development has been to widen the scope of this vision. See Ferguson (1990). For a review of related literature see Gardner & Lewis (1996).

During the rest of the year, the Governors communicate the wishes of their governments for the Fund's day-to-day work to their representatives who form the Fund's *Executive Board* in Washington. The 24 directors of this Board, meeting three times a week, supervise the policies set by member governments through the Board of Governors. At present, seven *Executive Directors* represent individual countries: China, France, Germany, Japan, Saudi Arabia, the UK and the USA. Fifteen other directors represent groupings of the remaining member countries—about 180 in all. Voting is weighted according to the value of deposits of the Fund. The Executive Board rarely makes its decisions on the basis of voting, but relies on the formation of consensus among its members.

The Fund itself is headed by a Managing Director, who is also chairman of the Executive Board, which appoints him. By tradition, the Managing Director is European, or at least non-American. Until recently, the reverse held true for the Managing Director's Deputy. At the commencement of the research, there was one Deputy. Since that time, that role has been expanded to require three people.

The Fund itself is divided into departments and bureaux. The departments are either *area departments* which are responsible for particular member countries divided up into contiguous geographic blocks (e.g. Western Hemisphere, Middle Eastern, etc.), *functional departments*, which either support and review area work (e.g. the Policy Development and Review Department), or other service or information bureaux. The Bureau of Computing Services, for example, supports the mainframe and networked server systems within the Fund, as well as economists' workstations. The Bureau of Language Services translates the Fund's most important documents into English, French and Arabic, as well as translating various memoranda, letters of agreement and other documentation into the specific languages of member countries as required. There are a number of other elements of the Fund's activities, such as the IMF Institute which is responsible for training economists in macroeconomic affairs, especially economists from the former Soviet Union. Figure 4.1 shows a simplified diagram of the main sections of the Fund with which I will be concerned.

Each area department consists of a *front office* and several *divisions*. In each front office are the senior staff, consisting of the director, senior advisers and division chiefs. Divisions have responsibility for certain groups of countries within the department.

In turn, within each division, and for each country, there is a *desk*.

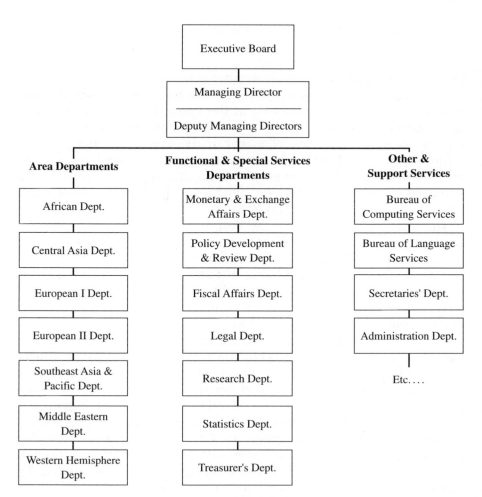

Figure 4.1   A simplified organisational chart of the Fund

All the information a member country sends should go in the first instance to the desk, and any information the Fund uses for its own decision-making purposes or publications should derive from the desk. Similarly, all communications, except formal requests for Fund resources which are addressed to the Managing Director, should go through the desk.

For each desk there is (more or less) one *desk officer*. Desk officers are economists who develop and maintain expertise on any particular country. A division chief will manage several countries and desk officers, and hence will be responsible for the information the Fund has about any particular set of member countries.

The chiefs and their desk officers are the main mechanism of information gathering and production at the Fund. They are not the only such mechanisms, however, nor are they able to operate without relying on other important elements of the Fund. All policy-related information, or at least all of that which goes into staff reports and other consequential documentation, is thoroughly examined and reviewed by what are called the functional departments, most especially Policy Development and Review.

The work of the chief and the desk officers, and allied to that its reviewing mechanisms, are tied to a number of major processes including the *Annual Meetings* and the *mission process*. It is this mission process that is the bread and butter of Fund work, and it is this process that is the main focus of the rest of this book.

There are two main types of mission, a routine *Article IV surveillance* mission and a *Use of Fund Resources* mission.

Article IV surveillance missions are undertaken more or less on an annual or semi-annual basis. They are undertaken by the desk officer and the chief responsible for the particular country, with the help of colleagues from the reviewing and functional departments. A mission team will visit the country to gather information, most importantly information relating to balance of payments, and discuss policy perspectives with the local authorities. On the basis of their discussion and data gathering, a mission team will prepare a staff report. Once reviewed, this is delivered to the Executive Board. The Article IV mission process and the related staff reports are key elements in the Fund's surveillance activities.

A *Use of Fund Resources* mission is undertaken when a country requests a loan from the Fund. A mission team, constituted along similar lines as above, will go to the country and, as with an Article IV mission, focus on the balance of payments. However, in this case the mission will try and understand the causes of the country's particular difficulties (the immediate reasons why a member has requested Fund resources). In concert with the authorities, it will then create a plan or set of recommendations for policies that will remedy these problems. These policies frequently include the use of Fund resources on a temporary basis. These recommendations are also outlined in a staff report.

The staff reports that derive from both types of mission (the routine Article IV type and the Use of Fund Resources mission) are circulated amongst all senior staff of the area department concerned, to the reviewing departments (including the already mentioned Policy Development and Review Department, but also to Fiscal, Monetary and Exchange Affairs), and to directly affected functional departments (such as the Treasurer's Department, if funds are to be released). They are then circulated to senior management: the Managing Director and Deputy Managing Directors. Once "cleared" by all these people, the staff reports are then presented to the Executive Board. These Executive Directors send the reports to their authorities (i.e. the member governments), await their comments, and then deliver those comments as appropriate at the relevant Board meeting. At these meetings, the Board then agrees or rejects the recommendations of the staff report. In terms of volume, the Fund as a whole will produce up to something like 300 staff reports a year.

The Fund also engages in the collection and analysis of economic and statistical data and presents these in numerous publications. These include the Fund's monthly *International Financial Statistics (IFS)*, which is prepared by the Statistics Department. The Research Department also produces the bi-annual *World Economic Outlook (WEO)*. Both the IFS and WEO are important resources for macroeconomic policy-making throughout the Fund's membership as well as for scholarly research. The area department desk officers are required to participate in the production of these publications.

Finally, the Fund also engages in technical work, offering training and guidance to all the membership through both *technical assistance missions* and training either in Washington or at the Fund's Institute in Vienna.

Conclusion

This then is the Fund. I have been at particular pains to emphasise how the Fund is now more involved in its membership's decision-making than ever before. Changes in the structure of the Fund, in the resources it has available, and in the procedures whereby those resources are made available to the membership all reflect this. The shift towards participating in the membership's decision-making has occurred along-side other developments in the Fund's role as an information provider. I have mentioned the WEO and the IFS, but the Fund has also been instrumental in developing standards for comparable international financial statistics and for the determination of such things as national income. All of this has been very important in the development of macroeconomics.

My main concern in this book, however, is with the policy function of the Fund rather than its information gathering and production. There are a number of reason for this, not least the practical limits on the amount of time I had available in the field. But in any case, this policy work, whether undertaken under the auspices of the Article IV surveillance process or when a member uses Fund resources, is the most important element of the Fund's work. It is not by any means all that the Fund does, but it is the most crucial aspect. The following chapter looks at elements of that work.

CHAPTER 5
The machinery of policy work

In this chapter I start developing an analytical conception of the Fund. In particular, I highlight some aspects of the *organisation* of the organisation. This may seem a curious way of putting it, but I want to draw attention to how the Fund organises itself to do certain tasks. I want to set up some of the Fund's organisational problems or, rather, features of its *organisational problematic*. By "problematic", I do not mean that the Fund is suffering from chronic disorder or is fraught with tension. I am simply wanting to characterise the relationship between what members of the Fund do, and the materials they have in hand. My main focus will be on the area departments, the associated review functions and those elements of the organisation involved in the Fund's policy work.

Of crucial importance in this chapter will be such matters as temporal constraints. At the most obvious level, this will involve a concern with how much time is required to do certain tasks, and how some tasks can arrive "out of the blue". It will also mean drawing attention to how there needs to be a balance between all the work that *could* be done and what it is practical to do. But I shall also be concerned with temporality in the following, deeper sense: with how Fund staff organise themselves so that what they will do in the future is planned out and agreed in the present. Furthermore, I shall discuss how the achievement of their plans is conducted in a fashion whereby that achievement can be examined and commented upon. Above all, I shall draw attention to how certain documents are key in this. By this I mean that documents such as *briefing papers* provide resources through which users can specify what their current activities should involve, and what their future activities should be. Briefing papers are resources whereby actions in the past can be re-evaluated, assessed and, if need be, brought to account.

These investigations will lead me to point out how briefing papers (and other documents I shall describe) are mechanisms whereby members of the Fund constantly reiterate and substantiate the organisation of the institution. This is why I call this chapter the "machinery" of policy work, since I want to begin elaborating the claim that certain of the Fund's documents are not mere descriptions of work done nor are they constructed for ritual purposes. The documents I have in mind instruct as well as explain, they predict the future as well as account for the past; these documents demonstrate the rationality of the organisation as well as provide resources for the investigation of that rationality (i.e. accountability). These documents are important elements in the *machinery* of the Fund's work. In a phrase, these documents speak for the organisation in the very process of organising the organisation.

But—and this is very important—these documents cannot be understood, nor the role they play recognised, until they are placed within the context of the Fund's policy work. It is only knowing what this work consists of, how it is organised and routinely structured, and, finally, what the problems are that it poses that one can understand how these documents have the role they do. It is only by understanding this context that one will begin to tell the difference between the things that documents need to say and those that can be taken for granted; between the things that need to be documented and those that can be ignored. For it is my view that users of Fund documents need to be familiar with the life of the Fund for those documents to instruct them about that life. They need to know what the Fund is about to enable them to use Fund documents as guides to correct procedure or as resources to make bare some set of policy problems. According to this view, documents and understanding of the setting in which these documents are used go hand in hand.

In this chapter I shall begin specifying the exact form of this *reflexive* relationship. In addition, and as I argued in Chapter 2, such an investigation provides the opportunity to map out the assembly of contexts that makes up an organisation as a whole. It needs to be made clear that I shall not be able to complete the task of that specification in this chapter alone. Notwithstanding what we have learnt previously, there is still much more that needs to be understood about how the Fund conducts its business. In this sense, I am beginning the task of uncovering the relationship between documents and the action of Fund staff. This chapter is intended to provide further materials, and more background for the detailed discussions later on in the book. This purpose is also reflected in the manner of exposition: as the reader will find, I do not offer much in the manner of ethnographic detail. As I progress in subsequent chapters, so this detail will start to appear, particularly by the time I describe the mission to Arcadia.

Overview of the chapter

So, more specifically, I organise my discussions in the following way. I begin with what may be thought of as the beginning of the "process" of the Fund's policy work: how the institution organises its policy information production and decision-making processes. In particular, I shall outline how the Fund organises itself year by year to produce policy analyses, and to present these at the right time to the right people (specifically, to the Executive Board). This will involve looking at the planning and management of the Executive Board agenda and what is called the "tentative schedule". This schedule ties the mission process to the Executive Board process. I shall argue that one needs to understand how the tentative schedule procedure is part of a larger scheduling process that involves the constant marshalling of persons, documents and processes. This will provide me with an opportunity to underline how policy work involves not just analysis, but effective control over the "when" and, to a lesser extent, the "by whom" of information delivery.

I shall then begin the task of characterising policy work and say something about what it involves. This will lead me to explain why review is so important. I shall outline elements of the Fund's review processes and draw attention to the key role of briefing papers. I shall explain how reviewing in policy work is not just retrospective or post hoc, but is part and parcel of the "work" from beginning to end. One of the crucial features of these review procedures is to ensure that the policy analysis presented to the Executive Board contains no surprises. Analysis of any and all countries should be organised so that "what it ought to be" is what was predicted beforehand. The reviewing procedures are there to ensure this. In later chapters I will explain how this has important implications for the nature of how facts are understood within policy work, for the nature of adequacy and objectivity and for what is meant by a staff report "warranting action". Ultimately, this has implications in terms of how the Executive Board has to invest trust in those who are responsible for the documents it is asked to consider.

The tentative schedule

So, I shall begin with the first stage of how the Fund does its policy work and, specifically, with how it schedules its activities into some kind of coherent whole. Of importance, clearly, is how the Fund links its policy information-gathering, production and reviewing processes to its executive decision-making by the Executive Board.

How the Fund manages all this is quite complex. As noted in Chapter 4, the Fund has to conduct its routine surveillance work and review the resulting staff reports. There are over 180 member countries, so there are at least that number of related Article IV (surveillance) staff reports the Board will have to deal with[141]. But there is also a great deal of other business. Of most importance, of course, are responses to ad hoc requests for Fund help. In 1994 (when the field work reported here was under way), about 70 countries were receiving some kind of Fund assistance (albeit not all financial). The Fund also has other work to do related to technical assistance, broad Fund policy issues, research, administration and other matters. Consequently, there is not only a problem getting all the work done, there is also a problem balancing what can be predicted and planned, with what is unpredicted and unplanned. This balance is achieved by creating a general framework. This is called the *tentative schedule*.

The tentative schedule is constructed on a semi-annual basis—at the watershed of the Annual Meetings and six months later. Each area department submits provisional plans of its surveillance and other missions. The submissions are collated, and any conflicts resolved. Many of the missions are conducted at more or less the same time each year, and this eases the task of scheduling them somewhat. But there is always some negotiation that has to be done. Once these negotiations have been completed, a tentative schedule is issued. This schedule specifies the agreed dates when staff reports will be on the Agenda of Executive Board meetings, along with other papers which are expected to go for Board consideration. It is the dates on this tentative schedule that the area department chiefs use to finalise when their own respective missions should occur, provided substantive reasons for change do not arise. More specifically, the chiefs work backwards from these fixed dates (when the staff reports are to be

---

[141] Though some of the Fund membership are on a bi-annual surveillance cycle.

presented to the Executive Board) to work out the actual dates of the missions. So, in effect, the planning of missions and the planning of work for the executive function is an iterative affair, the dates of missions being provisionally determined, ordered, collated and then fixed, and this worked out hand in hand with the workload for the Executive Board.

There is more to the process than this, however. For the tentative schedule needs to provide sufficient space or enough gaps to allow unplanned work to become items on the agenda of the Board. There are a number of reasons why unplanned work appears. The most important of these has to do with how balance of payments problems are, to some extent, unpredictable and how their onset can be rather rapid.

So, for instance, variation in the international price of some commodity can have an almost immediate impact on an economy whose main export is that commodity. A large reduction in price can transform a balanced balance of payments position and a balanced government budget into *imbalances* calling for a corrective policy response almost overnight. This means that the Fund has to be able to respond rapidly to problems amongst its membership. This in turn leads to unexpected missions and associated staff reports and these in turn generate unexpected items on the Executive Board agenda. To deal with such contingencies, those who manage the tentative schedule have to re-configure the schedule at very short notice.

But such changes are constrained by the following factors.

First, there are *time limits* on staff reports. After a certain point in the information production process, there is less room to manoeuvre the date when a staff report can be presented to the Executive Board. For staff reports have to be delivered within a certain period. At the moment, the Fund takes the view that a staff report should be reviewed by the Board within 60 days of a mission returning from its member country. There is some small leeway here, but by and large this is a principle that is adhered to. In other words, staff reports must be used, acted upon and dealt with by the Executive Board at the appropriate time and cannot be put off indefinitely. Space in the agenda has to be made at the right time—even if this means complex shifting around of other items or even extremely long working days for the Executive Board.

That staff reports have to be used within a certain time period may seem simply a matter of courtesy. But it is more than this. It is a reflection of some of the fundamental features of staff reports, and especially the time-related nature of the information they convey. I will be saying more about this. The point of concern here is that this makes the management of the tentative schedule more difficult than it might otherwise be.

Second, staff reports have to be presented *in person*. Typically this will mean presentation by the chief of a mission, but sometimes it will mean a chief's deputy. The desk officer will normally be present too, although he or she may or may not be asked to contribute to any discussions the Executive Board has when a staff report is presented. Given that the chiefs, their deputies and the desk officers will be involved in other activities (most importantly other missions), there is a considerable logistical problem getting the right persons on the right day to the Executive Board[142]. This problem should of course be dealt with by the time the tentative schedule is released on the six month cycle. But the issue here is that even if this has been achieved, the vagaries of balance of payments crises—as just described—can cause changes in the dates of missions. This may make it difficult, if not impossible, for certain persons to attend a Board meeting at the planned time. Furthermore, it is sometimes the case that efforts to do so are constrained by the 60 day time limit on staff reports. That is to say, the shifting of the dates of an already planned mission so as to allow an ad hoc mission to deliver its report may mean that the time limits for the delivery of the planned mission are broken.

This particular need for authors to present their reports is sometimes viewed by the administrators of the tentative schedule as merely a result of the respective chiefs, their deputies and desk officers wanting to give themselves some profile. Although there certainly is some of this, I will argue later on that *authorship* and the delivery of staff reports in person is the legacy of the role of authorship in earlier stages of the production and review of staff reports. The personal delivery of these documents is a ceremonial display of the importance these individuals once had in the reports they authored, though by the time they actually stand up at the Board, that importance has diminished so much as to be virtually inconsequential.

These then are two of the reasons why managing changes in the tentative schedule is difficult. Such changes derive from the nature of balance of payments crises. The upshot is that those who plan the

---

[142] Members of the Board itself will also want to be present for certain staff reports (the representative of the member reported on, for example).

tentative schedule leave gaps in the Board's agenda. These provide opportunities to allow for these crises and for the complex task of integrating the various processes, documents and persons involved.

But in addition to this, the tentative schedule process is undertaken with reference to a preference to keep individual work items on the Board's agenda as short as possible. There is a similar preference to have as few of these items as possible. This preference is not, I should say, one generated by those who manage the schedule wanting to ease their own predicament. It comes down from the highest levels in the Fund: from the DMD's offices, the Board of Directors, and others.

But irrespective of the source or motivation, the upshot is that there is a normative requirement that staff reports be no more than about 15 pages long (excluding appendices). Of more importance, there is also a preference to ensure that the reports (however long) do not cause difficulties for the Board. It is thought that such difficulties—irrespective of what they might be—could result in the Board taking longer to process those documents than is manageable within the Board's time constraints. The tentative schedule administrators discuss with senior staff in the area departments what are likely to be difficult reports and organise the schedule accordingly. The result is that there are normally about four or five agenda items per day, unless a "difficult one" is involved, in which case the number is reduced to two or three.

Taken as a whole, the management of the schedule is an ongoing affair, with a constant juggling of persons, documents and processes. Almost as soon as it is agreed and issued at the six month period, the tentative schedule has to be changed, and each change is followed by more and more changes, in an endless cycle. In practice, the release of the semi-annual version serves as a straw man device that all those involved (the area department chiefs, the administrators of the schedule, etc.) can use to negotiate and renegotiate the actual schedule on a month by month and week by week basis.

But beyond the specific methods whereby the Fund organises its intersection between the policy investigations and the executive function, the important point is that the activity of policy work needs to be *flexible*. This is because it needs to be organised in such a fashion that what is planned to be done at one moment can be changed at the next; because it needs to accept and respond to the changes in international economic circumstances yet be able to continue "routine surveillance" work; because it needs to deliver policy work within time constraints;

and finally because it needs to be organised so that those who author documents can personally deliver them.

The tentative schedule process is, of course, "merely" the administration of policy work, rather than the work itself. One needs to understand what this work consists of to appreciate why those who administrate it need to worry about the things they do. This is not to suggest that these administrators do themselves have a deep understanding of policy work. One administrator said to me that he would like to know more about policy work but that his own work responsibilities were such that he never had the chance to do so. The Fund's missions were as opaque to him as they are to much of the general public. My point is that the concerns he had to deal with were the outcome of the character of policy work.

An introduction to policy work

At this stage in the argument, one needs to understand two aspects of policy work: first, something about the organisation of that work (its logistics if you like); and second, what it involves as an intellectual exercise. I will deal with the logistics aspect first.

In the previous chapter I noted that there is a *desk* for each member of the Fund. One feature of desk work is that it tends to be sequential in nature: first one task will be concentrated on, and then another. Some of these tasks require almost complete dedication, others less so. For example, mission work involves almost complete concentration, in part because of the workload and in part because of the physical separation from other work sources. Other kinds of work (for instance *World Economic Outlook* (*WEO*) submissions) can be done while some time is given to the routine administration of the desks: sorting out the letters and dealing with information requests.

But whatever the particular concern at that moment in time, a feature about desk activity is that focusing on one task and the creation of task sequences results in something of a compromise. Concentrating on one thing means neglecting other things. The actual amount of work that will be neglected at any point will vary enormously depending on the tasks in questions, the member countries involved and the point in time in the mission cycle. So, for example, some of the larger desks involve so much work that more than one economist manages it more or less "full time"; for some of the smaller members, the desk work is so little that those responsible for it frankly admit that they have only a half time job on their particular country (though in the latter case these individuals will find themselves giving more time to other countries and missions than those on large desks would be required to do).

Be that as it may, what I want to draw attention to is how it is there is some tension between the need for continuous information gathering and production, on the one hand, and concentration on specific information tasks on the other. In many ways this tension is an unsurprising feature of Fund work. After all, in nearly all organisational settings, some things have to be done at the expense of other things. But the point here is that the Fund does not produce information about *all* of its membership *all* the time. It may receive that information all the time, it may be able to sort it out and marshall it rapidly, but at any particular moment in time, policy work involves focusing on some sequences of tasks and not others.

Of paramount importance is how the sequences of work involved with missions dominate this organisation. Fund economists will complete one mission sequence before they go on to the next sequence of tasks. In practice, this next sequence nearly always ends up being *another mission*. In short, policy work involves moving from one mission sequence of tasks to another in a never-ending cycle of first this mission and then another. One consequence of this is that work related to such things as the WEO (i.e. non-mission related) tends to get pushed aside. It is not unusual for desk submissions to WEO to be done very late, and then only with much complaint[143].

Now of course there are many teams, and so, many individual missions are being worked on at any one time. But nonetheless, there will be periods when the Fund does not have at hand information about a particular country. My point is to suggest that this reflects the fact that the Fund does not need information about a particular member all the time. Whenever there is such a need, the area departments ensure that it is satisfied. I have shown in part how they do so: they change the tentative schedule so that there is a constant *reorganisation* of Fund

---

[143] These complaints are partly because those involved have so much other work to do and partly because those who manage desks view the production of the WEO as "someone else's job" (namely the Research Department).

activities to ensure that what is needed is just that which is produced and delivered to the Executive Board[144].

These logistics are of course wrapped up with the nature of policy work itself. Before I can explain how this is so, let me now sketch out this work. In the previous chapter I suggested that there is a Fund *interpretative schema*. My concern now is to begin to specify what use of that schema involves.

The first thing I want to draw attention to is how mission teams need to describe and characterise the current economic circumstances of a member country. Doing so can involve a range of tasks dependent upon the quality or extent of information processes in the member country. A large number of countries generate sufficient information to enable area department desks to complete a description at almost any time. Many other countries do not have the wherewithal to do so, and the only way the desks can get the information is by helping those members to produce it. This involves a great deal of technical assistance work. Sometimes this shows itself in special missions and sometimes in a large amount of information production and gathering work on Surveillance or Use of Fund Resources (UFR) missions.

But the problem of description is not simply one of collecting information. It is also about how to *interpret* data. This is not to say that there are many interpretations to choose from. It is rather the opposite: to know what is the correct interpretation. This requires deep understanding of what the "raw data" mean. This is one of the key reasons the Fund sends missions to its member countries. They can thereby learn from those who are immersed in the information production processes, what it is that is conveyed by any particular set of figures.

Let me illustrate. Most central banks will calculate deposits on a daily basis. This provides an up-to-date and accurate representation of the government's deposits. Members of a mission will want to know this. Amongst other things, this accuracy or "up-to-dateness" will

---

[144] By way of aside, the constant keeping an eye on what is needed and re-ordering work accordingly results in the chronic unpredictability of area department work, and thus also of *desk officers'* work. A desk officer may go on four or five missions a year. Only the mission to his or her own country is likely to occur at a predicted time. The desk officer is unlikely to get more than a few weeks' notice for other missions he or she will participate in. I shall remark on this again when I discuss an example of an Article IV mission in Chapter 8.

mean the mission economists can use central bank deposit "actuals" to reconcile other figures whose provenance the economists cannot be so sure about. Such figures may come from customs and excise institutions. These institutions may collect figures for the values of exported and imported goods but may produce these only on a quarterly basis with annual corrections. Consequently, the actual figures for international trade at any particular moment in time, or more exactly, for the current period (the period the mission is concerned with) may be inaccurate. Eventually customs and excise will complete production of the figures (i.e. issue correct figures), but mission economists may not have time to wait. They want the current figures and they want them immediately. Consequently, mission economists will have to make estimates for these figures. Those numbers that the mission economists are sure about, such as a central bank's daily *foreign currency deposit figures*, can be used for this. In particular, it is likely that these deposits will indicate what are the actual sums of cash coming in and out of the country as a result of foreign trade. These figures can be used to anchor and correct the estimates that customs and excise generate.

This then is how a mission constructs a descriptive interpretation of the current economic circumstances. In addition to this, missions need to construct an *analytic* picture or framework of the foundational relationships in the economy. With this framework, projections of the likely results of various policy initiatives can be undertaken. These projections are made in the short and medium term. Central concerns will be balance of payments positions, fiscal policies and monetary policies. Key targets for achievement of policy goals will typically relate to inflation rate, growth, employment, foreign currency reserves and gross domestic and foreign debt. The mission teams have to provide recommendations in relation to these targets and outline what they think are the appropriate policies. As with the description of an economy, the determination of such recommendations involves considerable interpretative skill. For, along with all the econometric and economic skills members of missions will need to employ, there will be the need to interpret what are the realistic assumptions for projections and what would be the probable economic and political circumstances that a government will find itself in. It is all very well predicting low inflation rates but these will stand no chance of being achieved if, say, the government exercises no control over monetary policy.

The main outcome of the mission is, of course, a staff report. An Article IV staff report usually contains four main parts: a synopsis of the member's relationship with the Fund, a review of developments in the preceding year or so with particular reference to the immediately preceding quarter, a report on discussions with the authorities (with particular reference to the major sectors and related policy initiatives) and a staff appraisal. Staff reports also contain numerous tables on economic and financial indicators and a medium-term outlook or framework.

What is important here, though, is how a staff report is an *artfully* created document. By that I do not mean it involves sleight of hand or tricks of the trade. I mean that it involves considerable skill in its construction. To begin with, and speaking at a general level, a staff report does not contain everything the mission team knows about a country. Nor does it explain all the criteria used in the various interpretations central to both the analysis and the staff appraisal. Nor yet is it a complete description of everything done on a mission. A staff report is a selection of the evidence, argument and recommendations which are sufficient unto themselves to enable the Executive Board to make its decisions. Furthermore, it is so composed and expressed briefly to enable the Executive Board to deal with the report expeditiously.

This brief description of some features of policy work is intended to underline how it includes a mix of both analytic and interpretative skill. One can capture all of this under the term *professional judgement*. I now want to show how this impacts upon, and is bound up with, the logistical side of policy work, and how this results in a certain form of organisation to the Fund.

Judgement work

There are a number of ways in which logistics and professional judgement are bound up with each other. To begin with, and as I have been at pains to point out, policy work is not simply a matter of getting data, tidying them up and presenting those data in a staff report. Rather, policy analysts have to be sent to member countries to learn about how to interpret the data. Only then can they adequately describe current circumstances. They also need to develop their own analytical model. This enables effective discussion and analysis of policy. As it happens, this is in large part a social process, though I will not say anything more about that at this point.

Related to this is the fact that in each mission the kinds of concerns are unique. It is not the case that missions always do the same thing, gather the same data and create the same analytic view. Instead, there is variation in what missions uncover. I do not want to exaggerate this. I am not saying that missions come back to Washington with incredibly diverse findings. Analysis of balance of payments problems tends to generate similar materials and requires similar sorts of techniques for their analysis and solution. It is rather that what this means in any *specific instance* will vary. These differences show themselves in the details rather than in the generalities. The problem is that the investigation into these specifics requires endless new forms of analytic interpretation, and thus heavy reliance on professional judgement. The upshot is that the Fund cannot know in every detail what judgements its mission teams will need to make. It has to trust those teams to make the right ones in each case.

A further aspect of the role of professional judgement is that, whatever the missions uncover, the mission teams have to generate reports that facilitate the functioning of the Fund as a whole and the Board in particular. For there are hundreds of missions a year. The result is, as I say, that staff reports need to be artfully created documents. They have to be concise and to the point. But more importantly, they should not present information that makes the reviewing function within the Fund pause and hold its breath; they should present what I have described as a "no surprise" analysis. By this I simply mean they should present an analysis that is reasonable, in accordance with Fund views, and so on. I will need to say more about this in later chapters.

And finally, all of this needs to be done within time limits. These time limits are in part bound up with the practicalities of review (e.g. how much time there is for the Board to review documents). But more importantly they are bound up with the fact that the problems the Fund's members have are current problems to do with current circumstances. Consequently, missions (and indeed member authorities) are not interested in what happened last year or the year before (though this will be useful to know). The Fund is interested in "real time" data analysis, and this impacts upon how much time the Fund has to do its work. Missions have to work within very strict time constraints, and their output—the staff reports— have to be processed within tight time schedules.

These then are elements of the Fund *problematic*. The Fund's policy work cannot be organised as a sequentially constant process of information gathering and production. Rather, it requires flexibility both in the temporal organisation of work (i.e. when missions occur) and in the outcome of that work (the variation in the details of balance of payments problems). It needs to have processes that ensure that this indeterminacy does not get out of hand. It needs to do its work quickly, reflecting the real time nature of its concerns. And, finally, it has to deal with great volumes of work.

The Fund has various tools and mechanisms to deal with these "facts of life". Documents are part of this. Amongst the most important of these are briefing papers. Of less significance, though nonetheless vital, are back-to-office reports. These are key tools in managing the tension between indeterminacy and smooth working; between the exercise of professional judgement in endless new ways and the need to qualify those judgements; and between the need to plan future activities and the vagaries of the present. To understand how they do so requires an understanding of the nature of review at the Fund.

The review process

The review process at the Fund consists of a system that includes the area department front offices and specific reviewing departments. The key elements of this review process revolve around certain types of documents, in particular the briefing paper already mentioned, the back-to-office report and the staff report itself. Each of these has a distinct role to play in review.

Reviewing occurs both before a mission leaves and subsequent to its return, and is sequential in nature. First of all, a *briefing paper* is prepared before a mission departs. Once this is cleared, the mission can commence. On return to the Fund, the mission chief (it is usually the chief) produces a *back-to-office* report. Thereafter, a draft of the *staff report* is prepared and reviewed. Once cleared, this is then sent to the Executive Board (subject to the administrative and clerical processes).

I want to focus on the briefing paper. The following procedure occurs when a briefing paper is reviewed. First of all, the briefing paper is reviewed within the area department responsible for it by the front office's senior staff. In effect, this reviewing is intended to ensure that problems are sorted out "in house" before they get to the reviewing departments. Once the front office has completed its review, the document is sent to the functional departments, most particularly the departments of Policy Development and Review (PDR), Fiscal (FAD) and Monetary and Exchange Affairs (MAE). It will also be sent to the Legal, Treasurers', Research and Statistics Departments. For an Article IV mission, only PDR will have to "sign off" a briefing paper, the remaining departments only having a right to read and comment. In Use of Fund Resources missions, the Legal and Treasurers' Departments will also have signing off rights.

A briefing paper is—in simple terms—a detailed discussion of important background data and issues that will be discussed in the mission and will appear in the final staff report. It is often similar in length to a staff report, contains some of the key elements of the analysis, contains something of the assessment the staff will make of a country's economy, and outlines what agreement is likely to be made as regards policy benchmarks. In a rough sense, the briefing paper is a "prediction" of what the staff report will look like. But the relationship between staff reports and briefing papers is much more complex than the word prediction conveys.

A primary concern in review is to comprehend what may be specific to the tasks a mission will undertake. The concern is not to make sure that a mission will do more or less what all missions do. The task is to determine whether in any *particular* set of circumstances a mission team will do what *any* mission team ought to do. To grasp these specifics, reviewers want thoroughness. Accordingly, a briefing paper will have to detail more or less all the important economic information that is currently available and which the mission team believes will form the basis of discussions with the authorities.

I can illustrate this using the case of the Arcadian mission described in Chapter 8. Here, reviewers perceived the briefing paper as lacking in this thoroughness. In particular, it did not contain a medium-term projections table for the balance of payments. The complaint about this partly had to do with the fact that such a table is normally required in briefing papers, but more importantly it had to do with the fact that "it would help provide sufficient detail" as the reviewers themselves put it. This detail would relate to the economic circumstances of Arcadia at that time. Although the table would not provide everything that the Fund would ultimately need to know about Arcadia, reviewers argued that it would be illustrative of these details and thereby allow them to determine what would be unique and specific about the work that the Arcadian team would need to undertake.

By way of another example, again taken from the Arcadian briefing paper, PDR wanted the mission team to include a specific list of all the liberalisation initiatives the Arcadian authorities were planning for the forthcoming year. PDR also wanted this to be combined with a list of those that had been implemented in the previous year. Only in this way would PDR feel confident enough to know what would be the exact nature of the policy discussions the team would undertake with the Arcadians.

Taken as a whole, the idea of a briefing paper is to use its review as a process that acts as a normative "checks and balances" restraint on mission teams. It works not only through the delivery of reviewers' comments on briefing papers, however. As one chief put it to me:

The review process acts like a ghost in the team. The ghost ensures that what we produce in the brief is what will be acceptable.

In other words, teams devise—or at least attempt to devise—briefing papers that pass muster first time round. Not only is there a ghost in the workings of the team, but also a team would prefer this situation than to be asked to revise later. In part, this reflects a bit of team pride, desk officers and chiefs particularly wanting to show how on top of things they are. It also reflects a practical preference for getting things reviewed and signed off as quickly as possible.

This is not say that these checks and balances always work. Sometimes mission teams do fail to achieve what they set out to do; at other times they find themselves in situations that no amount of preparation could have predicted. But, by and large the review process does work, or rather, what the mission comes back with is what was predicted in the briefing paper. One of the ways missions can do this is to use the briefing paper for themselves. For though a briefing paper exists primarily to enable external review, it becomes of use to them because it acts as a set of terms of reference—though precisely what this means needs some explanation.

A briefing paper is something that mission teams orient to. During missions, the mission team will look at the briefing paper again and again. Even if they do not actually look at it, they will constantly bear it in mind. They do so because they want to ensure that what they *said* they would do is indeed *what* they do. They want to ensure that the findings they are gathering, the interpretations they discuss, and the agreements they make, are the ones they described, predicted and proposed—or, if not, that they will make sure they have substantive reasons based on new information for making changes.

This orienting is also, in a sense, a guide. The team will encounter materials that were not noted as a topic in the briefing paper. If these materials are significant, then a problem does arise for a team: the team will not have got its predictions "just right". The team will have to adjust its position accordingly, based on the thrust of the briefing paper. But those materials that the team encounters which are viewed as of no "material significance" are effectively left aside or "walked around", since they make no impact on the state of affairs on which a team will report.

There is yet another component to the relationship between the doings of a team and a briefing paper. It is important to recognise that in being a guide or an orienting device, the briefing paper is "designed" in the first place to outline activities that can be realistically and practically oriented to. It outlines what a team can be expected to achieve on a mission. So, if a briefing paper makes predictions, then the team that wrote it knows that they must live up to those predictions; if it is a guide, it must be something that they can follow; if they are to orient to it, then it must outline activities that in being oriented to, will result in a staff report which is adequate.

These then are the ways that the mission teams use a briefing paper to organise their work. The same briefing paper will have been previously used by the reviewing function to control, measure and qualify the proposed work of mission team. In this way, the future of the Fund's work is planned in the present, and that future turns into a reality which is predetermined to some extent. At least, this is the hope. Sometimes mission teams find themselves in situations that no amount of preparation could have predicted.

To deal with such eventualities there is yet another organisational process in place. When a team returns to the Fund, the mission is required to submit the previously mentioned *back-to-office* report. This document, of one or two pages, is sent to the front office of the area department from which the team is drawn, to PDR, and to the senior management of the Fund. This explains whether the mission has been able to abide by the briefing paper or, if not, why not. In nearly all cases, the contents of the back-to-office report are affirmative (i.e. it affirms that a mission has achieved what it set out to do). But, occasionally, a back-to-office report contains bad news.

Amongst the problems that may arise for a mission team is the conduct of the authorities in the member country. For a whole range of reasons, they may make it difficult for the team to accomplish its work to an adequate standard. This may have been due to a major event occurring, such as a war. Another, much less dramatic problem may have to do with poor preparation on the part of the member authorities.

Irrespective of the particular cause, the back-to-office report alerts the Fund if problems of these kinds were encountered by the mission team. This gives the organisation time to set in motion possible remedies. These remedies can vary from giving the mission team more time to complete a staff report through delaying a staff report's presentation to the Board, or even arranging for another mission to be sent.

The important point here is that the back-to-office report is an instrument that points towards whether the Fund should use the flexibility its procedures allow. This flexibility shows itself in other ways too. For, even after a back-to-office report has been submitted and a staff report cleared for presentation to the Board, the organisation can still adjust itself. This is bound up with the concern with contemporary economic circumstance and with real time data. For example, a mission team can decide to issue a supplement just hours before a report is due if they think significant changes have occurred since the mission was undertaken. Sometimes a mission will request that the presentation of its Article IV report be halted altogether if they believe significant changes in the country in question have occurred since the mission was conducted. A staff report can be taken out of the agenda just hours before it is due to be discussed (although this is very rare indeed).

This does not necessarily result in the report never getting to the Board. Typically, a mission will choose to delay presentation of a report until amendments can be made. Sometimes these can be done very quickly with minimal alteration of the text and data in the reports. Sometimes it takes longer, and may even require another mission. Once amendments are made, some reports are changed from Article IV to a joint Article IV–UFR report just days before they are delivered.

The purpose, then, of back-to office reports, and these opportunities to delay, supplement, amend and abandon staff reports, is to ensure that, if anything is going to go to the Executive Board, it is appropriate. By this I mean that the right information is delivered at the right time (i.e. with up-to-date data). This in turn requires the appropriate policy analysis (i.e. reflecting the current circumstances).

Of course, this is normative, and there is not, in practice, a clear distinction between good and bad reports, between ones that can be processed with ease, and those that will cause hiccups in the orderly running of the organisation. Sometimes "bad" or "bad-ish" reports do make it to the Board. As I noted, one of the practical devices used to ensure the smooth running of the Executive Board despite this is to arrange its agenda in such a way as to ensure that there will be only one problem a day to deal with; the other issues being "straightforward". At times, this hidden management of the Board's agenda breaks down when faced with the practical exigencies of unexpected requests for Fund resources or the illness of staff.

Talking texts

Briefing papers and back-to-office reports are not the only documents that support the *organisation of the organisation*. Nor are they the only documents constitutive of the review process. They are, however, amongst the most important. What I have been wanting to suggest is that documents like briefing papers are not simply catalogues of things planned. They are a part of the way in which the organisation *talks to itself*. In this case, not only are the mission teams using the briefing papers to talk to the reviewing function, but they are using those briefing papers to talk to themselves in the future.

Other documents, illustrated by the back-to-office report, are opportunities not for the organisation to talk to itself, so much as opportunities to talk *about* itself. These are opportunities for self-commentary and all that implies: excuses, self-criticism, reflection and, of course, self-congratulation.

In speaking for the organisation in these ways, documents are also reflecting a division of labour. For instance, when a mission returns to Washington and a back-to-office report has been circulated, the briefing paper no longer talks to the mission team. Instead, PDR uses the briefing paper to talk *about* the mission. By this stage a mission team can no longer use a briefing paper as a resource for its work. The opportunity to do that work will have been passed by the time a back-to-office report is done. Instead, PDR will have the briefing paper as a resource to tell it whether the mission team has done as expected; that is to say the briefing paper becomes an opportunity to investigate questions of accountability. Such investigations are particularly important when a back-to-office report has indicated that a mission has not achieved what it set out to do. In these circumstances, PDR needs to revisit the goals outlined in the briefing paper and assess whether the mission was right to have "failed".

The role of the briefing paper is illustrative of how the same document varies the role it plays as it moves through its career and reflects a division of labour. Part and parcel of how a division of labour manifests itself is how certain thresholds within this career seal off one set of doings in a division of labour from another. So, in the case we have been discussing, the return of a mission and the presentation of a back-to-office report seals up the work of the mission team, but opens up new avenues of work for PDR.

The connection between briefing papers, the return of a mission and the issuing of a back-to-office report is illustrative also of how documents do not always operate alone but sometimes in terms of one another. Specific arrays of documentation enable individual items of documentation to do certain things including, as I have illustrated, shifting the onus of work within a division of labour. Often that equates to shifting onus through time.

For documents to do these things requires more than the documents themselves, however. For it is only by knowing what any particular set of documents are intended to do that users can place themselves in a position to make effective use of those documents. Though I have been saying that documents talk for the organisation in various kinds of ways, what is meant by this talk is often only transparent to those who expect and understand the role of the documents in question here. A back-to-office report does not say "the issuing of this report places the onus of concern with the related briefing paper on PDR". But those who receive that document in PDR will know that that is what it conveys. Knowledge of the circumstances of use, then, allows documents to have the voices that they do. But they can speak for the organisation only because members of that same organisation know how to hear those voices.

Conclusion

I have not by any means mapped out all of the salient properties of the organisation of the organisation. In the next chapter I will contrast some elements of the organisation of policy work with that of statistical work. This is intended to further highlight and deepen our understanding of those features that I think are important and which I will come back to in Chapters 7, 8 and 9. For now I want to conclude by returning to some of the discussions in Chapter 2.

In Chapter 2, I discussed Karl Weick's suggestion that documents are one of the mechanisms whereby members of an organisation come to share reality. This view would seem to imply that members of organisations can exist in wholly different worlds and to avoid the clash of outlook that might result, agreements as to "common ground" have to be struck[145]. I want to distinguish this view from the one I am outlining.

When a mission team submits a briefing paper, it is not doing so as a way of creating a shared world view, or an ontology if you like. Rather, it is sharing knowledge about the specific, practical problems it has in some particular case. The general reality these problems are part of, the world view if you like, is not in doubt. A briefing paper is not an opportunity for a mission team to share with PDR what it thinks is the reality of the Fund's situation. It is a chance to share the details that the mission team thinks will characterise the work the team needs to do in the mission they are about to undertake. The world of policy work, I am suggesting, is *already* shared or known in common before briefing papers are written. That is to say, mission teams and PDR (and indeed other policy analysts within the Fund) know what their business is about, and that does not need to be restated. What does need to be mentioned—and indeed documented—is what the operations of this policy work will mean in any particular instance. The question that is solved with briefing papers is this: "How do we deal with this case?" It is not: "What is something PDR and the mission team can agree to?"

This leads me on to how the process of constructing the briefing paper and having it reviewed results in certain things being brought in and some things driven out (i.e. moved in or out of the domain of concern). For this harks back to Bruno Latour and his claim that documents are one of the ways institutions drive out competing views of the world. Latour's thesis is that this destruction of alternatives was essentially a moral task, rather than an empirical one (though empirical materials would be marshalled to service moral ends). His view is that questions of reality and empirical fact are subordinate to questions of

---

[145] See Weick (1995).

power and status[146]. My case has been that though issues to do with morality are involved, they are intimately and indeed inseparably bound up with hard fact.

By using the term "moral" here I am alluding to the question of what is practical for the Fund to do as against what is ideal for it to do. This may be thought of as moral insofar as judgements about this involve assessments of what is "too little", what is "too much" and what is "just about right." These are normative judgements (i.e. what is good or bad, done well or done poorly) and hence moral. But at the same time, these judgements are firmly based on what the mission team and the reviewing functions know as the facts of any case. Only in understanding these facts can an effective judgement about what is or is not enough be made. In this regard, my view is that when one is considering the Fund one should not make a contrast between the empirical and the moral, as if one *competes* with the other. They are distinct elements, but they are married.

This is not say that questions of power and status do not come into it. They certainly do. For it is a function of someone's status within the Fund that they are entitled to judge what is enough and what is too little; it is this status that also entitles them to judge what is adequate fact and what is inadequate. Here, being a chief holds more weight than being a desk officer when it comes to deciding what is sufficient evidence and what is appropriate policy. But this status is bound up with socially recognised expertise. This is a very different argument than the one Latour puts forward. I shall come back to this in later chapters.

Part of how this marriage between fact and morality is dealt with is through the Fund's division of labour. This itself plays out through time so that what is one group's problem at one moment in time becomes another group's later on. For instance, the marriage of fact and morality starts off being the concern of a mission team when they draft a briefing paper. But by the time a back-to-office report has been delivered, that concern becomes PDR's, especially if there has been some difficulty on the mission. In moving through its career this way, the active readings that are undertaken transform a briefing paper and the users of that document. At one moment its existence and use are bound up with one group's responsibilities (the mission team's); by the

---

[146] See Latour (1990).

time they have discharged those responsibilities, the document is transformed into the responsibility of another group (PDR's).

This linking of tasks sequentially leads me on to my last concern in this chapter which has to do with what is implied by the suggestion that documents constitute some of the mechanisms that organise the Fund. For this implies that the Fund is *machine-like*. The ways I have been unpacking how this might be so has, I hope, not been too contentious. But the use of the *organisation as machine* metaphor has caused considerable controversy in the past[147].

As I noted in Chapter 3, those concerned with computers in the workplace have argued that the use of this metaphor has led to computer systems that have failed to deliver the promised goods. The metaphor exaggerated sequentially ordered processes and undervalued the ad hoc, the flexible and the contingent. This resulted in systems that were too rigid and over-emphasised the linearity of work processes. The result was that users of these systems had to devise "work arounds" that could deal with the non-linear, ad hoc and the contingent nature of their work[148].

As regards management and organisational theory, criticisms of the "organisation as machine" metaphor have focused on a host of particularly controversial manifestations. For example, classical management theory seemed to endorse this view and this led in turn to scientific management and its derivatives—Taylorism and Post Fordism[149]. These undervalued the role of people in the workplace, their skills and their needs. A number of contrasting schools of thought have emerged that have tried to correct these mistakes[150].

Then finally there were those ethnographic studies of work practice that emerged during the 1980s which drew attention to the inappropriateness not just of the regimes that resulted from the "organisation as

---

[147] For discussion and review see Morgan (1986).

[148] See Hirschheim (1985).

[149] For classical management studies see, for example, Mooney & Reiley (1931) and Fayol (1949). Taylorism is derived from scientific management's most famous exponent, Frederick Taylor. See his *Principles of Scientific Management* (Taylor, 1911).

[150] Examples include the Human Relations School, the Socio-technical School and most recently, the Labour Process theorists. These latter have flourished since the publication of H. Braverman's *Labour and Monopoly Capital: the degradation of work in the Twentieth Century* (Braverman, 1974).

machine" metaphor (i.e. scientific management, Post Fordism, etc.) but of the claim that work processes can ever be conceived of in ways susceptible to representation in machine code. The target of their critique was, of course, primarily artificial intelligence where, here, it is the mind rather than the organisation that is a machine. The main thrust of the ethnographic criticism was that the meaning of any action could only be understood with reference to the context of that behaviour. In this sense, behaviour was situated. Machine action could not replicate this situatedness, or at least not in the ways that human action is bound to particular contexts[151].

But what lies at the heart of much of the criticism of the machine metaphor is really that its use has been too pedantic, or too mechanical. The view of what a machine is has been much too limited. There has been too much emphasis on sequential machinery, and none on what one might call reflexive machinery. But similarly, criticisms of the metaphor have tended to exaggerate the difference between the systematic (hence mechanical) properties of organisations and the unsystematic (hence non-mechanical) properties of social action. In so doing they have underplayed the systematic in social behaviour and the reflexive in the mechanical.

What I have wanted to show is that an organisation like the Fund is not organised like a machine that supports a sequential production-like process. The organisational machine I have in mind consists of a matrix of activities intersecting in complex ways through time. The Fund is a machine that manages certain sequential processes whilst intersecting them with other processes that allow movement into the past, observation of the present and glimpses into the future. Documents are key to this.

My argument has been that the use of documents allows a movement between various points within the *temporal matrix* of organisational action. Within this matrix, a document can allow someone to measure the future, another person to specify what needs to be done in the present, and a third to account for the past, all with the same document. This is bound up with a document's career. In short, the matrix allows an organisation to talk *to* itself and *about* itself. But, as in the talking of people, the *tense* of these activities will vary according to what needs to be done at any moment or place in time. It is in this way that the organisation organises itself.

---

[151] The key text here was Suchman (1987).

This view may seem very like the view developed within cybernetic theory. According to this position, organisations are self-referential and inform themselves about the effectiveness of their operations as they adapt and evolve to their external circumstances. This theory has been very influential in a variety of domains, not just in organisation theory[152]. My view is distinct, however, partly in how it emphasises the situatedness of conduct highlighted by the ethnographers of work practice in the 1980s and partly because it emphasises the role of background knowledge or understanding. That is to say, I have been wanting to emphasise how artefacts like documents can be mechanisms supporting the organisation of the organisation because users' background knowledge enables them to recognise what they can do with some document. At the same time, the documents in question provide resources to help users make such distinctions. In this sense the machine I have in mind is reflexive.

It may be that in having this organisation, institutions like the Fund may be better thought of as ecologies: consisting of mutually interdependent entities, reciprocal relationships and adaptive processes. This is a much more popular metaphor in current organisational literature[153]. But, even if one does adopt that coinage, one should not forget that within an ecological system there are mechanisms that allow the ecology to keep going. Whether one thinks of these as mechanical or biological, it is these that I have wanted to examine in this chapter.

---

[152] The main text here is Wiener (1948).

[153] For a good review see the introduction of Star (1995). Also see Altheide (1995).

CHAPTER 6
The use of information

Policy work is only one part of the Fund's business, or more precisely, one part of its set of purposes as described in the Articles. Its mandates in surveillance of the international monetary system and in the development of economic and financial adjustment programmes require that the institution generates both information for its policy work and information for more general use. It is perhaps worth reminding ourselves of those aspects of the Fund's Articles pertinent here (discussed in Chapter 4). Section C of Article VIII states that:

The Fund may arrange to obtain further information by agreement with members. It shall act as a centre for the collection and exchange of information on monetary and financial problems, thus facilitating the preparation of studies designed to assist the members in developing policies which further the purposes of the Fund.

The same Article specifies what kinds of information this will consist of (see pp. 102–3 in Chapter 4). In brief they are as follows:

- its holdings of foreign exchange;
- total values of exports and imports of merchandise;
- international balance of payments;
- international investment position;
- national income;
- price indices and thus measures of its inflation rates;
- and what, if any, exchange controls a country has in effect.

These data are used for a number of purposes by the Fund. One purpose is associated with policy analysis in the area departments which I have begun to describe; another is for the bi-annual World Economic Outlook (WEO) prepared by the Fund's research department with submissions from the desks; and a third has to do with the provision of various statistical compendia and manuals by the Statistics Department. My purpose in this chapter is to sketch out some of the work related to this latter set of tasks, and to use that as an opportunity to contrast what goes on there with activities within the policy branch of the Fund.

More specifically, I want to suggest that the relationship between users and documents that I began to highlight in the previous chapter is not the only relationship that one might find, even within the same organisation. The varieties of this relationship will depend upon a number of factors, the one I have been focusing on so far being the "organisational problematic". Now, the fact that the Fund has the mandate to gather and disseminate statistical information as well as to undertake policy work means it has at least two problematics.

I want to investigate this second problematic and draw some contrasts, such as comprehensiveness as against methodical consistency, timeliness as against periodicity, and collaborative as against autonomous work. These dimensions distinguish statistical and policy work, and this in turn is reflected in the role and nature of the documents produced under the auspices of each. My concern in this chapter, however, is not to investigate fully both sides of the Fund's work, but to use comparison to point toward how certain sorts of information and certain sorts of documents enable the Board to act. In particular, I am interested in the moral implicativeness of staff reports. I shall explain what I mean by that in the conclusion.

Overview of the chapter

My analysis is constructed in the following manner. First, I outline (albeit rather simply) the organisation of the Statistics Department, including the divisional structure and the division of labour within it. I then describe some of the various tasks individual economists undertake. These include work related to such things as the monthly publication, *International Financial Statistics* or *IFS*; participation on methods standards committees; and completion and publication of various "manuals" such as the *Manual for Balance of Payments*. I shall also discuss the department's mission work, both the role of technical assistance and involvement in the area departments' Article IV missions. I shall then explain how these tasks fit together, and describe some of the working routines of the Statistics Department.

I then construct an analytical view of statistical work. I begin by noting the apparent anonymity of statistical information and how this contrasts with the kind of information delivered by mission teams in policy work. I then remark on the importance of periodicity in statistics and how this too is different from the importance of timeliness as it manifests itself in policy work. I draw out some of these features by discussion of omissions in the Statistics Department's monthly publication, the aforementioned *IFS*.

This provides the empirical background for discussion of the main distinctions between policy and statistical work. I shall group these into three: first, relating to the temporal organisation of the two sets of activities; second, relating to how individuals work within the two domains; and third, relating to the role of documents.

The Statistics Department

The Statistics Department has four basic concerns:

1. to routinely collect, collate and publish statistical economic data;
2. to define and sanction methodologies for codifying these data;
3. to offer technical assistance to the membership as regards the preparation of this statistical information; and
4. to contribute to policy analysis.

To achieve these goals, the department has a total staff of about 160 individuals, of whom 100 are economists by trade[154]. Its structure is very similar to that in area departments and thus consists of divisions managed by chiefs. Its divisions are organised to reflect the geographical partitioning of the area departments matrixed with concerns for specific types of data. So, for example, of the two financial institutions divisions, one concerns itself with members dealt with by the area departments for Africa, Middle Eastern and Western Hemisphere; the other for data deriving from members dealt with by the Asian and European area departments. But both financial institutions divisions deal with data related to money, banking and interest rates.

To sketch out the work of the department, let me describe it with regard to the four concerns outlined above. The first of these relates to

---

[154] The department was undergoing change during the field work period which resulted in an expansion of the numbers of divisions and in the numbers of staff. This primarily reflected the changes in Eastern Europe and the former Soviet Union but was also bound up with the increasing volumes of technical assistance work the Fund undertakes. Here I report on the department as it was at the start of my research rather than as it has become since.

the *routine collection, collation and publication of statistical data.* Economists in each division are responsible for information relating to several countries, but only those aspects of economic information relevant to their division's area of concern (Figure 6.1). So, for example, one economist will deal with balance of payments figures in a selection of countries; whilst another will deal with, say, real domestic sector figures.

There is not necessarily any obvious relation or similarity between the countries an economist may be responsible for—the countries may be both geographically and economically distinct. Rather, allocation of countries is based on the total amount of work that results. So, as an actual case, one economist was, at the time of the field work, responsible for monetary and international reserve figures for the following: Bhutan, Croatia, Eritrea, Guinea, Ireland, Saint Helena, Israel, Mozambique, Switzerland and Swaziland.

The information that any individual economist needs derives from two sources: either it is collected on missions (whether it be technical assistance, Article IV or Use of Fund Resource missions), or it is submitted directly to the Statistics Department by the membership in accordance with the members' obligations. These latter submissions are usually in response to questionnaires sent out by the economists on a monthly or quarterly basis. Responses are conveyed in a variety of forms: by floppy disc, email, magnetic tape, telex, fax and surface mail.

Much of these data (whether collected on a mission or sent directly) will not be in the form that the economists need. They will have to

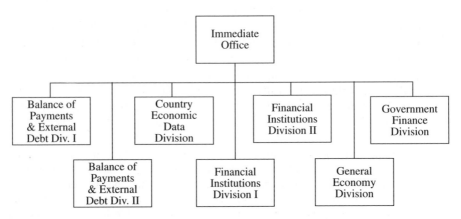

Figure 6.1 The Statistics Department

transform them into the appropriate aggregates. The actual work involved will vary between countries as well as between types of aggregates. There is, for example, some international consistency for the calculation of balance of payments and national accounts, but much less so in relation to government finance statistics.

Once economists have completed their work, the resulting figures are sent to research assistants. These assistants also have the onerous job of entering the data on to the department's mainframe storage system, the *Economic Information System*, or the EIS. The EIS consists of various file databases, including time series, equation, transaction, and key-word files. I say that data entry is an onerous task because data entry works on a batch system which requires some considerable degree of familiarity with system interaction protocols[155].

The EIS is reputed to have the world's largest economic database. It is used for nearly all of the department's publications. These include the *Government Finance Statistics Yearbook*, the *Balance of Payments Statistics Yearbook*, the *Direction of Trade Statistics* and the afore-mentioned *International Financial Statistics* or *IFS*. This latter, the IFS, is the most central to the department's activities. In one way or another, the majority of economists in the department are involved in the provision of data for this publication. Servicing this need is funda-mental to the statistical function. The *IFS* is the standard source of international statistics on all aspects of international and domestic finance. It includes all the relevant data for the analysis of balance of payments problems (including inflation rates, international liquidity, money and banking, international transactions to name but a few). It has been published since 1948.

The second main concern of the department is *defining and sanctioning methodologies*. Accordingly, it participates in various working parties and committees drawing up methodological prin-ciples. These include the *Working Party on Measurement of Inter-national Capital Flows* and the *International Working Group on External Debt Statistics.*

It is worth mentioning that the statistics function has been central in the creation of methodological consistency, most especially in relation to national accounts. Indeed one often hears it said by department staff

---

[155] At the time of writing, plans were being made for migrating this system from an IBM 3090 mainframe currently being used onto a server-based environment on a Novell network. This was expected to result in a much improved "interface".

that before the Fund was created (and hence its responsibility for statistics), there was no way of making international comparisons for the calculation of national accounts.

However, despite the efforts of the Fund, there is not consistency and agreement in every area of methodologies. As I have already noted, there is still no consistency in relation to government finance statistics or for the calculation of monetary and other financial statistics. Partly, this is because there are historical precedents for the calculation of such things, making change and international consistency difficult. No such precedents, or rather very few, existed in relation to national accounts.

Be that as it may, the outcome of these methodological activities is incorporated in various publications which, as their name suggests, are treated as manuals for statistical method. They are the manuals for *Balance of Payments*, *Government Finance Statistics* and the *System of National Accounts*. Economists in all the divisions may be involved in one way or another in the creation of these manuals, depending upon status and experience.

These methodological concerns also show themselves in the Statistics Department's third main concern, namely, its *technical assistance* to the membership. This assistance shows itself primarily in technical assistance missions to countries needing help in learning the appropriate methodologies. Many underdeveloped economies have very little professional economic expertise and rely on the Fund to help them create it[156].

A large proportion of the department's economists will be sent on technical assistance missions each year. Typically this will be to countries they are responsible for in their division, although this is not always the case. One might note also that methodological issues tend to be dealt with sector by sector, so necessitating separate missions for each sector. There will be a mission to a country to work on, say, balance of payments methods, and another mission to the same country at some later time for government finance issues.

In addition, many Article IV missions under the aegis of the area departments incorporate a technical assistance element. Members of the Statistics Department provide this assistance. This work has grown in importance recently, especially with the joining of former Soviet Union (FSU) economies to the Fund. Though FSU economies have

---

[156] The Fund's Institute also has an important role here.

plenty of technical experts themselves, this expertise is in methods and analytical techniques that are no longer in use. They need to learn what may be described as essentially capitalist (or "market economy") techniques for accounting. It is the Statistics Department's function, alongside the Institute's, to provide the suitable training and guidance for this.

Last, but by no means least, the department is required to *contribute to policy work*. Such contributions are both direct and indirect. On the direct side, its most obvious manifestation is in the Statistics Department's participation on area department missions. This will occur when there is a technical assistance component to the mission in question. Such technical assistance has been especially common in relation to FSU countries, as has already been remarked, but has also been important historically in missions to Latin America.

On the indirect side, the contribution the Statistics Department makes derives mainly from the large number of technical assistance missions organised by the Statistics Department itself. The purpose of these is to enhance members' provision of data for the Statistics Department's own data production tasks. This work enhances the quality of the department's main publications but in addition, the production of data in accordance with international standards will benefit the area department desks.

There is one other set of benefits, at least in theory. For the information presented in the *IFS* can be used by the area department desks for their policy work. I say theoretically for there are a number of reasons why many desks do not do so. I shall come back to this.

Working routines

Having outlined the main tasks, I now want to describe briefly how they fit together. I shall do so by using members of the department's own characterisations.

So, one might begin by noting that there is "information work", most importantly for the *IFS*; second, that there are methods and other related jobs; and third, that there is mission work, primarily for technical assistance.

The first of these, information work, has the following character:

For the *IFS*? It is routine, predictable. The amount of work remains more or less the same. There is some change over time but it is more or less the same on a month by month basis.

The importance of this work also results in it providing something of a bedrock to all Statistics Department work. Other tasks have to be superimposed on it:

You know how much to do for this (the *IFS*) and everything else is fitted around it.

One might note also that many economists claim that once they are familiar with it the work can be completed without too much difficulty. It does not require a great deal of creative energy on their part nor does it involve devising new analytical tools and techniques:

It is very regular. You get to know what changes you have to make. It doesn't require a lot of creativity. Once you get to know it. Ha! That makes it sound boring. It isn't, well not generally. Maybe I have been here too long!

Further and closely related to these latter features, research assistants can have an important role here, since they too can take on some of this work. This can be important when the economists are away:

Interviewer: What happens when you are on a mission? Who does the *IFS*?
Division economist: A lot of the work can be done by research assistants. Not all of them but some are very good. I mean, if there is any problem they can't deal with I can always deal with them when I come back. In any case there are plenty of other economists in the department who could do my work.

The second set of tasks consists of work on the methods committees and the various methods manuals and publications. This is necessarily more diversified. The exact involvement of any individual economist will also vary enormously dependent upon the issues of concern and the economist's expertise. Furthermore it often involves travel.

However, it is apparently the kind of work that cannot be easily described:

How can I describe it? It is a lot of meetings! I think you would have to participate.

I did not have such a chance preferring instead to focus on policy work. But irrespective of what it involves, this work has to be super-imposed on work for the *IFS*—the "information work" as I have called it.

The third set of tasks relate to missions. Mission activities neces-sarily take the economists away from the office. Moreover, Statistics Department economists may go on a large number of missions over a year. This may seem surprising since face-to-face discussion is crucial to policy work as I have remarked, but one may not think it so important in statistical work. But, in fact, the technical assistance missions do necessitate a visit to the country in question and a great deal of person-to-person discussion. This is because the Statistics Department's economists need to familiarise themselves with the methods and procedures of the member authorities, as well as the persons who have responsibility for these procedures, before they can make proper recommendations. It is only through spending time *in situ* that this be achieved.

The increasing volumes of technical assistance missions combined with an increase in the keenness of the area departments to request technical assistance in their own missions has resulted in considerably more logistical problems for the Statistics Department. When I explained to one of the senior staff within the department that I thought of its work as much more desk-bound than area department work he replied:

Well, that might have been true but these days we are travelling almost as much as anyone else. It has become quite a logistical problem here since we all have other work that needs to be done irrespective of whether we are in the building or not. The area departments don't have those problems. When they are away (i.e. when they are on mission) everything gets put on hold . . . the work members of the mission team would otherwise do, I mean. We can't do that. We don't stop an edition of the *IFS* because we are on mission.

Comment

These then are some of the key tasks and concerns of the Statistics Department's economists, albeit simplified. Taken together, they add up to a great deal of work. Though they may be divorced from the kinds of pressures and deadlines of those in the policy area of the Fund, they have pressures of their own kind and often find that there is not enough time to get everything done. This is not to say that things go unfinished but, rather, that their job, like those on the area department desks, requires judgement about where to draw the line between what is practically possible and what is ideal; between what could be done in a world where there are endless amounts of time and a world where there is never enough. These practical realities have a bearing on the nature of the work, and indeed on the nature of the information the Statistics Department produces.

The features I draw attention to here are more subtle and symptomatic of the tasks in question than the formal structures of the department might indicate. My concern is not just to note the obvious fact that the Statistics Department is made up of a single department whereas, say, the policy area of the Fund is made up of a selection of area departments, intersecting with various functional and administrative services. I am concerned with the *problematic* that underscores the organisation of the Statistics Department. The resulting organisation of the organisation, I want to suggest, highlights a number of important issues that distinguish this statistical work from policy work. These distinguishing characteristics include much more than just differences in formal apparatus (i.e. the numbers of departments, and structure and goals of the divisions within). They have to do with questions about the nature of the information produced, why that information is produced and the manner of its production.

One may begin to unravel the differences between statistical and policy work here by noting that, although much of the data used in policy work and, say, presented in a staff report may look more or less the same as that found in some edition of, say, the *IFS*, the data themselves have a different epistemology.

One issue I am drawing attention to is that statistical data are, in a sense, anonymous. No one cares too much who put together the information in the *IFS* (or indeed the other publications of the Statistics Department). This is, I believe, a significant feature of statistical information. This significance shows itself in the fact that, for example, the Statistics Department can, to some degree, swap around the actual persons working on some specific set of data. The question of who does the work is of no fundamental interest or import. In contrast, the area departments cannot readily swap persons around; those who start a mission cycle and commence the writing of a staff report must complete that task.

A second epistemological feature distinguishing statistical from

policy work has to do with timeliness. What is of importance here is
that policy information has a pertinence at a particular moment in time
whereas statistical information has a permanent utility just as long as
(a) it is updated on a regular basis and (b) consistent methods are used.
These are the requisites of information that is used for comparative
purposes. To state the obvious, with consistency of method, classifica-
tions and categories of data remain the same year in, year out, and this
allows those data to be examined historically. With updating on a
regular basis—or "periodicity" as the Statistics Department itself
would phrase it—historical comparison can be made between fixed
points in time. In some ways it does not matter greatly what period is
chosen for updating and revision (i.e. whether weekly, monthly or
annually), just as long as the period remains consistent.

This is just to sketch out the two issues. They can be brought into
further relief by looking at *omissions* in the statistical data. For, if one
looks at almost any page of the *IFS* one will find certain "fields"
empty: i.e. there are omissions in the data sets (Table 6.1). Although
the staff of the Statistics Department would feel very uneasy at mention of them, I would like to suggest that their existence in the Statistics
Department's information base, and hence in publications such as the
IFS, attests not so much to a failure on the part of the Statistics
Department to do its job but to fundamental features of statistical
information. These features are linked to the organisation of how
that information is produced.

To explain, there are a number of reasons why omissions exist.
Perhaps the most important relates to the fact that some of the membership constitute their economic data according to different methods
from those used by the Statistics Department. Sometimes the Statistics
Department finds it impossible to recalculate those data according to its
own methods. Naturally the Statistics Department does not want to
enter wrong data into its database, so it simply does not submit anything at all in the relevant fields. Hence omissions in things like the
IFS.

As already noted, the Statistics Department's involvement in various
kinds of methodological work, including technical missions, means
that the number of these omissions is decreasing. But the issue here
is not that the Statistics Department is reducing the number of omitted
data points, the point is that it is the existence of *methodological
criteria* that provides the objective basis for assessing the correctness
of data. It is the existence of these criteria that allows for—and one

Table 6.1 A sample from the IFS showing omissions for Arcadia. In this case, most omissions relate to the most current reporting periods

Arcadia	Previous year				Current year									
	I	II	III	IV	I	II	III	IV	July	Aug	Sept	Oct	Nov	Dec
of Period														
Exchange rates														
Market rate	31	1.4586	1.4155	1.4134	1.4118	1.4171	1.4158	1.4158	1.4375	1.4006	1.4020	1.4158	1.4157	1.43
Period		*Period average*												
Market rate	50	0.9298	0.9397	0.9508	0.9662	0.9818	0.9836	0.9997	0.9557	0.9618	0.9836	0.9789	0.9889	0.999
Market rate	86	0.9328	0.9381	0.9435	0.9663	0.9806	0.9676	0.9785	0.9704	0.9616	0.9708	0.9635	0.998
of Period														
Fund position														
Quota	5.0	206.0	206.0	206.0	206.0	206.0	206.0	206.0	206.0	206.0	206.0	206.0	206.0	206.0
SDRs	1.5	20.3	17.5	4.7	16.0	21.9	16.2	11.1	18.5	16.2	16.2	16.2	1.1	11.1
Reserve position in the Fund	–	–	–	–	–	–	–	–	–	–	–	–	–	–
Total Fund credit and loans outstanding	7.3	207.3	207.3	197.1	194.0	181.1	178.0	165.0	178.0	178.0	178.0	178.0	165.0	165.0
of Period														
International liquidity														
Total reserves minus gold	4.8	1,447.5	1,760.8	1,605.3	1,259.9	1,429.3	1,807.4	.....	1,423.0	.....	1,807.4	1,778.2	1,804.6	.....
SDRs	7.9	31.8	26.4	7.0	23.3	31.6	23.3	15.9	27.1	23.6	23.3	23.4	1.5	15.9
Reserve position in the Fund	0.1	0.1	0.1	0.1	0.1	0.1	0.1	0.1	0.1	0.1	0.1	0.1	0.1	0.1
Foreign exchange	6.9	1,415.6	1,734.3	1,598.2	1,236.5	1,397.6	1,784.1	.....	1,395.8	.....	1,784.1	1,754.8	1,803.0	.....
Gold (million fine Troy ounces)	0.216	0.216	0.216	0.217	0.217	0.217	0.217	.....	0.217	.....	0.217	0.217	0.217	.....
Gold (national valuation)	4.7	4.8	4.7	4.8	4.7	4.5	4.5	.....	4.6	4.6	4.5	4.5	4.4	.....

Deposit money banks: assets	7.0	529.8	497.8	154.6	387.8	375.3	555.1	....	451.1	499.3	555.1	564.7	541.0
of which: Claims on non-banks	2.5	328.6	302.6	249.5	210.7	191.0	334.5	....	213.0	281.9	334.5	297.6	274.7
Deposit money banks: liabilities	6.2	1,695.2	1,749.9	1,740.8	1,726.0	1,665.0	1,841.1	....	1,782.0	1,771.0	1,841.1	1,882.6	1,895.7
of which: Liabilities to non-banks	1.5	1,442.4	1,449.8	1,497.2	1,440.7	1,440.2	1,461.2	....	1,552.5	1,491.3	1,461.2	1,477.4	1,474.6
Other banking institutions: liabilities	–	–	–	–	–	–	–	....	–	–	–	–	–

of Period

Monetary authorities Foreign assets	397	1,356	1,669	1,536	1,231	1,415	1,755	....	1,373	1,547	1,755	1,770	1,803
Claims on central government	63	76	83	85	56	55	54	....	59	48	54	58	51
Claims on deposit money banks	941	1,031	860	829	1,208	1,132	1,081	....	1,281	1,298	1,081	903	746
Reserve money	583	1,632	1,697	1,667	1,728	1,779	1,923	....	1,930	2,019	1,923	1,878	1,780
of which: Currency outside DMBs	194	1,242	1,286	1,315	1,313	1,365	1,431	....	1,459	1,499	1,431	1,388	1,413
Foreign liabilities	332	328	319	304	315	295	306	....	292	295	306	301	274
Central government deposits	83	189	286	137	124	177	310	....	162	251	310	201	161
Capital accounts	129	129	128	128	133	133	133	....	133	133	133	133	133
Other items (net)	274	184	183	214	196	218	218	....	197	195	218	219	252

might say even leads to—these particular omissions. Without these criteria, there would be fewer omissions since they could not be recognised.

I say "fewer" because there are other sources of omissions. One source has to do with the fact that some countries do not submit data on a regular basis. This may be for a variety of reasons such as lack of staff or political turmoil. But whatever the cause, some countries go months without sending information on certain sectors and there is very little Statistics Department staff can do about it. Unlike policy analysts, they cannot use their professional judgement to make estimates. They cannot put their name to some figure and say, "I used my professional skill to determine this". For statistical information does not allow such practices. If it were to do so, not only would the importance of methodological criteria be diminished, but there would be a need for the review processes of policy work. As should be clear, statistical information work does not incorporate those review processes[157].

This point can be further underlined. For omissions do not just derive from inappropriate methods or even from the tardiness of some countries in supplying the Statistics Department with data. A further source of omissions is that the Statistics Department only collects what it calls "ex-post facto" data (or data produced "after the event"). Unfortunately, these data are not always available: sometimes members send estimates instead (e.g. budget estimates), or they send forecasts or provisional data. Such data are unusable for the purposes of the department.

My case is that all of the above points relate to the question of anonymity in statistical information. Statistical information has no author because it does not involve the judgement of policy work. There is, if you like, no need to point the finger at the person who calculated the statistical information since it is the *methods* that determine that information, and not an individual's (or a team's) interpretative skills.

Furthermore, and this may not seem such an important point at first, these criteria can be applied by anyone familiar with them. One is

---

[157] Though it is checked. So for example, once data has been entered into the EIS, assistants will print out hard copy for the economists to check. The draft versions of submissions to the *IFS* are also checked by senior staff within the division. But this work is essentially administrative I am suggesting, rather than analytical, as is the case in policy review.

reminded here of Egon Bittner's observation that the notion of a formal organisation can be invoked to enable organisational incumbents to point towards their compliance with organisational protocols[158]. In the case of the Statistics Department, statistical methods can be invoked as a guide to the work of the economists within it. What is crucial here is that invoking these methods does not necessarily mean discussion with or the seeking of agreement with other persons (although it might). My point is that an individual need only refer to the manuals (if they cannot remember the methods themselves). Contrast this with policy work. Here, assessments of "adequate fact" are based on what may be described as a complex social organisation. Here I have in mind the review process that is part and parcel of all policy work. This review process requires the elaborate interlinking of individual work practices with those of other individuals and groups—a process of collaborative activity that bolsters and checks "individual judgement". The long and short of it is that statistical information can be processed effectively by individuals; policy information requires collaboration.

The issue of omissions in data is also pertinent to a discussion of the second issue that distinguishes policy work from statistical work, namely, the *timeliness* of the data the Statistics Department must produce. For even though statistical economists may work very hard to get things finished, sometimes they do not succeed. They are of course responsible for such failures, but this responsibility is subordinate to a greater one: the responsibility to get such things as the *IFS* published on time. Statistics Department economists cannot hold up publication of the *IFS* because some of the figures are not complete. Such delays are, one might say, a luxury they cannot afford. One might put it more strongly: the point of statistical work is to complete it on time, or at least to get the bulk of the work done on time—even if that means one of two pieces are left out. For, the utility of the entire corpus of statistics information resides, in part, in the continual production of it according to agreed time-scales. It is in this sense that statistical data have to be produced on a timely basis, and it is in relation to this fact that some omissions do arise.

All of this is not meant to give the impression that the Statistics Department is not working adequately. Rather, I am arguing that omissions are, for the most part, the manifestation of the *proper application of statistical method*. Furthermore, those which slip

---

[158] See Bittner (1965).

through because of "practical realities" may be thought of as the "cost" of ensuring that the bulk of the work is done on time. Getting the bulk of the work done is more important than fussing about one or two particular numbers. Besides, there are very few omissions that derive from such practical exigencies. In any case, omissions are often treated as things that can be rectified "next time round", i.e. next month. And lastly—though I have not mentioned this up to now— ensuring a complete and correct database is viewed as a goal that will be attained in time (and with many technical assistance missions!) and not in the here and now.

As I have said, staff of the Statistics Department may feel ill at ease with these discussions of omissions. This is not because they would want to claim that they never occur but because they would rightly recognise that the casual reader of such discussions might get the wrong impression. As I have explained, the great bulk of omissions arise precisely because correct procedures have been applied, and not because of improper procedures. Those which do slip through are the cost of ensuring the adequacy and the timeliness of the greater bulk of the data. Omissions from this view reflect a job well done, not a job poorly done. My concern with this issue has been to deepen my analysis of statistical work and associated organisational structures. It enables me to now specify some of its salient features.

First, in statistical work individual contributions cannot be identified when a task is complete, nor is it requisite that they be identifiable. For statistical information disguises the authorship of that information. Perhaps that sounds too conspiratorial. What I mean is that authorship does not matter. It is not relevant. Consequently, the task is such that trained individuals can be moved around, more or less flexibly, along what one might think of as the production line for such things as the *IFS*. This enables managers to re-allocate individuals as and when logistical problems arise in any particular part of the work cycle.

Second, statistical information has metrics for the assessment of objectivity that enable individuals familiar with those metrics to process that information autonomously. Although there will be a need for supervision and administration of their work, there is no need for elaborate review and checking procedures. Thus, the Statistics Department can process data rapidly and without the burden of the review process that is so conspicuous in policy work.

Third, the metrics of statistical information are grounds for the incompleteness of data. That is to say, whereas in policy analysis there is a need for some kind of completeness and hence the necessity of making judgements, in statistical work absences in the data are treated as a natural outcome of the proper application of analytic principles.

The use of documents

There are a number of implications that follow on from these characteristics. One has to do with how this limits the kinds of actions that can be based on the data the Statistics Department produce. The most important for our concerns is that these elements show themselves in relation to the Fund's policy work.

For the Fund's Executive Board operates its policy decision-making on the assumption that those decisions are based on "adequate" descriptions and analyses. One element of this adequacy is bound up with "thoroughness", as explained in the previous chapter. What is meant by thorough or alternative formulations like "sufficient" or "complete" is complex and I have not provided sufficient materials in the preceding discussions to specify what it means. By the end of the book I hope to have done so. But if the reader can bear with me, what I am wanting to draw attention to is that such thoroughness cannot be guaranteed in statistical information; indeed omissions in that information are a manifest demonstration that it is not designed to provide such thoroughness. Therefore the Executive Board cannot use that information for its policy work[159].

A second and clearly related point has to do with how the area departments and associated policy functions cannot rely on the information produced by the Statistics Department either, and this is for the same reason. Instead, desk officers and the chiefs of missions rely on their own information production since this can ensure the "adequacy" they require. Their task is, after all, to deliver what the Board thinks is appropriate. In this way, the Board's judgements as to what is required spill down to policy workers at the coal face.

---

[159] As it happens, those same omissions display the fact that statistical information has been designed to be *methodologically* right. This includes concern with due periodicity, or time-scales (every month in the case of the *IFS*) which of course is different to the thoroughness. What is interesting about this is how documents like the *IFS* are self-explicative insofar as they indicate how they have been put together and what one can do with them.

It needs to be made clear that the Board could choose otherwise. In other words, there is no absolute reason why the Board should opt for thoroughness over methodological correctness. The view it has adopted is essentially normative, or to do with what it perceives as the best way of doing things in the circumstances. From this perspective, the Board is not abandoning any concern with methodological propriety, it is placing less emphasis on that than on thoroughness. Policy work consists of articulating judgements as regards these matters and manifesting this articulation in the production of certain orders of information. There is a different amalgam of concerns articulated in such things as the *IFS* and in Article IV staff reports.

One result of this is that the two functions that are involved in the respective production of such things as the *IFS* and Article IV reports have different relationships to the Board: the area department missions are closely tied to the Board's policy decision-making; the Statistics Department is much more closely linked to the Board in terms of its concerns with the dissemination of statistical information—part of the Fund's articles as I remarked at the outset of this chapter.

That there is a different set of relations between the Board and certain departments causes considerable comment within the institution. The issues have to do with what is perceived as the "correct" balance between such things as thoroughness and methodological propriety. The debates are about what is perceived as proper, best, ideal or most appropriate. In debating these things, members of the Fund are demonstrating and displaying the very expertise that is required to make such normative decisions.

The flavour of these debates can be quite intense. One reason for this is that the balance between methodological correctness and thoroughness varies in every instance: some countries generate data that is in nearly all respects methodologically sound, whilst other countries, typically the less developed, do not generate such data. Those who deal with the latter kind (i.e. the desk officers for members with what one might call "poor" data sets), find that their work takes them away from the data the Statistics Department generates. When I brought this subject up with such desk officers, many remarked that though they would like to use more *IFS* data, they did not have time. As one desk officer put it:

Yes, I am being pressured to use the *IFS* data, but I have got to worry about my work, what I can do, not what would be ideal.

He then picked up a copy of the *IFS* and having flicked to the page for his country, pointed out the various omissions in the table.

How can I use this? This is no good! I don't have time for these debates. Someone else needs to sort it out. I have my job to do.

A senior adviser in an area department offered a more sanguine view:

Look, sometimes the tension here arises because people forget that they have different jobs. Policy work and statistical work aren't the same. That slips from view sometimes.

This alludes to the question of what needs to be understood within a setting to enable some documentary artefact to be deployed effectively. This adviser was pointing out that knowledge of the organisational members is not something that once learnt is never forgotten. To the extent that this adviser's comments hold true, then one might say that these debates about the role of data from such things as the *IFS* and their use in policy work are not just a reflection of things that might get forgotten, but are also opportunities for these same things to be recalled.

Conclusion

Over the years, the Fund itself has had various formal examinations of the differences between the information generated by the Statistics Department and area departments as part of their policy work. None of these studies have offered ways of dissolving this difference but they have gone some way to understand it. So, studies conducted in the late 1980s, for instance, concluded that what distinguishes policy from statistical information is essentially a matter of scope, with the odd methodological difference built in.

My concern, however, has been to draw attention to the *moral implicativeness* of information. In this case, the information in question is embodied in documents: in documents such as the *IFS* on the one hand, and in Article IV and Use of Fund Resource mission staff reports on the other. What I mean by the term "implicativeness" is how a document like a staff report warrants action. By using the term "moral" I am alluding to how that warrant is based on assessments of what is practical, what is appropriate and what is preferred. Such assessments can turn out to be wrong. In this sense, the Board can be held accountable for its decisions. Its behaviour is then moral.

What I have been arguing is that the Board has over the years developed a certain determination of what materials are required to give its decisions justification. This is bound up with and constitutive of what I have called the Fund's organisational problematic. In this chapter I have noted that there are two of these problematics, reflecting the range of tasks required by the Fund's Articles.

I want to conclude this chapter by drawing attention to how these two different problematics play out in terms of time, and how this in turn has implications for accountability. I want to suggest that the relationship to time is more complex than it might appear. Or more precisely, documents such as staff reports offer one specific set of opportunities within the matrix of temporally organised action, whilst documents such as the *IFS* offer another.

For instance, if one treats the *IFS* and a staff report as providing views on the world, then the nature of that view evolves differently through time for each document. I have noted that the *IFS* provides only a partial view on current circumstances. It is therefore not an ideal resource for the investigation of the present time. However, with the passing of time, so the data available for the *IFS* increases. As there are fewer and fewer omissions, so the picture gradually completes itself. In this sense, the resources that slowly become available in the *IFS*—or rather a series of *IFS* reports—enable an ever better view of the past. As the past gets further away, so the picture of that past gets better and better.

In contrast, a staff report is designed to provide a view on the present which is rich enough to enable a determination of the future. As I say, this is how a staff report can support Executive Board decision-making. In complex ways, these decisions will affect and to some degree control that future. But the significant point is that once determination of that future has been undertaken, and once the future becomes reality, the report in question has outlived this role. By the time the future becomes the present, the materials a staff report present may have become out of date. Estimates will have been corrected by actuals, projections will have been altered by results.

The point may be clarified by putting it in terms of a career. A staff report terminates its career when it has facilitated the Board in making decisions. These decisions are about the future when viewed from the present. But as the Board moves into that future, so that staff report slips into the past. It becomes locked in that moment it was delivered.

This has implications for accountability. If this is the case that a briefing paper can be used by PDR to investigate the work of a mission retrospectively it can do so only because those investigations are constrained by a short time-frame—the few months during which the work in question was undertaken. If one expands this time-frame with a view to using such things as a staff report to investigate the past over a number of years, one will start to struggle. For what that past has turned into may only have become visible through the gradual accumulation of statistical and financial data. Much of this information may not have been available to those who composed a staff report. All they had was the materials in hand, not the materials that would, in later months and years, show themselves.

A paradox here is that it may be that to assess its past decisions the Fund would have to use such documents as the *IFS* rather than the staff reports actually used in those decision-making processes. Doing so, however, would be fraught with complexities. For they do not reflect the same relationship to the materials used to describe the world, to the division of labour they are part of and which construct that view, or to the temporal matrix within which they operate. With one, the Fund can look forward, but not back; with the other the Fund can look at the past but cannot measure the present.

CHAPTER 7
Desk officers

All buildings in central Washington have to be no more than a certain height. This is one of the reasons why Washington seems so unlike other American cities. But in addition, the road system is not based on the usual kind of North American grid system, but consists of a set of radial thoroughfares imposed upon a grid. These cross one another at various "circles", which makes driving around the city rather disorienting. Part of being an ethnographer, of course, involves learning the geography of a place. As it happens, nearly all Fund staff have offices in its main building, so I did not find myself getting lost on the streets of Washington[160]. But I did have considerable difficulty inside the Fund's building. About a third of the building is subterranean, consisting of various car parks (each floor being painted a different colour to identify it), archives, system administration offices, offset printing and copying facilities, telex and communications offices and much else besides. The above-ground floors, 13 in all, are organised in a way that reflects the hierarchy of the institution: members of the Board are spread out between the 13th and the 12th floors, with the Deputy Managing Directors (DMDs) holding office on the 12th floor. In between these and the ground floor are the various area departments and key reviewing departments. For example, European I Department (basically Western Europe) is on the ninth floor; Middle Eastern on the third; and Policy Development and Review (PDR) dominates the fifth floor. The floors themselves, however, are hard to distinguish from one another. The corridors allow no view onto the outside or onto the atrium on the inside. There are a handful of plants, but few notice-boards or other geographical markers. One can easily get disoriented.

Geography even in an anonymous building was, however, the least of my worries. For having tapped on the right door, I still had the hardest part of my job to do, and that was to uncover the nature of the work in question. This was particularly difficult at the Fund. For the kind of work that gets done, especially the work of *desk officers* is curiously

---

[160] Though certain important departments occupy buildings a block or two away. The Statistics and Research Departments, for example, are in "IS Square", a short distance up 19th Street.

difficult to specify. If one walks into a desk officer's room, all one finds is an individual, sitting at a desk with various papers and files lying beside a VDU. There is no work to observe, nothing demonstrable in the way there is with, say, air traffic control or hospital work. One cannot ask for the desk officer to explain how "this" or "that" is done—there is no action in particular that one can to point to. Nor can one ask about the key economic problems they are grappling with. For, because of one's trade (i.e. a sociological ethnographer), this is something that one is not expected to understand.

What one has to do instead is to coax the desk officers into talking about their work in simple terms, and to do so in a way that provides instructions as to what is important. Through these instructions, one is led to understand the details of their work and the practical realities that distinguish between what the desk officers might *like* to do and what they *actually* do. As I argued in Chapter 3, my concern with this difference is not to seek out irony and paradox, but to flesh out the facts of life that give the work in question its flavour, its situatedness.

In this chapter I want to describe some of those practical realities. I want to distinguish between what one might call the arcane expertise of area department desk officers (an expertise in such things as analysis of the aggregated money flows in economies), and the mundane, practical, organisational context in which that expertise shows itself. I shall describe the diversified character of the information they use in their work, as well as the practical time limits restricting the analytical endeavours they can undertake with that information.

But this chapter will be distinct from the previous one in that I shall attempt to deepen my characterisation of the work in question by considering the implications of technological change. More particularly, I shall report on my discussions with desk officers about the implications of providing networked access to the information they collect. Such enquiries led me to deepen my understanding of how their expertise is deployed within a particular division of labour. This itself is bound up with the temporal organisation of the tasks. These themes, of course, continue on from those I have begun to elaborate on in the previous two chapters. My concern here is not just to delve a little deeper into them, it is also to start reporting more ethnographic detail than I have hitherto thought appropriate. This will provide me with an opportunity for completing the background to the main ethnographic task of the book, a description of an Article IV mission.

Overview of the chapter

To explicate my arguments, this chapter is organised in the following way. I begin by describing desk officers' work at a kind of abstracted level. By this I simply mean the kind of level desk officers themselves typically offer as a first cut at describing what they do. These descriptions most often turn around the nature of economic reason, and as a consequence assume some kind of expertise in economics. Without wanting to pretend any such competence, I shall attempt to explain what I understood as the kinds of "economic reason" desk officers employ by reference to one of the tools of their trade, specifically, a "flow of funds" analysis. Such analyses are intended to enable economists to recognise the basic models that underscore how a national economy might be conceived of in policy work.

I then look beneath this abstract level, to find that such tools are used in a setting where other more fundamental tasks have to be undertaken. These tasks involve, for example, gathering and sifting all the information that is delivered to these individuals (i.e. the desk officers). This information arrives in a variety of forms: in paper mail, in email, in journal articles, in government publications and in spreadsheets from colleagues. Desk officers have to manage all these materials and work them up before they can turn to a flow of funds analysis. I will then note that this work is undertaken within practical time constraints. Desk officers cannot spend all their time dealing with the information that comes their way. Nor, even if they did, would it be certain that they would finish. For this work is never quite done; it is always being added to and worked on a little more.

I then go on to show how a concern with what kinds of processes technology might support provides another angle on important properties of the organisational action of desk officers. In particular, one learns that although desk officers do not "complete" their information gathering and analysis work for large periods of the year, when desk officers participate in the mission cycle they reorient their work to ensure that their data collection and analysis work gets completed. There is then a contrast between patterns of work (and associated information gathering and production tasks) associated with different points of the working calendar. Finally, though I shall only foreshadow the arguments here, if one focuses on the mission component of this calendar, one discovers that there is another set of basic parameters with regard to what is treated as information that is shared and distributed, and what is treated as private and unshareable.

The work of desk officers

I start then with the kinds of descriptions desk officers typically offered as an introduction to their work. I do not mean that they always offered the same accounts, only that in general terms these descriptions had a similar flavour. A quote from one of the 90 economists I interviewed will indicate what I mean. Having asked him to describe his job, he replied:

I see my responsibilities as being as informed as possible about the current developments (of my member country) and I think most importantly, to have a basically coherent, albeit explicit analytic framework of understanding. Without it there are a million and one different traps, but I think when you have it, you know, having put it together the pieces of the puzzle and having taken on the dynamics of the economy, you know what it is important and what is not.

What does this mean? What is an analytic framework of understanding? Another desk officer offered me some advice:

Look, read . . . (referring to a training manual), take the flow of funds bit, that will give you some idea of what desk officers mean when they talk about models.

And I duly followed his advice. Reading this manual did not by any means give me all the things I wanted, but it certainly helped me to develop what Geertz calls a sensibility for the kinds of things that the first desk officer I quoted had in mind[161].

The manual explained, and this is to paraphrase, that a flow of funds analysis enables desk officers to understand (at least in broad terms) which part of an economy generates resources and which consumes them. This, apparently, is fundamental to macroeconomic analysis and to understanding the financial imbalances that may lead a member

---

[161] By this Geertz was referring to a sensibility for any and all work, not just the work of economists. See Geertz (1983).

country to seek Fund resources. The manual went on to say that to understand how it does this, one needs to know some basic facts.

First, the Fund collates economic data (disregarding what that data might be or where it comes from for the moment) into four broad categories: data about the government or non-financial public sector, data about the non-financial private sector, data relating to the financial sector, and lastly, data about the external sector. The flow of funds analysis is an integration of these, showing to the desk officer the flows of revenue and expenditure between sectors. So, for example, it can show that investment in the non-financial private sector is financed by savings in the external sector. Thereby, it can highlight which sectors are running a deficit and which a surplus.

Furthermore, the manual outlined how there are certain key relationships between the sectors and the respective flow of funds between them and, ultimately, this is a reflection of the economic activity in question. These relationships, the reality if you like, include facts such as domestic savings depend upon the income of sectors as well as the desire or possibility to consume (and thus not save). Therefore, domestic savings are a function of and reflect wage policy, pricing policy, supply of goods, exchange rates, etc. Another fact is as follows: the gap between the resources generated in one sector and used by another, when aggregated at national level, is equal to foreign financing; at the sectoral level, it is equal to the financing from other sectors plus external financing.

It is these relationships, I learnt, that are important elements in what the desk officer quoted called an "analytic framework of understanding". There are, needless to say, other elements in this framework. As I continued the process of interviewing desk officers, of prying ever more deeply into their work, so I learnt that such an understanding is crucial in enabling desk officers to comprehend the authorities of the member country in question. It was explained to me on several occasions that it is no good building up a conception of how an economy operates if that conception—that analytic framework—does not allow for effective exchange and mutual understanding between desk officers and member authorities. This is not to say that there is only one analytic framework that needs to be shared by one and all, only that the conceptions must be significantly similar to allow sensible discussion, critique and exchange. As another desk officer put it:

Here is an important point—it reveals the way which policy makers think about the economy because that's the data set they work with themselves, and I have found—I think equally throughout Europe—that you have to understand the model that the policy makers have in their own heads. Otherwise you have, no em, the model (you have) is wrong . . . or it's a different model. You have to be able to argue with them about the economy in terms of their model.

Practical contexts

So when one starts to talk to desk officers, one is presented with remarks about analytic frameworks or models. If one burrows away into their explanations, coaxing them to say more, they will start to talk about the kinds of tools they might use to build up these models. What one learns thereby (about the desk officers) is still superficial. But such things are the stuff that is talked about when one first meets desk officers. This is the first cut they offer on describing their work.

Having gone through this stage, desk officers will typically start talking about the details of what they do or, as one of them put it, "what I actually do". I did not take this to refer to some platonic essence in their work so much as a reference to the mundane, everyday practical realities of their work, all too often dismissed as the things that actually get done rather than what ought to be done. Such a contrast can of course be misleading and many ethnographers, especially within the so-called constructivist camp, have turned this distinction into an excuse to ironicise the work they describe[162]. As I said at the outset, I certainly do not want to do so myself, being more concerned to take these partly self-mocking observations of the "real work" as pointing towards what for me are the interesting aspects of that work.

What this real work consists of, I learnt, has to do with questions such as where the numbers used in such things as a flow of funds analysis come from. I had presumed from the first that they did not come from thin air and, from more or less the first interview, I gathered that desk officers did not find these numbers placed on their desk first thing Monday morning (delivered from the hands of a research assistant perhaps). What I began to learn is that desk officers have to dig out

---

[162] For a discussion of this see Woolgar (1993).

those numbers from a variety of sources. They have to sift through various materials to get the raw stuff for their analytical work.

One desk officer explained this by starting with a complaint:

What do I actually do? I am a traffic cop. I get so much information here that I seem to spend all of my time sorting it and out and sending it on elsewhere.

What he was alluding to was the myriad sources and modalities of information that came his way. These materials consist of such things as newspaper editorials and articles in *The Economist*. There are also the documented analyses of other somewhat similar organisations to the Fund, such as the Organisation for Economic Co-operation and Development and, of course, across the road on 19th Street, the World Bank. Occasionally, scholarly work in economics journals is also collected. But there are also such terse texts as *government bills* for financial or economic legislation, Ministry of Finance *budgetary statements* and *financial statements* from commercial banks. Most desk officers also get such things as quarterly statements of *foreign currency holdings* from central banks, and a somewhat smaller group get *estimates of government fiscal revenues* faxed to them.

The desk officers have to juxtapose these bits and pieces, these newspaper reports and monetary tables, these faxed notes from central banks and editorials from the *Financial Times*, into a position where materials can be found that constitute the stuff used in such things as a flow of funds analysis.

Some desk officers keep notes or compilations of important economic information in what are often called "black books". Others keep AREMOS time series and Lotus spreadsheets. But during my discussion of what the "real work" consisted of, I was told that desk officers do not keep these artefacts continually up to date:

I try and update some of my time series when I can but to be honest I don't do that very consistently. It depends how much time you have. You know there are so many other things you have to do. In any case I don't give it much priority.

Additionally, desk officers do not aggregate their materials into some kind of whole. They may keep a variety of spreadsheets, notebooks and data, some of which are more up to date than others, but one will not find an integrated representation of any country, even an out-of-date version:

What databases? There is no database! This is something that people have to understand about operational countries (i.e Use of Fund Resources countries). Even for Article IV countries. Sometimes there may be some general time series but I have not seen any operational country with a database in the sense of a large composite file that has all the series for the country you may need. The thing simply does not exist.

The discussion in the previous chapter should provide some indication as to why this should be: it is in the nature of the kind of data that the Fund's policy workers use that it is, in a sense, ephemeral. By ephemeral here I mean that the data are bound to the time in which they are generated. The purpose of the data is, after all, to reflect the "current" period.

This is one powerful reason why desk officers do not keep an integrated representation of a country. For this would mean that they would have to amend and revise it more or less every week to keep it up to date.

Given also the fact that the Fund does not want information about the membership all the time but only when it decides to do so—and this means primarily during the mission process—then there is little incentive for desk officers to maintain such databases with all the work that this would entail.

It is in this sense that one should understand the conflict between what could be kept in a database and what is practical. It is not just that desk officers do not have the time. It is that in the circumstances in which they operate, a concern with keeping an up-to-date database takes lower precedence over other matters. So, and as a result, such things as flow of funds analyses are the kinds of undertakings that desk officers would like to commence but, for practical reasons, rarely complete.

It hardly needs saying that there is much more that one would need to understand about the organisation of desk officers' work to appreciate fully its complexity and organisation. But my point thus far has been to locate desk officers' work in a practical context where certain elemental features can be seen to be important. Issues of the amount of time that is available for work, and questions to do with the materials that desk officers have at hand and are required to be able to deliver, are all part of those elemental features. But in addition, further issues of salience and further elemental features of their work can be uncovered by reference to technological change.

New technologies and desk officers

By using the term technological change I do not mean that this followed on from my concern (outlined in the opening chapter) to use the present to map out the future. I mean that such investigations provided a vehicle to uncover further features of the work, and it did so irrespective of whether I was (am) interested in technological possibility. In any case, the present is never static or fixed. Work is always evolving and the tools that support work are always evolving too.

The interplay between work practice (social action if you prefer) and the tools that support it is part of the "natural" resource of organisational ethnography (as indeed it is for all ethnography). The interplay—or, as it sometimes manifested, the tension—between tools and work practice can draw attention to what I earlier called the organisational problematic. That is to say, it can draw attention to the way in which an organisation organises itself to do certain tasks. New tools and new technologies may change that organisation or may draw attention to elements of that organisation that need to be preserved.

So, returning to the research, it happened that my field work was carried out while the Fund was investigating a networked technology that had considerable potential to create change. During an interview with one of the DMD's special advisers, a workstation supporting this system was installed in his office. This became an opportunity for him and me to discuss at great length the problems of designing systems to support work, problems of culture in the workplace, and all those topics I remarked upon in Chapter 3.

The system itself, known as System X, was introduced with the hope of enabling the DMDs and other senior staff (including the special adviser just mentioned) to have direct access to area department desk officers' workstations.

System X was not developed as a demonstration of what future technology would look like, however, so much as it was an opportunity to highlight some of the forms that new technology might take. It was hoped that users' reactions to the technology would provide resources for designing something better in the future. The issues that were

expected to be uncovered related both to the rather complex technological requirements to ensure ease of navigation around the network
and what work practice features would be impacted upon by such a
system.

My own research became a major resource in helping explain why
System X was unsuited to effective work practice[163]. More specifically,
my discussions with desk officers made it clear—and I shared this with
those responsible for the system—that System X was inappropriate for
current work practices. This was not necessarily because of the compromised nature of the information on the system (i.e. because the
information was often incomplete and consisted of a collage of materials, bits and pieces)—a reason that might come to mind initially. After
all, lack of properly maintained and annotated data is often cited as the
bugbear of all those applications which are intended to support shared
data.

The issue here was rather different. It had to do with what was
wanted for sharing and what was not. As one desk officer put it:

You could make sure that all the data we keep on the workstations was up to
date and properly annotated. Doing that could be made a management priority
and data management could be something that we get measured on. I don't
think that would ever happen but in any case, even if we were required to do
that no one would use it, no one would use System X. The only person who
wants to use the information is the desk officer himself.

This struck me as peculiarly interesting for at least two reasons.
First, information is one of those categories of material that is often
spoken about as if any number of persons might become users of it.
This is especially the case when information becomes digitised, for this
creates a "new universe, a parallel universe created and sustained by
the world's computers and communications lines . . . the realm of pure
information" (Benedikt, as cited by Nunberg, 1996, p. 117)[164]. In being
"pure", anyone can have access to this information. According to this
vision, digital technology allows information to become free of the
physical fetters that bind it to its original creator. So, in this case, the
use of paper, filing cabinets, paper-based mailing systems and so on
might be thought of as constituting the fetters that tie information about

---

[163] See Harper (1996b) and also Harper & Newman (1996).

[164] See Nunberg (1996).

member countries to particular desk officers. Yet what I was told is that the information is indeed tethered to desk officers not because of its physical medium, but for other reasons.

Before saying anything about that what those reasons might be, let me remark on the second reason why I found this interesting. In my second week of interviews, one of the more senior members of the Fund said to me: "Look, have you ever seen a staff report?" I explained that I had not. He went on; "It's not the staff report that is so important, it's this bit." at which time he pointed out that on the first page of the text there was a footnote stating that the figures in the report were based on discussion with the authorities and staff estimates. He wagged his finger at the word "estimates" and said: "This is crucial, Richard. This makes the materials we use quite different, quite special. You have to understand this to understand the Fund."

I say this was interesting to me because it is almost commonplace to say that one of the outputs of bureaucratic life is a collection of anonymous documents; that a crucial achievement within bureaucratic organisations is to transform the materials gathered by unique individuals in unique circumstances into the objective, voiceless documents of modern bureaucratic enterprise. These are the salient claims of authors as distinct as Weber, Foucault, Giddens and Smith, as I argued in Chapter 2[165]. Yet here I was confronted with a document that specifically identified the authors and which linked the materials used in that document to those authors.

This, however, was still far from sufficient to explain why information on desk officers' workstations would not be used by anyone but the desk officer. So I asked the same senior member of staff if he was suggesting that there were issues of ownership as regards data on desk officers' workstations:

No. The data is shared but only in certain circumstances and in any case is never shared widely. What you have got to understand is how desk officers have responsibility for delivering the right information. They do so as part of the mission process, as part of the team that does that. You have to realise that is their job and not anyone else's.

---

[165] For a recent discussion of Weber, Foucault and Giddens on this issue see Dandeker (1990).

He then explained that I needed to learn more about the mission process and the patterns of information production and sharing that were constitutive of it. I subsequently did so through my observation of the mission to Arcadia.

Without wanting to elaborate too much at the moment (for obvious reasons), I learnt that during the mission process, desk officers will "work up" their individual data sets. That is, they will endeavour to complete their activities to produce the raw materials they need for such things as flow of funds analyses. But they do not do so alone. They collaborate with other mission team members (there are normally four economists working on each mission) who have also been "working up" their own data. Gradually, a commonly specified set of interpretations is agreed upon by the group. This is used to compile such things as the staff report.

One important feature of this process is that data stored on any individual workstation reflects that stage in the social process of agreement and iteration undertaken by the mission team. Hence at some point in the mission cycle, the data are rough and incomplete; the social process of figuring out the data being only begun. At another, later stage, the data are more complete, more effectively understood and developed, the social process of which it is part being nearer completion.

One can put this in terms of a document career. When a team starts work on a mission, when data have just begun to be gathered and the first meetings between the economists have occurred, data are too rough to be shared amongst the team, although each member will have some understanding of other team members' data. The document the team is working toward—loosely speaking the draft staff report—is, at this moment in its career, fragmented across persons. These persons are its authors. Toward the end of the mission cycle, data can be more readily shared, since by that time data will have been more thoroughly worked up, assessed and cross validated. At this moment in time, the document they are working toward can be brought together.

From this view, one should see that at any specific moment in time, the adequacy of data and the document those data are part of is only visible to participants in a mission team, since it is only they who are aware of what stage of completion the data and associated documentation has reached. All others outside the mission team and outside the mission cycle, will find those data, as well as the document in question, opaque and unsuited for use.

Deepening the characterisation of work

As I understood this, I began to shift my understanding of what desk officer work involves. I began to realise that their work does not just involve dealing with a variety of materials, nor is it driven simply by time limits. I realised that one also needs to understand the distinction between what they do in Washington and what they do on a mission. For, in a somewhat oversimplified sense, the process of gathering and analysing data in Washington is perceived as only producing partial, or more accurately, "provisional" information. It is only when missions are undertaken that these desk officers will endeavour to get the data required into what one might call a "complete" condition:

You can spend a great deal of time keeping all this stuff (information) but, in between missions, it kind of, look, you have got to realise that it's only during a mission that you really get to grips with this data.

And another:

You have got to distinguish between what they do during the mission process and what they do at other times.

From this view, I had been correct to understand that outside of the mission process, when economists are working on their own, the data they store will be very difficult for anyone to use but themselves, and even then it is often too rough and ready for desk officers to make use of. It is better thought of as a kind of residue of their work, the detritus from tasks that are all too often incomplete. This may be contrasted with their work during the mission cycle, where they orient towards working up their information into shareable material. But the sharing in question is strictly limited to their fellow mission members.

In understanding this, I also began to appreciate why it was that desk officers could not see what System X would be used for. From their perspective, the only people with an interest in accessing information are those they work with on a mission. Making information available to anyone within the Fund is unnecessary. Thus it made perfect sense for one of them to ask; "What would senior staff do with the information I have?" He posed such a question since he knew that senior staff would not be part of the mission process and thus would have no proper reason for accessing information.

This is not to say that senior staff are uninterested in that information. As should be clear from previous chapters, they certainly are. The point is that they are interested in it at the proper time. It has to go through a range of procedures that ensure its adequacy before they see it. When it does end up on their desk, it does so at the right juncture within the document career.

This may sound as if I am talking about a merely sequential process: first this, then that, then another step. In fact, the sequence in question is much more complex than this, involving a back and forth, a looking at the past as well as the future, such that the term "sequential" does it hardly any justice at all. As I argued in Chapter 4, such activities are bound up within a matrix of a temporally organised division of labour which allows a complex shifting of perspectives and systems of action. The trouble with System X was that it did not support or properly reflect the actual pattern of information production, sharing and delivery. It blurred important boundaries in the career of such things as staff reports. It enabled those who would properly have access to those reports at a certain time to have access much earlier than they were entitled to. In this, System X was not just a system that allowed a jumping of the queue; nor was it a system that allowed a blurring of a boundaries that served merely ritual import. It was a system that contradicted the fact that at certain times within the career of a staff report only specific "users" can effectively participate in the actions related to that report.

Conclusion

There is of course much more one could say about desk officers. I have skimmed over the distinctions between the kind of work done by desk officers for different members: work on a G7 desk (a "big desk" as they are called) is in many ways substantially different from that done by desk officers for a member using Fund resources. But my concern has been to emphasise the relationship between the work of desk officers and missions and to highlight the centrality of missions irrespective of the kind of member country in question.

I now want to conclude by returning to the remarks that opened this chapter. For it should be clear by now that not only did I need to learn my way around the Fund's building, I also had to learn the patterns of work associated with the mission cycle. This meant learning about *who* would be doing *what* at any moment in time and *where* they might be doing it.

Thus, by way of example from one day's interviews, in the morning, I found a desk officer I had agreed to meet working on amendments to a *letter of intent* specifying the conditions of a Fund loan. He was doing this (working closely with his chief) because the member authorities had failed to achieve their performance target with regard to inflation as agreed in the last mission. The desk officer was sitting in the chief's room discussing what might be the alternative ways they could formulate a new agreement. In this sense, the desk officer and his boss were trying to wrap up a mission cycle, albeit in this case the failure to achieve performance objectives made the end of the cycle somewhat ragged. The importance of this particular task resulted in the desk officer and the chief asking me to come back another day. A second desk officer, interviewed later on that morning, had just completed a G7 note for his country and was sitting behind his desk mulling over his next task[166]. This would be to draft out the main themes of his section of a briefing paper for the forthcoming mission to that country. This desk officer was then at the start of his mission cycle. He also had plenty of time to talk to me. In the afternoon, I met with a desk officer who had just returned from mission. He was trying to draft the back-to-office report for his chief. Though he was pressured for time, he was pleased to talk so that "he could see the wood for the trees".

In learning about the time-scales and patterns of mission activity, I was able to more effectively coax desk officers to talk about their work. On this particular day, my work was fairly successful—only one interview postponed. But other days it was much less so. Often, I could not find those I had agreed to meet. It was not that the individuals in question had an office hidden at the back of the area department that I could not find; it was that they were off somewhere at short notice, perhaps meeting with a new team for a mission they had just been told they would be participating in; or because the mission they were on had delayed its return (negotiations taking longer than planned); or because PDR had insisted that their briefing

---

[166] A G7 note is a more or less bi-monthly report circulated around the Fund describing the main features of the major economies.

paper be substantially revised and the mission chief had called a powwow. In understanding the importance, flexibility and vagaries of mission work, that is to say, why these kinds of things happen, I began to appreciate why an empty office was a sign of the natural order of the Fund's work.

CHAPTER 8
A mission to Arcadia

Throughout my sojourn in Washington, members of the Fund said to me "Look, to understand this place you have to go on a mission" and "Missions are what it is all about". Although my field work programme required that I observe a mission—missions are central to the document career—just why having to go on one, what it was about *being there* that would transform my outlook and identity was unclear. As I noted in Chapter 3, one possibility was that going on a mission would constitute a *ritual induction* that would transform my identity from an outsider to an insider. In any event, early on in my research, once I had understood the general parameters of the document career, I had made a request to observe a mission, but the likelihood of that request being accepted seemed remote. No one from outside of the Fund had ever been on a mission; missions often involve the handling of extremely confidential information. Yet, much to my delight, this request was granted and the Fund arranged for me to observe an Article IV mission[167]. My observation and experience of this led me to recognise, however, that there are indeed a number of important "facts of life" about policy work, knowledge of which does enrich one's perspective and does alter how one perceives the Fund's activities. In this sense, this event *was* a crucial induction to the setting, but the transformation achieved through being there was more than merely ritual, as was the case with observing the work of air traffic controllers on Saturday nights, or attending a "domestic" with the police. Here I really did learn things that I might have otherwise missed in my ethnography.

My task in this chapter is to elaborate just what these things were. This will involve some further description of the elemental mechanics

---

[167] What this meant was that the director of the area department gave his sanction for me to observe one, and pointed towards a suitable candidate mission. I then had to make the same request to the mission in question and this involved presenting to the chief and his deputy. Once they had given the go ahead, I then had to ask the member country's representative on the Executive Directors' Board. The extraordinary generosity of these individuals in supporting the research cannot be exaggerated.

of missions, and illumination of how the facts of life, as I have called them, show themselves in those mechanics. To do this will require me to cover a great deal of material and, furthermore, these materials will have implications for a host of arguments that I have been elaborating throughout the previous chapters and which I want to finalise in the remaining. My main concern in this chapter, though, is to describe how missions (at least, Article IV missions) consist of an iterative process whereby a mixture of arithmetical, econometric and meeting skills are used to create data that are reconciled and measured against the data collected by others within the mission. This process results in an overall picture of an economy being built up. This is then used as a basis for discussion with the local (or member) authorities, and ultimately is used to create various documents, including the staff report.

Running through these basic mechanics are a number of key facts. For example, the broad set of skills and techniques used on missions enable the economists to produce a staff report *come what may*, i.e. irrespective of the incompleteness of the data they have access to and disregarding (more or less) any contingencies they have to deal with. Further, data work on missions is a deeply social process and not just one that involves economic analysis. For, although data may be found in a variety of different places (namely, different offices within the various institutions of the member authority government agencies), only certain persons within those offices have the rank to sanction the relevant interpretations and associated numbers. These people provide the stamp of approval. The mission must seek these out. On the mission to Arcadia, one individual had a particularly important role in this. For though this individual was not able to give official sanction to every single number, his data, his views on that data, his explanations and accounts of policy, were treated as absolutely essential and vital to the mission's overall activities. Trust in this individual was crucial to the mission's work. The mission was not unusual in having a close relationship with one person in the member authorities. This is the norm in mission work (though it does not occur in every case).

I also want to describe some of the ritual elements of missions. One important aspect of ritual has to do with getting numbers and associated interpretations "signed off" by the right person (usually senior officials, as I have just described). Another has to do with the process of agreeing a basis for policy concerns in discussions between the mission and the authorities. Here the mission chief will make fairly ritualised orations to the local authorities; these commence and some-times terminate the discussion of policy. I shall not be suggesting that these orations are merely ritual or symbolic showpieces, or that they have no analytic value. Rather, I want to show that it is partly through ritual that the symbolic importance of the events is demonstrated. Further, it is through these same rituals that the symbolic status of the participants is also affirmed. Without ritual, the essential charac-teristics of the events—in this case policy discussions—would be changed. This character ensures that the outcome of these meetings is treated as consequential; or, put another way, ensures that these are meetings that *count*.

Of course in this setting, the word "count" has at least two relevant meanings, the first implying the significance of the meetings, the second pointing towards the fact that these events are in crucial respects about counting numbers. My view is that such countings are not simply arithmetical (although they do involve a large amount of that), but are also the final stage of a social process that transforms "speechless numbers" into ones that have a "voice". This voice is communicating something very specific: it enables the team to make warranted determinations of what the future will be. As I argued in Chapters 5 and 6, in the final analysis, the purpose of missions is to enable a mission team to divine the future in the entrails of the present. But such activities are not a kind of magic, something that is made up on the basis of witchcraft or sorcery. Rather, this predicting of the future is undertaken on the basis of materials that can be demonstrated to be "reasonable", "warranted", "accurate" and "objective". This is not to say that the team does in fact always predict the future precisely, but rather that they get themselves in a position where making predic-tions is a reasonable thing to do. In this sense, the team's predictions consist of a kind of science. This is a practical, "real world", hands-on skill. This is the heart of the matter. This is what policy analysis is all about.

Overview of the chapter

This chapter will be somewhat different from the others so far in one important respect. Hitherto, my descriptions have been at a somewhat abstract level, focusing on processes and the general patterns of work.

Here I shall describe activities in a much richer, more evocative way, and to some extent I shall try to bring the actors in question to life. I do not want to enable anyone to be recognised in what follows, nor am I too interested in the personal perspectives members of the mission brought to their work. But I do want to bring home to the reader something about what gets experienced on missions, since this will enable a better understanding of the issues in question.

My primary concern is to understand the social process that is mission work. A feature of this process has to do with how different individuals approach their tasks in ways that reflect a division of labour. This is important: I do not want to give the impression that mission work is all of kind; it is rather built up of various pieces, each of a somewhat unique character. The success of the team depends on all these parts coming together.

To convey the importance of this, I start my discussions by considering the approach taken by the most junior economist in the mission. This will provide me with an opportunity to create an ethnographic feeling for the mission, and also an opportunity to further deepen what I mean by the division of labour. For I shall be talking not just about different jobs but also about differences in understanding with regard to the tasks in question. I shall explain how this economist approached the mission knowing very little about Arcadia. This was only his second ever mission, his first to Arcadia. But I shall describe the kinds of things he had at hand to enable him to get his job done. Most importantly, he had previous staff reports and the mission's briefing paper. I shall sketch out how Arcadia is viewed in these documents, presenting the picture that the Fund itself creates of Arcadia.

I then describe the mission proper. I commence with a vignette of the first day's activities. Though little of consequence happened on this day, the activities that were undertaken point towards the main threads of activity in the following two weeks or so. I then focus on the activities of one economist, the "fiscal economist", describing the cycles of work he undertook through the bulk of the mission. Concurrent with the fiscal economist's activities were meetings between the desk officer, the deputy chief and the individual whose views I have noted were central to the mission's work. I shall describe the purposes and outcomes of these meetings.

By this point I will have covered enough to provide a sense of what is involved in the early part of the mission, and how this generated a growing body of information that allowed the team to deepen and affirm its views about the country's economic circumstances and policy position. This formed the basis of the discussions undertaken at the end of the mission. I describe one of these meetings in some detail. It was in these meetings between the mission and the authorities that the chief made his orations, but it was here also that the hard work of determining policy was worked out collaboratively.

Attitudes towards mission work

To start, I shall discuss the various ways individuals on the mission approached the task at hand. There are many things that might be encompassed by such a concern, not all of which are pertinent. There is a sense of pressure and anticipation just before a mission and, particularly for a desk officer, in the "annual cycle" the mission is effectively the centrepiece of his or her work. This is what they prepare for and this is effectively where they have to measure up to what the Fund requires. This frame of mind may be contrasted with that of the chief. For chiefs will lead several missions a year, and in each case will find themselves in the "thick of organisational life", dealing with the review process, presenting to the Board and more. In contrast, desk officers may be so busy with the details relating to some mission report (for example, a RED or a policy framework paper[168]) that they will not have time to surface and observe a Board meeting. These differences in perspective reflect differences in concern, desk officers having one set of tasks to do and chiefs another. In this sense, there is a practical basis for the differences in outlook of the participants on a mission. For want of a better phrase, one might call this a *natural attitude* to work[169].

One has to be very careful when one unpacks this attitude. Some things are pertinent to our concern, others are not. Let us illustrate this with the perspective of the junior economist. Consider first that this

---

[168] A RED is an appendix which goes along with a staff report. It contains mostly statistical data. A Policy Framework paper is a document typically prepared prior to negotiating missions.

[169] This particular notion is developed in Schutz (1962). Some ethnomethodological commentors have refined this notion and labelled the ways in which individuals approach their responsibilities within a division of labour as *egological*. See Anderson et al. (1989).

young man was an "EP". An EP is an individual who has a two-year
appointment during which both he/she and the Fund can assess whether
the EP's future should (or indeed could) be bound up with the Fund.
The *Economist's Program*, as it is called, is one of the main procedures
for recruitment to the Fund.

One aspect of being an EP is learning about the life experience that
comes with employment at the Fund. Key to this is the fact that not
only are extended periods of time spent away from home, but that these
periods can be at short notice, as happened in this case. For the EP had
only few days' notice of his participation in the Arcadia mission. Such
short notice is not unusual. The kinds of pressures that the Fund is
placed under, and the number of missions it has to undertake, result in
there being a constant manpower distribution problem. Individuals
drop out of missions unexpectedly, others get pulled in the night
before. This is a fact of life.

There are a number of consequences that derive from this. One is
that individuals cannot always plan their work in such a way as to
ensure that they finish one set of tasks before commencing another. In
this case, when the EP got a call from the chief saying he was to go
to Arcadia in a few days' time, he was still working on sections of a
RED for a mission he had returned from some weeks before. To
prepare for Arcadia, the EP would have to suspend work on the RED
and start reading old staff reports and the latest briefing paper for
Arcadia. Consequently, he would be unable to complete his RED as
planned.

Leaving aside the question of how he dealt with this delay (presumably explaining this to the other chief he worked for, amongst other
things), the bottom line was that the economist's heavy workload
would continue. Thus, instead of being in the position of happily
explaining to his wife and friends that the long hours he was putting
in to complete the RED would soon be over, he now had to explain that
these hours would continue, albeit for another purpose. Worse still, if
his immediate experience was anything to go by, there was a chance
that these long hours might never end—his life might become just one
intense blur of one mission after another. In short, this economist was
experiencing the fact that life in the Fund can involve considerable
personal cost.

This naturally was of concern to him. Indeed he became quite
worried. His worries were not related to the melancholy of professionals who are disenfranchised by bureaucratic life (written about so

eloquently by Merton)[170], nor the dismay of professionals who remain unsure of what questions their research will be put to[171]. His was the doubt of an individual who is unsure whether the rewards of a particular career would justify the personal sacrifice involved. His wife was about to give birth, and he foresaw the possibility of rarely being at home and having little chance to share in the upbringing of their child. At commencement of the Arcadian mission, his choice as to whether to stay at the Fund after his two years were up was far from certain. It was hardly surprising that the prospect of having to choose between worldly influence (through policy analysis) or domestic salvation with more regular work elsewhere (academe for example) loomed large in his private conversations both with me and others on the mission.

But this is not the concern I have here. Though important to this individual, though naturally what one would expect him to be concerned with, I want to focus on another aspect of his attitude to work. Two elements concern me. The first is a frame of mind that enables economists to cope with the sometimes fraught and intense work schedules. This intensity has a number of consequences on such things as the extent of routine data collection undertaken on each desk. As noted in Chapters 5 and 7, desk officers tend to be demand-driven, and this is a reflection of the relentless pressures they are placed under.

A second fact I am concerned with is how it is *natural* for them to take on work at short notice. What do I mean? Consider how, in the case of the EP, he was expected to be able to participate effectively in the mission despite the brief period he was able to get up to speed. He took on the work despite being a *naïf*. This should not lead one to think the Fund has say, poor resources management (though, as I have described, it does have a complex logistical task involving the allocation of jobs at short notice). Rather, it points towards the fact the some of the work undertaken on missions can be done by those who cannot claim to be experts. At the same time, other work requires individuals to be deeply immersed in the understanding of a country. I shall describe these different tasks shortly. For the moment, let me focus on the fact that individuals are able to take on work at short notice. They can do so because there are resources at hand that help them.

---

[170] See Merton (1957), especially pp. 195–225.
[171] See Feldman (1989).

Approaching Arcadia with understanding

Various documents enable a group of individuals who may have different understandings to come together and work effectively as a team. Staff reports and the most recent briefing paper are, in this respect, a *set of tools* that enable a social coherence and a solidarity of purpose. They do so in a number of ways as I have already remarked in Chapter 5. Here I draw attention to another aspect of their tool-like nature.

For staff reports and briefing papers present a certain view of the country, but not a static picture. When, for example, the EP read the old staff reports and the current briefing paper for Arcadia, he was able to see what would be the framework of action that would guide him during the mission. The descriptions in these documents were bound up with *courses of action.*

Now not only can an EP use documents in this way (i.e. as a resource and a set of instructions on what to do), but these documents also provide a resource for the reviewing function within the Fund. That is to say, that just as the newcomer was able to read through the old staff reports and the briefing paper to learn about what was going to be done and why, so too could the reviewing function rely on these documents to provide them with the same. The reviewers (in the functional departments) will have other resources as well. A good PDR economist, for example, will have his or her own data to refer to and comparative information that enhances his or her ability to read staff reports and briefing papers. In this sense, these individuals are not newcomers to the issues. But what I am pointing towards is the basic function of documents in the Fund: they are the method whereby organisational purposes and actions are specified, accounted for and controlled. It is through documents that the Fund is able to cohere its actions.

Now, I have been concerned with the EP's relationship with the Arcadian mission because his ability to use the related documents highlights the power of documents. Later, I shall describe some of the activities that he undertook as a result. But now I want to draw attention to the relationship others have to the mission and associated documents. For if the EP approached the Arcadia documents from the outside, others approached them from within. The desk officer, for example, along with the deputy chief, had been working on the analysis provided in the briefing paper for some weeks, and both were aware of the host of background materials that made their understanding of that document richer and deeper than that of the EP. This was reflected in their orientation to the briefing paper and ultimately in the tasks they undertook on the mission.

One can begin to unpack this by first looking at the picture of Arcadia as presented in the old staff reports. Here one will see that things are implied in terms of courses of action, but the picture is rather general. This may be contrasted with the briefing paper. Here things are more specific: the relevant doings are described. To understand this properly, however, to grasp what a briefing paper means for those who use it, one also needs to comprehend what the briefing paper went through during the process of review and iteration. For it is through this process that the picture and the associated doings are worked up, detailed and refined. Of particular importance here is how the desk officer, the deputy and the chief were involved.

A picture of doings: the Fund's view of Arcadia

I shall start with the general picture in the staff reports. These were the documents the EP read to get a sense of what the Arcadia mission would be about. According to the view presented in these reports, Arcadia is not a cultural, religious or military entity, although it is all those things in part. It is an object that is looked at in a particular way. This interpretative schema, as I called it in Chapter 4, is all about the balance of payments position and, related to that, such things as: government finance and its impact on those balance of payments; questions to do with what are perceived as factors that restrict or distort the economy adding pressure to the balance of payments; and, finally (although I could add to the list), the policy strategy that will ensure the joint goals of long-term growth and balance of payments stability. Within a staff report, these are presented in a historical perspective, the policies and economic situation of the past being used to explain the present. So, more specifically, Arcadia is described as follows:

In the mid-1950s, Arcadia embarked on a programme of intensive government control of the economy. This involved the establishment of a large state sector and pervasive controls of "the mechanisms of the economy". These controls affected the production and sale of goods and services, investment and savings, and so on. Towards the end of the 1960s, Arcadia shifted its polices towards encouraging more private enterprise by providing substantial protection (tariffs, import restrictions) from external competition. Although Arcadia had modest petroleum deposits, these were sufficiently large to enable the government to expand its own investment levels (into state industry, infrastructure, etc.) and to strengthen and maintain the protective policies it had instituted. However, in the 1980s, the fall in petroleum prices, combined with depletion of petroleum reserves, forced the Arcadian government to cut back drastically its investment and to slow down wage increases. By the middle of that decade, gross domestic reserves (i.e. the cash the country has to pay for imports) had fallen to barely a few weeks of imports and unemployment was rising rapidly. To deal with these problems the Arcadian government had to deal with the following more specific concerns:

- *a budget deficit;*
- *an expansionary monetary policy ;*
- *large and inefficient state enterprises;*
- *a distorting system of price and investment controls restricting growth and change;*
- *a widening current account deficit;*
- *and finally an increasing external debt (necessary to pay for the budget deficit and the current account deficit).*

The Arcadian authorities began to deal with their problems by dismantling controls in the economy and reducing government investment. It was hoped that this would remove "the structural problems" in the economy. But during this "transition period" the Arcadians also received support from the Fund (and the World Bank). The policies that were adopted were jointly worked out by the Fund and the authorities and stated in their various Memoranda of Agreement *related to the disbursement of Fund resources. By the early 1990s, the Arcadian economy was in a much better position than it had been, although there was still a precarious balance of payments position and a residue of controls in the economy.*

The specific concerns of the mission

It needs also to be remembered that this is a *sketch* of the Fund's view—much more was actually said in the staff reports. But this gives an idea of the vision of Arcadia as seen from the Fund.

The second component of the materials I want to focus on was embodied in the briefing paper. Here I am concerned to describe some of the components of that paper and to link those to particular courses of action—both activities undertaken during the review of the briefing paper and those marked out for the mission itself.

The briefing paper more or less reiterated issues that I have just described: namely to do with balance of payments, but focused also on a number of particular issues. Amongst these were:

- an apparently sluggish export performance for manufactures in the previous year;
- a larger than expected growth in internal consumption over the same period;
- the government's measures to reduce the budget deficit and, in particular, investigations of the mechanisms the government was using to finance itself.

These concerns were marked out by the desk officer, the deputy and the chief in their first draft of the paper, and were related to particular doings.

For example, with respect to the last of these concerns, the mechanisms the government was using to finance itself, the brief specified that the mission would undertake investigations of these mechanisms. These were to be undertaken bearing in mind that the Arcadian government had, until recently, a tradition of state control of the banks, and thus a monopoly of access to credit. In recent years, the government had begun to spin-off some of these banks into the private sector, but this process was not complete. There was also a residue of controls on credit and investment. As a result, the exact status of some banks and their relationship with the government was unclear.

Accordingly, an investigation of the mechanisms of government finance meant an investigation (amongst other things) of the relationships between the banks and government. As it happened, this turned out to be the task of the EP (though this was not known when the paper was first drafted; his identity became clear during the briefing paper review cycle). What is important here is the fact that it was these kinds of activities that the desk officers, the deputy and the chief recognised as the doings in question that were pointed towards in the briefing paper.

There were other subjects or courses of action that were not detailed so comprehensively in the first draft of the brief. With regard to some of these matters, the desk officer, deputy and chief assumed that it would be better to determine these in reference to the reviewers' comments.

For example, the team were unsure why manufacturing sector export growth had been sluggish. They knew that there could be a variety of reasons for this. The most simple might be a reduction on demand in export markets. An alternative could have been excessive credit within Arcadia. This may have been absorbing resources that would otherwise have gone into expanding exports. A third was that Arcadia might be losing some of its competitiveness.

In the first draft of the briefing paper, the one sent out for review, they explained that they would investigate the reasons for this sluggishness. However, as a result of discussions with PDR, the brief was changed to specify investigation of the impact of internal credit and external competitiveness. The mission team agreed to this, knowing enough about Arcadia to be able to determine what these courses of inquiry would involve. More specifically, this would involve detailed discussions with one particular individual in Arcadia who would be able to provide information about the sluggishness of exports and whether competitiveness or other factors lay behind it. In other words, in agreeing to make these topics more central to the brief, the desk officer, the deputy, and the chief knew what this implied for the courses of action on the mission.

Another issue related to this had to do with the regulatory framework and whether this impacted upon manufactures. The team made little direct mention of this in the first brief, except to say that the Arcadian authorities had been reducing them. They expected that PDR would want to discuss this, but were unsure what implications those discussions ultimately would have on the final briefing paper. The team's expectations proved correct, and PDR did want to meet. After these meetings, it was agreed to investigate in detail the process of deregulation and to enquire as to what were the specific changes undertaken in the previous year. The mission team mapped out what these activities would be. In this case, the team planned a series of meetings with selected officials who would provide more facts on the changes in the regulatory framework. The team would make detailed minutes of these meetings and PDR would be able to see these after the mission.

These are just some of the issues that were worked up and documented in the briefing paper and associated processes. There were others. Whether this particular briefing paper was accurate or not is not my main concern. Rather, I want to focus on the relationships various members of the mission team had to the documents in question, to the understanding that would be required on mission, and how this played out in terms of a division of labour. I want to underline how some members of a mission are on the inside of the process, are immersed in understanding about the country in question, and are familiar with the courses of action that would need to be undertaken if one set of activities are proposed as against some other. These individuals, the desk officer in this case, the deputy and the chief, had a different relationship to the briefing paper than the EP. But this reflected the organisational features of mission-related activity: such activities are organised through documents and around a division of labour. In the next few pages I describe some of these various activities and then elaborate the relationship between these actions and the documents produced during and after a mission.

The mission

I now move to the mission itself. Here my method of exposition will increasingly use impressionistic description, but this will be interlaced with commentary. First, I present a vignette of the team's arrival. This will provide me with the opportunity of illustrating how the team began to warm themselves up to the work at hand. This involved, in part, mapping out in their minds the social process they would be under-taking—a process that was not just about collecting numbers but also collecting "readings" of these numbers by a predetermined set of officials. I will also draw attention to the kinds of assumptions the team made about the provenance of the materials made available to them. In particular, I will discuss how they assumed that these materials are generated in processes that have understandable problems: things get lost, numbers get added up incorrectly and mis-categorisation occurs. These too, are facts of life in mission work. Finally, the vignette will provide me with an opportunity to evoke Arcadia as a place more richly than the Fund's view on the country would allow.

Day one: a vignette

The team left Washington together except for the chief and the admin-istrative assistant who were to follow later. The departing team consisted of four economists and myself. Their behaviour on the plane reflected pretty much what I have described: the EP was trying to complete his understanding of the main issues by re-reading the pre-vious year's staff report and the desk officer and deputy were mulling over what would be the issues related to manufacturing exports and competitiveness. The fiscal officer, whom I have not mentioned yet, was using the flight as an opportunity to relax, and spent it mocking my explanations of what he called my "science of ethnography".

The first view we had of Arcadia came with a parting of clouds as we approached the airport. We could see a blue sea, smooth coastline and ochre landscape pockmarked with little confusions of grey and white villages. In the distance, slowly emerging in the haze, was the great swathe of the capital city of Arcadia itself, a muddled warren of creamy white buildings at its heart, wide sweeping roads and modernist blocks in the suburbs, and dusty olive green mountains behind.

On arrival, the team were the first to depart the plane. They were greeted with swoops and bows by a smiling official and a coterie of uniformed customs officers. The official directed the customs officers to remove the team's luggage and to lead them to passport control. There, he shooed the passport officials away, explaining to them that the team had diplomatic status and therefore did not need visas. The desk officer pointed towards me. After some confusion, it was decided that I be given a tourist visa. Meanwhile, another smiling official arrived and presented the desk officer with a huge stack of documents. We were then introduced to two more individuals who would be our chauffeurs. Whilst negotiations were undertaken about how to load us and our luggage into the cars, the desk officer started to browse through the papers he had been given. His head began to drop as he looked more closely and he glanced at the rest of team with an expression of glee and concern.

Look, here are two copies of the budget, some other tables. I don't know what they are, but there are also four sets of the national accounts, all with the same bottom line, but look: they have different numbers. What is this?

The rest of the team looked at each other and the deputy said:

Don't worry just yet! We haven't even got to our hotel. Let's start work later!

We were then driven down a broad avenue towards the centre of the city. There was a strong smell of eucalyptus and spice, mixed with the occasional waft of kerosene from the airport. After about 15 minutes, the drivers swerved off the road into a small lane leading up to a towering cement hotel set in its own formal gardens. A fountain trickled in front of the main entrance. This was to be the mission's home for the next two weeks. During the check-in, the deputy announced that the team would be given half an hour to unpack before the first team meeting.

My own room could have been a smart hotel room anywhere: an anonymous but luxurious box with a large bed and too much furniture. But from my window I could see the city: nearby some small terraces of whitewashed warehouses and then behind, jostling each other, flat roofed houses and tenements with an occasional dome and here and there a minaret. Further off, silhouetted against the setting sun, banks of awkward looking tower blocks. In the other direction was the sea, or at least what I took for the sea, for there were no waves, only a strange grid of dikes and sluices going along the shore in either direction, and disappearing into the evening gloom. I opened the window and the sounds and smells of the city poured in. The spices were stronger now, but combined with the smell of decay. There was also a dustiness and heat that was absent at the airport.

By the time I had arrived for the first team meeting, the deputy chief was already discussing with the desk officer the papers that he had been given at the airport. These had been spread out over the bed. The desk officer pointed towards them and was saying:

Well these are what we want. I have sorted them out. I assume that they must have included some early drafts. It is not a problem. It is the bottom line that matters at this point. Besides, I can see from the way they have been working which is the most recent so I will use that. I can clarify things with officials later on. Still, here are some materials that each of you can use to help build up your tables.

At which point he started sorting out the tables and giving them to the rest of the team, explaining as he did so:

These won't be completely right but you can use them to set up the spread-sheets. You can start entering them straight away. Here, use these numbers and these.

The deputy then took over the meeting:

Okay let's not worry about that at the moment. Let's try and plan out what we have to do.

She then outlined what meetings had been arranged and a list was handed out. She pointed out who amongst the team would be meeting with which official and when. She turned to ask each economist:

Do you know what you can get out of this person? What information will you still need after this meeting? Do you know who you will need to meet afterwards? Can I have those meetings arranged for you now?

She took particular pains to explain what the EP would be doing, listing the officials he would be seeing and explaining why he would see them:

The first person you meet tomorrow at the Central Bank will give you the latest figures on the monetary sector (the EP's concern) but you should get a lot from her because she knows more or less everyone you will need to deal with. She will give you a lot of advice on what you need to find out. She is easy to get on with so don't worry, you will be all right.

Meanwhile the desk officer kept interrupting with a kind of bubbly enthusiasm. He knew both the lady in question and most of the other officials that the EP would meet in the next few days:

Yeah, don't worry, don't worry! They will tell you all you need to know. I'll help you also.

The deputy then made a little speech. She explained that, in her opinion, the "shift in credit towards the government" would be the crux of the staff report (by this she meant the question of how the government was financing itself, the mechanisms for this and the resulting influence of this on investment in the economy at large, including exports of manufactures). She wanted to reiterate (it had been stated in the briefing paper) that it was therefore going to be the main focus of the mission. She concluded by saying that she was expecting the Arcadians to supply most of the relevant facts in the next few days and that they would enable the team to get most of the materials "into a fit condition for the chief's arrival".

Once the meeting was over, the team met downstairs in the hotel restaurant. They knew that their rooms would be their main workplace for the next two weeks or so. They knew also that the work would increase as each day passed, and that eventually they would become increasingly tired and irascible. The first evening was a chance to relax and be lighthearted, to renew friendships and, in the case of the EP and myself, to get to know some new "colleagues".

This social side of a mission is one of the curious features of Fund life, curious in the sense that although the Fund is relatively speaking a small organisation, the nature of its work is such that individuals may not see much of each other for months on end. Then they are suddenly thrown together for the intense experience of a mission. So it was here. The desk officer and the fiscal economist had worked together six months previously, the deputy chief with both of them in the previous year, but in between times none had had the chance to catch up with each other. And so the evening was whiled away getting acquainted again, recounting tales from intervening missions, offering advice for the EP and myself, and pondering whether the team's view of Arcadia as presented in the briefing paper would turn out to be correct.

Comment

So, in many ways the first day was not consequential. But there are two telling aspects of the day's events on which I want to reflect: first, the attitude of the desk officer to the materials he was given at the airport, and second, the deputy's concern with whom the mission members would be meeting.

As regards the documents given the desk officer and their apparent oddness, essentially what he found was that four sets of national accounts did not consist of the same individual numbers. How did he view this problem?

I think it is extremely important to grasp his perspective on this. For example, a conspiratorial desk officer might have contended that the oddity was a reflection of deliberate obfuscation on the part of Arcadian officials. But this desk officer did not think this. Rather, his assumption was that the problem in the documents had to do with the nature of the material that is used in policy analysis. To paraphrase, his view was that this material had to be worked up, crafted and polished. Further, in this process mistakes can be made, sometimes simple and sometimes more complex. In this case, the oddness was actually the result of a clerical error: "some early drafts of the tables had been picked up". In other words, he did not view the material of policy analysis as existing in some tidy, clean and perfect world; a world say, akin to a scientific laboratory. Instead, he assumed that these materials are produced in the ordinary world of offices, over-filled with paper-work and filing cabinets. In a phrase, these materials were produced in the mundane world where simple mistakes get made for all too ordinary reasons.

A lot turns around this. For when one is trying to understand a "real world", practical activity like policy analysis, it becomes all to easy to make misleading comparisons between what one might call the "dirty facts" one finds in that real world and what one might call the clean, tidy facts one will find in the confines of, say, pure research. Such comparisons, wrong in my opinion, are commonplace, especially in relation to activities that involve numbers.

For example, in "The values of quantification", Jean Lave argues that there is a common-sense ideology that contrasts mathematics by mathematicians as it exists in an ideal, "other worldly place", with the kinds of mathematics used in real situations by ordinary persons[172]. This ideology leads people doing such things as adding up prices in a supermarket to believe that their mathematical reasoning is inferior to that done by "real mathematicians". And so it could be here. It might be argued that there is a difference between the "real", "proper" economics undertaken in research settings (an economics which uses pure facts, unsullied by error or administrative mishaps), and those of the other, mundane world—the place of missions where facts are muddied by clerical errors, and where the problem is to clear away the "noise".

But I think it important to view such a contrast as overexaggerating if not misrepresenting the issues in question. For this desk officer, and I would claim that this holds for all members of the mission, did not have a contrast of this order in mind—namely, a contrast between platonic essence (the pure, the clean) and (sophist) practical reality (the dirty, the messy). It was rather that they knew there would be practical difficulties in their work. They did not bemoan this. Their problem, if that is the right description for it, was not that these difficulties would arise, so much as they could not predict when these problems would show themselves. This was almost entirely contingent on circumstances. And as this first instance indicates, these contingencies did indeed show themselves at unexpected times, even before they had managed to unpack their bags.

The second issue I want to raise relates to the social process aspect of missions. I want to draw attention to this for two reasons: first, because one needs to understand it to recognise some of the essential

---

[172] See Lave (1986).

properties of mission activity, and second, because if there is a common-sense view (a wrong one as I have argued) that distinguishes between proper and improper mathematical reasoning, then there is scholarly confusion about this particular issue.

The issue I am thinking of here has to do with how and why the mission team displayed a concern with how its work involved a *social process*. The fact that the deputy wanted to talk about which meetings were arranged with whom, and therefore what would be the outcome of those meetings was not, I would argue, a reflection of the mere fact that data have to produced by someone. It is rather a recognition of the fact that in policy work, *numbers and persons go hand in hand*.

There are a number of issues here, but of importance is that the team were recognising and depending upon the relationship between an individual's role in an organisation and the understanding that individual will have as a result of that position. This may seem a banal point, but it is fundamental to mission activity. It is also something that researchers on knowledge-based activities seem to misunderstand.

For instance, consider some of the recent research into the kinds of knowledge used in engineering. Here, Louis Bucciarelli has claimed to have discovered that engineering is in fact a largely social process and not one that is "just about engineering"[173]. Predating this work, the French sociologist, M. Callon has also "discovered" that most engineers have to engage not only in engineering, but also in the social process of ensuring their engineering projects survive the vagaries and politics of organisational life[174]. According to this commentator, engineers are "lay sociologists" deploying their theories about society to accomplish their engineering goals. But both authors misunderstand the work of engineers in the first place. For it was they (i.e. Bucciarelli and Callon) who assumed that engineering was not a social process only to discover that it was in their research. I would suggest that engineers themselves, in contrast, are all too aware of this plain fact: engineering is in part a social process—it always has been and always will be. I say this without particular reference to studies of engineering (though I have undertaken them myself). My point is that all work of

---

[173] See Bucciarelli (1988, 1990, 1994).
[174] See Callon (1990).

whatever kind involves social process and this is a mundane fact known to anyone who works.

Therefore this is also the case in policy analysis. The work does not involve analysis of disembodied, transcendental entities (i.e. entities beyond the grasp and contamination of an individual's subjectivities). Rather, it is all about creating analysis through the social process of agreeing and determining the facts in question. What is of concern to members of a mission is not that this is so. It is rather what *in practice*, this means: which people and in what ways can these things (agreement of the fact and determination of policy) be achieved in any particular instance.

And this brings us back to the EP. One of his difficulties was that he was naive as regards these matters. He did not know who to ask about the relevant materials, and perhaps even did not know what would be the right questions to ask even if he did get to the right person. These things he would of course learn through the advice he was given and through the experience that he would slowly accumulate journeying around Arcadia's government offices. But that would take time. In the beginning he would find these things difficult.

Nonetheless one should not exaggerate the importance of this knowledge. Understanding of who one gets information from is not something that can be learnt once and then relied upon ever after. Understanding about who knows what and how to find out more is rough and ready knowledge—something that could be shown to need revision for a whole host of practical, contingent reasons. The people within the authorities might have changed, retired or moved on (even taking up jobs at the Fund). Or it might be that the issues of concern for any particular mission have never been investigated before, and as a result, no one in a mission may know "where to start" or "who to start with". The point, however, is that these are just practical realities; something that has to be dealt with, something which is just a *fact of life*.

Ordinary work

These arguments beg the question of exactly what economists ask and of whom. So I will now describe some of the things that get done in the early stages of a mission.

The first few days of the mission were spent marching around the various buildings of the Arcadian authorities, gathering more information and more numbers, and discussing with those responsible for their production issues to do with how to interpret those numbers and, on that basis, how to use them. Each member of the mission would have his or her own "circuit" of meetings, numbers and officials to work around.

More specifically, it will be recollected from Chapter 7 that the Fund separates economies into various sectors. This is reflected in the organisation of the mission process. In this case, the desk officer concentrated on the national accounts, prices and wages; the fiscal economist concentrated on public finance; and the EP concentrated on the monetary sector and financial reforms. The deputy chief had responsibility for the external sector and the balance of payments.

This data collection process consisted of various sections or stages which are akin to the peeling of an onion. First, there was the collecting of the first set of data. This would supplement the data the desk officer had already collected over the year or via the questionnaire he had sent to the authorities prior to the mission[175]. These data would be collected in meetings at such places as the *Central Bank* for balance of payments and foreign currency holdings data, and the *Ministry of Finance* for fiscal figures. At the end of each day, each economist would add the figures to his or her increasingly extensive spreadsheets. The figures for one sector would then be reconciled with the figures in the other sectors (how a flow of funds analysis works will give some idea of this procedure). When there was a problem of reconciliation between two or more sectors, the team would decide what might be the cause. They would conjecture, say, that the numbers collected for the fiscal sector were not up to date in comparison to figures from other sectors. To investigate this, the fiscal economist would be asked to enquire into when the figures were calculated in his next round of meetings. This may be thought of as the further stage of the mission, a further peeling of the onion.

Reconciliation, both between and within sectors, is an iterative process. The amount of time taken will also vary, according to the differences I noted elsewhere in the book. In some countries, the bulk of the mission will be given to building up the data, in other missions, much less of this will happen. In this case, and for a variety of reasons, gathering data in Arcadia took much longer than planned. I will not describe or account for this delay. But I do want to convey a sense of

---

[175] This is normal practice for all desk officers.

how the data are collected and who they are collected from. I will illustrate this with reference to some of the tasks that the fiscal economist undertook in the first period of the mission.

A vignette of collecting data: the fiscal economist's work

The fiscal economist's work during the first week took the following form. In the morning, he would go to the Ministry of Finance and gather some figures and revised figures. At lunch he would go back to the hotel and add these to his tables. In the afternoon, he would return to the Ministry with questions relating either to figures outstanding from his inquiries in the morning or relating to the data entries he had made to his tables at lunch time. In the evening, he would return to the hotel to meet with his colleagues and attempt to reconcile the various sectors that each had been working on during the day. This then would highlight more "oddities" in the numbers which would then need to be discussed with officials at the Ministry the following day.

This was exhausting, tiring work, not only for himself but for the officials at the Ministry. One problem was that these officials had their own work to do; another was that these officials were not always able to help answer some particular question.

For example, on the fifth day, the economist arranged to spend all morning with a senior official. He had already spent several hours over the previous two or three days with the same official, but wanted another meeting to revisit some numbers that were turning out to be awkward. These meetings had been very pleasant and relaxed. One reason for this was the delightful room the official occupied. It had enormous high arabesque windows, and these allowed a gentle flow of cool air bringing in the sounds and smells of a nearby bazaar; the discussions had often been punctuated by the calls of hawkers advertising their wares. Furthermore, the room was unusually ornate for a government office. Although it was cluttered with paper and filing cabinets reached up to the ceiling, there were elaborate ornaments on the walls, and delightful, rococo covings on the ceiling. This office had obviously seen more aristocratic days.

However, on this particular day, rain was pouring down. The windows were closed. The air was stuffy, and there was a damp musty smell (partly generated by the fiscal economist and myself, since we had got soaked running from the car to the Ministry first thing in the morning). Most of the meeting had been rather frustrating for both parties. The questions the economist asked mostly turned out to be ones that the official could not answer and instead had to direct the economist to some other, more junior official. On several occasions, the official asked for his more junior colleagues to come and make arrangements with the economist for meetings when the numbers in question could be discussed.

After about two hours or so, the economist got to the subject of the projections for credit to the government for the forthcoming quarter (these were important to the mission so the economist wanted to get them right). The economist started to list the categories of numbers one by one. The economist would say a category and the number and the official would give his reply:

Okay; for that number, that is Mr Smith. You saw him earlier. Add that to your list of topics.

The economist would say another number.

Okay; that is Mr Jones.

Then in response to a query about the next number:

Mr Smith again.

And so on.

One or two numbers the official did not know whom to direct the economist to. He wrote down the category and said:

I will have to get back to you on that one.

This went on for about 30 minutes or so during which time the official had been unable to answer any of the economist's questions directly. Eventually, the economist asked for an estimate of revenues from the sale of a specific type of government bond. The official bent forward and gently put both hands on the table. He sighed and then stood and turned to face the window.

Look it's raining today. Do you expect me to be to predict whether it will rain tomorrow? Who knows!

The economist looked at me with a frustrated expression, and then turned to gaze at his notebook. The official then laughed and turned round.

Don't worry! I am teasing! I just can't do this anymore! I need some tea!

Meetings! More meetings!

I present this particular vignette to give a flavour of the piecemeal work of gathering information. The official's playful outburst at the end was a reflection of how arduous this can be for all involved. But beyond the interactional details, there is a sense in which this kind of work can be thought as auditing—the pedantic gathering of numbers from those who produced them and a simple test that those numbers add up[176]. But there is more to it than this. For one feature of auditing is that it is essentially a ritual with no purpose, making no difference to the numbers or persons in question, and leading to nothing—no analysis, no product; only the rubber-stamping of the processes examined. By contrast, although the fiscal economist was certainly interested in the mere arithmetic of the fiscal numbers, this interest was driven by a desire to understand the mechanics and purposes behind those numbers. This in turn would allow the economist to assess whether these numbers could be used by the mission or would need some translation. Let me explain.

The Arcadian authorities separated tax revenue into two parts: first, the tax paid directly on earnings and transactions, and second, the tax that was outstanding or "due" on those activities. It was necessarily difficult to tell whether taxes that were outstanding (or due) would ever be paid or, if so, when. Yet the Arcadians merged the actual receipts (the "actuals") with the estimates for retrospectively outstanding taxes (i.e. taxes owed to the government by individuals and companies) into its figures for revenues and projected revenues. The Arcadians' view on this was that, although in any particular case there could be no

---

[176] There is now a considerable literature on the "sociology of accounting" and of auditing in particular. Amongst the issues this research has pointed toward is both the practical techniques used in auditing and the ceremonial or symbolic side. The latter are important in justifying high auditing fees and the patterns of power between those who audit and those audited. Such issues show themselves here too, as we shall see. For studies of practical reasoning in accounting see Harper (1988).

guarantee that an outstanding tax would be paid (for example a bank-rupt is by definition unable to pay any outstanding tax), at a population level it was predictable what amount would be received. Therefore, the Arcadians believed it made practical sense to assume that a certain amount of taxes to be paid would come from outstanding accounts each quarter. As a result, the Arcadians' figures for total tax revenues merged *actuals* for tax paid with *estimates* for taxes to be paid retro-spectively from outstanding accounts.

The fiscal economist needed to know that this was how the Arcad-ians added their figures because he could then assess whether he could use the same in his work. As it happened, in this case he could not use these merged or aggregated figures. He needed figures for taxes "actu-ally received" which disregarded estimates for retrospective payments. He also wanted projections for the forthcoming quarters which separ-ated any estimates for revenues deriving from outstanding taxes from estimates for direct revenues (the Arcadians merging these two cat-egories in their projections). This was how the mission team was going to put together their view of Arcadia.

For our purposes, it does not matter greatly who was right and who was wrong (even if there is such a thing). The issue I want to focus on here is that the fiscal economist needed to undertake meetings with the authorities to learn about how they made their revenue calculations because it was only on that basis that he could assess what recalculation (if any) was appropriate before figures could be entered into the mission's gradually emerging view of Arcadia.

Another example, related to the above, will further illustrate the need for so many meetings. This example has to do with what one might call organisational perspectivalism. For not only did the Arcadians deal with tax revenues and audited taxes differently from the mission, but they also separated the departments which dealt with them. This had implications for the numbers each department generated.

To explain, the *tax revenues department* generated accurate figures for taxes actually received and projected to be received ("direct taxes" as I have labelled them), but at the same time they also calculated figures for the revenues that would derive from taxes outstanding. But these latter figures were rather rough. The economist needed to find this out because when he first went to the Ministry he was given the figures for both categories of revenue by this department. The next day he went to the *tax auditing department* and was given a different set of numbers. For this department did the reverse: it generated "good numbers" for its

Inside the IMF

own concerns, namely tax outstanding and projected to be received, but fairly rough numbers for direct tax revenues. The fiscal economist naturally found this confusing. After two days of meetings he had two sets of numbers. Whose should he use? Which were correct?

By having more meetings, the fiscal economist was able to discover the mundane reasons for the existence of these two sets of numbers. For he found that each department generated the figures it needed for its work, but at the same time generated figures representing the other department's work. It was not clear why they calculated these latter sets of numbers. But in any case, for practical reasons the numbers they generated to represent the other department's work were not "as good" as the figures each department generated for itself. Essentially this had to do with the fact that each department did not have all the relevant numbers to assess what the other was doing. What the fiscal economist needed to do was take the best from each of the departments (this is in fact what the Arcadian authorities would normally do but had failed to inform the economist).

The point here goes back to my remarks about the desk officer's attitudes to the four sets of national accounts he was given at the airport—that the material of policy analysis is produced in a world where ordinary problems or "ordinary oddness" show themselves. These problems, however mundane or ordinary, make work for the economists. They have to gather numbers and understand how they are put together, and they often have to revisit those who produced them, asking again and again how they might be revised, worked up and made usable. That this process has to be undertaken is another one of those facts of life on a mission.

Numbers as doings

Ultimately, this work is not just about learning about issues of categorisation, or which calculations are rough and ready. The goal was also to unravel the various purposes the Arcadian Ministries had, and to determine what figures, recalculated or not, could be used for the mission's purposes.

In this regard, one might view his work (and indeed that of his colleagues) as a kind of archaeology[177]. The mission team was trying to recreate the context that the numbers had originally "lived in"—a

---

[177] See Lynch et al. (1983).

context which was not visible in the numbers themselves. According to this view, the numbers were the kind of objects archaeologists deal with: only fragments deriving from the society that produced them. The numbers that confronted the mission were incomplete pieces of evidence, and the mission team needed to use them to build up the context in which those numbers had a proper life. To define this context required definition of how the numbers were part of a set of tools—tools that enabled the Arcadians to do something.

One can be reminded of how the two tax departments generated two sets of numbers to clarify this. One set of numbers represented their own activities, and the other represented the activities of the other department. As tools, these numbers varied in efficacy. Numbers generated by the auditing department to represent audited tax revenues were a good measure of those revenues (i.e. a good tool for that), but the figures the same department made for direct tax revenues were rather less accurate (in other words, a poor tool for that measuring job). The point is that the numbers were tools for certain kinds of things and not others. It was knowing this—discovering what the officials did with the numbers—that the fiscal officer had to uncover.

Thus, one might characterise the fiscal economist's job as one that involved recognising what (possibly broken, and rough and ready) tools confronted him when he looked at the numbers. He had to discover, if you like, what tools lay hidden beneath the surface of the aggregated figures. Once he had found this out, the fiscal economist could generate his own tables, the purpose of which would be to represent the current fiscal circumstances of Arcadia.

This, in turn, was another job. Mapping out policy alternatives would itself impact upon the materials the team would want to gather. The numbers presented in the staff report, for example, would have to be suited to that particular job.

Thus it was that toward the end of his work, many meetings with officials in the Finance Ministry involved the fiscal economist presenting drafts of his own tables and discussing with the officials whether they perceived that the tables would be an adequate tool for the mission's job. Problems with the tool(s) would show themselves when, for example, discussions with some particular set of persons had led the economist to alter that total for one category of numbers and this in turn had impacted upon the totals for all the numbers. This new total might contradict what the authorities had, up to that time, believed was correct. When this happened, the fiscal officer would discuss with the officials what to do. Sometimes the officials and the economist would decide that he should go back to the original officials who directed him to make the changes and enquire whether the number may be revised yet again. Sometimes they would decide that the consolidated total had been in fact wrong, and the new version was correct. Gradually, the fiscal economist completed his tables (Table 8.1).

Sorting out the facts in the facts

In my discussion of the EP's tasks at the outset, I drew attention to the division of labour on a mission. I argued that this division consisted of more than simply a distribution of jobs, but was bound up with different understandings about Arcadia. This was reflected in the work of the deputy chief and the desk officer on the mission. Like the fiscal economist, they would be undertaking some of the archaeology I have described; but in addition, they commenced the mission with meetings with one key official in the Ministry of Planning. Their understanding of Arcadia made these meetings worthwhile.

More specifically, the official in question had an almost unique insight into the economic position of Arcadia. This was based, in part, on years of work in various ministries and in part on his current role in the Ministry of Planning. His connections with missions in the past had also resulted in the growth of considerable trust between him and Fund staff. The deputy chief and the desk officer wanted to talk with this individual not only to gather certain figures as part of their archaeology, but also to get some guidance on how to read and interpret the figures that the team as a whole were gathering. From this view he was the mission's "chief informant".

They were after two things. First, they wanted some advice on how to separate the flotsam from the main body of economic fact, for the figures that would be collected in the archaeology consisted of both long-term trends or "underlying movements" and elements reflecting one-off events. For instance, the Arcadians had bought two Airbuses in the previous year and doing so had impacted on the current account and ultimately the Arcadian balance of payments. But the mission needed to separate out this fact since this was unique, or an exceptional item as it is sometimes called. It did not reflect the underlying trend. The mission was of course after this trend in the current account and in

Table 8.1 A table by the fiscal economist

Arcadia: consolidated revenue and grants of the central government
(*millions of X*)

	Yr 1	Yr 2	Yr 3	Yr 4	Yr 5	Yr 6 Est.
Revenue	*2,532.8*	*2,713.1*	*2,928.0*	*3,286.2*	*3,491.4*	*4,031.2*
Tax revenue	1,896.8	2,002.8	2,257.9	2,551.4	2,874.6	3.290.0
Taxes on income and profits[a]	335.0	325.9	378.2	404.7	501.2	560.4
Of which: petroleum sector[b]	(52.2)	(55.5)	(56.9)	(50.3)	(82.2)	(74.7)
Social security contributions	220.9	227.7	325.3	391.9	426.3	502.3
Taxes on payroll	44.1	27.6	31.3	39.4	33.9	38.1
Property taxes	48.6	52.6	52.2	64.9	69.0	76.7
Taxes on goods and services	572.5	585.0	607.0	715.4	834.9	940.2
Turnover taxes and VAT[c]	(273.9)	(252.5)	(209.7)	(272.2)	(316.7)	(371.4)
Excises	(226.0)	(256.1)	(291.0)	(327.3)	(402.1)	(445.2)
Other	(72.6)	(76.4)	(106.3)	(115.9)	(116.1)	(123.6)
Taxes on international trade and transactions	632.4	730.6	816.8	888.5	954.5	1,111.9
Import taxes	(599.6)	(710.4)	(794.0)	(868.0)	(935.3)	(1,094.0)
Export taxes	(10.0)	(7.7)	(9.5)	(9.4)	(11.7)	(9.5)
Other	(22.8)	(12.5)	(13.3)	(11.1)	(7.4)	(8.4)
Other tax revenue	43.3	53.4	47.1	46.6	54.8	60.4

(*continued*)

Table 8.1   (continued)

Arcadia: consolidated revenue and grants of the central government
(*millions of X*)

	Yr 1	Yr 2	Yr 3	Yr 4	Yr 5	Yr 6 Est.
Non-tax revenue	635.9	709.8	668.6	727.9	609.6	737.2
Petroleum sector	352.3	388.3	393.9	392.9	254.4	296.3
Other non-tax revenue	283.5	321.5	274.7	335.0	355.2	440.9
Capital revenue	0.1	0.5	1.5	6.9	7.2	4.0
Grants	*16.0*	*30.4*	*143.2*	*70.1*	*32.5*	*54.1*
Total revenue and grants	*2,548.8*	*2,743.5*	*3,071.2*	*3,356.3*	*3,523.9*	*4,085.3*

Source: Ministry of Finance.
[a] Effective for Yr 4 incomes and profits, new tax rates were applied to individuals and companies.
[b] Effective with the Yr 5 budget year, public sector petroleum companies are subject to the normal tax regime.
[c] Effective 1 July, Yr 2, the value-added tax (VAT) replaces turnover taxes.

the balance of payments. The official in the Ministry of Planning could provide this "inside information".

This element of these discussions was crucial for how all the numbers collected by the rest of the team were used. In particular, to ensure the suitability of the numbers not only required investigations of how the Arcadians calculated and used their numbers (as I have just described), but it also required investigations of what numbers "merely" described circumstance and what could be used in the production of the team's projections. There can be some difference here. Some facts about the present are not necessary when describing the future, and can indeed be misleading. For the mission team a problem was that they needed a set of facts which would describe both the present and the future without compromising the adequacy of either goal.

The second element or purpose of these meetings related to the fact that the official could share with them the perspective the authorities had on the current economic trends. Here the concern was for the mission to understand the weight given to some issues, and the indifference felt towards others. Ultimately there would be a good chance that these views would be shared with the team during the policy discussions that concluded the mission, but the team wanted to get an understanding before those events so as to tailor their investigations in such a way as to enable them to "talk to those views".

The trust between the official and the team was also such that the official could offer frank remarks that might be more difficult to make in the formalised and partly ritual events of policy discussion. For example, the official was quite willing to say the authorities "really didn't know" why some trend was manifesting itself in the figures whereas in the policy meetings such admissions would be difficult. It is important to realise that such frankness was not pointing towards failings on the part of the authorities. By and large they had a view and considerable understanding about the matters at hand. It was just that there were a few issues that they were unsure about. This was a fact of life.

The understanding that the desk officer and the deputy chief had at the outset meant that they could direct enquiries into what was mere flotsam and what was significant. They did not want the official simply to list all the oddities of the preceding months, but wanted—indeed needed—to work through these in reference to what they perceived rightly or wrongly as the salient issues with regard to the economy. Some flotsam did get in the way, some did not; some of the views the Arcadians had were relevant to the mission, and some were not. Only by having a deep understanding of Arcadia could they undertake such investigations with any hope of success.

Essentially the process in question consisted of a series of meetings during which the numbers (in the national accounts, the monetary sector, and so on) were briefly analysed and discussed. These meetings went on throughout the mission as the team gradually revised and built up its own tables. The process itself involved going through the individual numbers (or category of numbers) one by one, while the official simply outlined what he thought the team ought to know about that category and presented the Arcadians' view on those numbers. Sometimes the members of the mission raised their own concerns about a number, requesting the official to explain some issues there and then, or to investigate those numbers for discussion later on.

Discussing the facts amongst the facts: a vignette

I can illustrate this with the first of these meetings undertaken on the second day of the mission. The topic of this first meeting was "the macroeconomic framework and review of overall developments". The official had already supplied some tables to the mission and these formed the basis of the meeting. These tables consisted of a consolidated balance of payments table for the previous four years (including targets), as well as detailed tables of exports of goods, services and transfers, and the equivalent import tables.

Much of the data on these tables would be very important at a later stage in the mission, but at the outset, these data could not be used. As the desk officer put it, they needed to learn "How to read these tables". Their concern was to know something about "What lay behind the figures", to understand what they meant. It was through discussion with the official that they could learn this. Only in this way would the team be able to determine how to use the figures for their own purposes.

There were two components to this concern. The first was understanding what the figures for actuals represented, and the second was understanding the relationship between the actuals and the related projections. The tables that had been supplied consisted of two columns for each year, one with the actuals and the other for the projected or estimated figures. So constructed, any contrast between the actuals and the projections was easy to see. Most of the meeting was conducted in reference to the contrast between these two orders of numbers.

There are a number of things I want to pick up about these discussions. For now I want to underscore how the discussions had an eloquently simple character. To illustrate, once formalities had been completed, the desk officer said that the mission wanted to get some explanation as to why there had been a lowering of export volumes and an increase in imports over projections in the most recent quarterly figures. He pointed towards the relevant numbers in the tables. The official responded by saying the answer(s) lay not in the general but in the particular, and suggested that they go through each sub-category of exports and imports. This indeed was how they proceeded.

The first of these happened to be textiles. It also happened to be the case that this particular category bucked the general trend, since here had been an increase in textile exports over and above projections. The desk officer asked if the official could explain this.

I suppose shirts are in demand!

He then smiled and said:

I cannot fully say why textiles have been doing so well. The manufacturers are reporting that business has never been so good. They claim that their designs and quality makes for a good product. I don't think there is anything else I can say on that number.

The desk officer made some notes, turned to his colleague to ask if she had any questions, and then they both agreed to move on.

Desk officer: Mechanical and electrical goods: these are down on projections: why?
Official: There is poor demand for these goods. It reflects the general weakening of demand in the world economy.
Desk officer: But if this is the case why has there been an increase in imports of raw materials given that there appears to be a slow down in the economy as a whole?
Official: Well, because there has been an increase in investments in tourism. This has caused an increase in imports of raw materials—building goods. This is seasonal: it is the time when many buildings need rebuilding. It is not a trend.
Desk officer: Okay, whilst on the subject of tourism, let's move down the table to numbers for tourism: how is that there has been a decline? Or rather, how is it that there has been a reduction: receipts for tourism are down.
Official: Tourism? There are more tourists this year but they spend less. I think it is that we went down market a bit. The tourists who are coming this year spend less than those who came last year. This is a potential problem: if the hotels go down too far the quality of the resorts goes down and the appeal to tourists reduces further. We are trying to ensure that we avoid that. We don't want to go through the crisis in (a nearby country). They found that they went down so far that the market for tourism collapsed. They built so many cheap hotels that they destroyed the reason for going there.

On certain categories of numbers the discussions became even more detailed. Partly this was a reflection of what numbers were available. For example, the imports numbers had the following categories which led the deputy chief and desk officer to ask for quite specific accounts:

Desk officer: Why has there been such a large increase in agriculture and foodstuffs? Look, this figure here: milk and yoghurt.

Official: Well, it has become fashionable. I think it is to do with healthy eating.

Desk officer: But this is a huge increase, this is millions of litres. No, seriously!

Official: Yes, what can I say? People in Arcadia didn't used to drink milk. It's not traditional. This year everyone is drinking it. I think young people think it will make them look like athletes.

The official then patted his stomach and said:

I've not been drinking it!

The desk officer and deputy chief looked at each other and laughed. The desk officer then said:

Okay, let's not worry about that one, it won't show itself in the final total anyway.

At other times the questions started out being rather more general but ended up being specific:

Desk officer: Can we consider the totals for consumer imports for this period compared with the previous quarter. According to the tables you gave us there ha, been a large increase in demand.

Official: No. Look, one problem is that the figures for the last quarter can't really be compared with the previous quarter because this quarter was Ramadan. So imports for consumer goods and agricultural goods will go up in Ramadan. It is a period of celebration.

Desk officer: I thought Ramadan was a period of fast.

Official: Yes it is in (a neighbouring country) but not in Arcadia. It is like your Christmas here.

Desk officer: Except that it lasts a month!

Official: That's why it is such good place to live!

Desk officer: Okay. So anyway that is warning us about reading a trend into this.

Official: Correct.

Sanctioning numbers

As the week passed so the focus of concern changed in these meetings. Gradually, the team began to build up a higher level picture where things like the oddities in the current accounts disappeared from view. Discussions were also undertaken on fairly complex problems such as how to determine the Arcadians' international competitiveness, and hence the optimum exchange rate for the Arcadian currency. A focus here was on the selection of the so-called "basket of currencies" used to calculate these matters. The Arcadians opted for a different set than the mission team.

I do not want to describe these discussions, however, since the main point I want to draw from these meetings with the official in the Ministry of Planning is how he was able to give inside informa-tion—information that derived from his location within the govern-ment and at the centre of information production. Meetings with him were an informal nexus whereby the team were able to sort out the "facts amongst the facts" and to learn about the authorities' perspect-ives. The many years of contact between members of the mission team and this official also gave the meeting an informal character, where matters that were of little importance were treated as an opportunity for jocularity. But this should not distract from the serious intent of these meetings nor the extent of professional understanding and expertise deployed in them.

It is important to note, however, that as the team moved towards completion of the data-gathering stage of the mission and began to reconcile the tables they were generating (i.e. for the monetary, the real, the fiscal and the external sector), so they embarked on another cycle of activity. Here the role of this official changed. For though he was able to give very useful comment on many of the numbers in question, he was only able to *sanction* a sub-set. The team needed to get all of its figures sanctioned before they could start on the analysis of policy and prepare their efforts to discuss policy with the authorities.

By using the term "sanction", I am pointing toward the fact that the Arcadian authorities had to agree to a number being used by the mission. To illustrate with the fiscal economist's activities: in the vignette of one of the meetings he had with a senior member of the Ministry of Finance, I drew attention to how he was directed to other, more junior officials. These individuals, the persons who had calculated the numbers in question, were then given an opportunity to explain their purposes in doing so. Thus one might characterise this part of the fiscal officer's activities as a process of going to the horse's mouth: i.e. getting to the person who was responsible of the production of the numbers in question. Now going to the horse's mouth is not all that the fiscal officer had to do. For once he had understood what the purposes were, once he had revised his own numbers, once he had worked up the picture as he understood it, he then had to go back to the more senior official to get that individual to "sign off" the numbers.

There are a number of reasons why he had to do so. First, he had to make sure that the numbers he had got from the junior official would not be contradicted by numbers generated elsewhere. A senior official may be more likely to know about the contradictions.

Second, some of the figures he ended up using in his tables were the product of calculation prompted by his own questioning. Therefore the more senior official may not have seen these numbers beforehand. Since this official would ultimately be held responsible for these numbers, it was therefore proper that *he* signed them off. Part of the protocol of this meant that the junior official showed the newly calculated numbers to his senior colleague before the fiscal economist did so.

Another reason had to do with the fact that the view that the fiscal economist was constructing was slightly different to the one the Arcadians themselves constructed. Partly this was because of the fourfold sectorisation characteristic of mission work, and partly it was a reflection of the mission's concern with balance of payments issues. Taken together, this resulted in a view which, to some extent, bridged the concerns of the various Ministries and institutions within Arcadia which generated the source materials for the mission. To be sure, these Ministries and institutions did have a concern with balance of payments—some more than others. But this was, to some extent, perspectival. One can think back to the example of the two tax departments here to remind oneself of the basis for such views. This is not to say that the mission's perspective was, by contrast, objective. For it too was based on a kind of perspectivalism, one which reflected the Fund's concerns. I have remarked on how this is manifest in such things as the Fund's staff reports.

The issue for the fiscal economist as regards these matters was essentially a practical one. He did not want to construct a view that would shock and surprise the officials in the Ministry of Finance. He wanted a view that all recognised as *reasonable* and *accurate*.

In these respects, the process of social agreement confirms part of the thesis put forward by Theodore Porter in his *Trust in*

Numbers[178]. According to Porter, the use of numbers and their collaborative investigation, their construction by various parties in government and other powerful institutions, is a means whereby the individuals involved come to display the objectivity of their work. The evidence I have presented thus far confirms this view. But Porter goes further and argues that the need for this display is related to the fact that the individuals (and the institutions they work for) have no other way of justifying their social authority. According to Porter, numbers are a method to manifest and justify positions of power. From this view, the purpose of sanctioning numbers is to provide a device that justifies not only the numbers themselves, but also the status of those involved. Evidence from mission work, however, suggests that this is not the reason why numbers are agreed to. The evidence here suggests that given the nature of the material in policy work, its mix of high-level numbers, estimates, projections and so on, it is necessary for all those using those numbers to agree what they might be. Agreement between the Arcadian authorities and the mission, as in this case, was the basis of the policy analysis, not a means whereby the power of those involved was justified to the outside world.

This does not mean to say that power was not involved. It certainly was. But it was involved in a different sense to how Porter construes it. Here power was at issue since the participants to these meetings—members of the Fund, senior officials in the Arcadian authorities—were socially sanctioned by their status to discuss these matters. Their positions in power enabled them to do so. From this view, it is the assumption of and the fact of power that allows the work to be done, rather than the work justifying that power.

Building up a picture

By combining the product of these meetings with the products of the archaeological work, the team constructed a basis upon which they could start making some concrete determinations of policy alternatives. More specifically, the team gradually aggregated the numbers in the tables for the four sectors, cross-checking and validating them, until they were confident enough to use the sector data to build integrated representations of those data. One of the most important of these

---

[178] See Porter (1995).

representations was the *key economic indicators table*. Others were the *medium-term projection tables.*

At this stage, the figures for the key indicators were still, to some extent, being worked on and revised. Working through the medium-term projections was a way whereby the need for revisions could be uncovered. Ultimately the work undertaken with these tables, both the key indicators and projection tables, enabled the team to embark on the last component of the mission—the policy discussions with the Arcadians. They still had to collect some data. The deputy chief was still awaiting some figures on external reserves, for example, and the fiscal economist was still making some final revisions to his tables. But they had enough to achieve their purpose: to gather and create sufficient materials to present persuasive views on the economy, views that highlighted the basis of policy decision-making.

The team's construction, built out of the residues of the hours they spent in meetings with various officials, deriving from their spreadsheets and elaborated in such things as the medium-term projections, was not "merely" a description of the economy. The output of their work could not be measured on, say, the basis of completeness, comprehensiveness or accuracy alone. Rather, the product of their activities was a perspective about the present from which to reason through policy alternatives into the future. This is ultimately the purpose of missions: not description, not reporting, but enabling policy. That this is so is shown in the fact that the main event of the mission was the policy discussions that concluded it. As the deputy chief put it, these were "What it is all about", "The thing that matters".

Before I go on to the meetings themselves, it is important to understand that their exact character varies according to a number of factors. In some countries, the meetings are held between the mission and a group of officials representing all the Ministries and institutions concerned, while in other countries these meetings are fragmented. This was the case with Arcadia. Here, meetings were held with the Ministry of Finance, the Ministry of Planning and the Central Bank.

Policy meetings are also affected by the extent of the information and expertise the authorities have available to them. Some member countries can find it difficult to keep abreast of their economic situation, simply lacking the institutional and human resources to do so. These members often depend upon the Fund to help them determine their situation and guide them in policy. Although Arcadia was rich in data, it was somewhat lacking in human resources, and so this was one of the roles of the mission.

These two factors, namely who the meetings were with and the distribution of expertise within, had a number of consequences on the meetings. Two are of concern. First, in Arcadia, the mission would present a view on data collected from all the Arcadian sources, and not just to the individual Ministry being presented to in any one meeting. It was likely that the mission's view would transcend the view of the Ministry in question.

Second, and related to this, the team were able, to some to extent, to determine aspects of the economic situation that would not have been perceived by the individual Ministries. In this case, the mission had uncovered the fact that one part of the government was incurring expenses while another was receiving much less revenue than projected. Combined, this would have an impact upon government finance and ultimately on the take-up of credit in the economy. From the mission's understanding, it appeared that the various Ministries and institutions were not generally aware of this. The team knew this when they had been preparing for these meetings. Not only would they be presenting some news, but what they would present was not necessarily good news. This also played itself out in terms of the kinds of power relations displayed in the meeting. For in this case the mission would be *telling* the Arcadians something they needed to understand; the Arcadians would be obliged to *listen*.

Mindful of these matters, the team worked hard to prepare themselves. The tables upon which the discussions would be based were examined again and again. They attempted to determine what the figures still being crafted "would turn out to be". They spent a great deal of time considering how to express and articulate their views. It was particularly important that the team got the tenor and emphasis of this "just right". For they did not want to misrepresent the authorities' intentions and past policy motivations. Questions included whether they should *recommend* the authorities to pursue such things as restraint on credit to the government or should be *forcefully urged* to do so. Such distinctions were important in conveying the extent of understanding the team had of the Arcadian authorities' past conduct and current intentions. For example, to *forcefully urge* would give the impression that the team believed the authorities were unwilling to pursue this policy; *to recommend* would give the impression that the authorities were more willing to do so. The latter was deemed more

appropriate since it reflected what the mission believed were the
Arcadians' genuine attempts to keep government credit within practical limits. It also reflected the particular form of relations between the
authorities and the mission. The mission had a role rather like that of
external auditors: they enquired into how things were done, then
offered correctives, encouragements and advice for the future. The
Arcadians were in this sense the audited; the authorities on show.

That language reflected the particular relations between the mission
and the authorities was not simply a concern for those directly
involved, however. It was also a very serious concern for later on,
too. Further down the line, in the various documentation produced by
the mission, infelicities of expression could be even more consequential. For example, in the staff report, nuances of language could impact
upon how a report was read by the Executive Board. The Board too
was cognisant of the kind of relationship it had with any individual
member.

I do not want to go into all these issues of meaning now, nor describe
all the activities the team undertook to prepare themselves for the
discussions. What I do want to do is present a cameo of one of these
meetings. My concern here is to highlight the ceremonial and ritual
aspects of these meetings and also to draw attention once again to the
practical ways in which the participants "worked through the numbers". But I shall also draw attention to how, through the process of
investigating future policies, the salient aspects of the current situation
would come more clearly to the fore. Whereas up to now I have been
highlighting how the mission team's goal was to use the present to
divine the future, I now want to note that they also used reference to
that future to further refine what the present may be.

A vignette of policy discussions

When the team gathered in the hotel reception early in morning of the
first day of the policy meetings, there was an atmosphere of relief—the
worst was over. For, by this time, the economists had become
exhausted. As each day of the mission had passed and the amount of
data they had collected had increased, so they spent more and more
time on data entry tasks and spreadsheet analysis. This work had
reached such a fever pitch that in the days immediately prior to the
policy discussions they had had little sleep, instead working late into
the night keying in data, and finding the task taking ever longer as their

minds and fingers became increasingly tired. But the atmosphere of relief was tinged with a degree of apprehension. For policy discussions can also be difficult occasions, not only in themselves, the local authorities being surprised and worried by the issues the mission presented for example, but also because the upshot of these discussions can be that a mission team has to go back to revisit its calculations. This was an outcome the team were loath to consider. It would mean more late nights, more exhaustion and further delays before they could get home.

Hence, they loaded themselves into the official cars with a strange mix of smiles and weariness. The economists knew that they would not be doing much during the discussions and that the chief would be the centre of attention. This was his day. But they knew also that the outcome of these meetings could be either the completion of the mission on schedule or the need for more work and delay.

On this particular day, there were to be two meetings: the first with the Ministry of Finance, the second with the Central Bank. I focus on this latter one.

Meeting with the Central Bank

Officials were waiting for the delegation at the entrance to the bank, and led the team into a meeting room. The chief entered first, followed by his staff. Whilst waiting for the bank officials to arrive, the chief asked for his economists to sit either side of him. He took some spreadsheet tables from his briefcase and placed them on the desk in front. He began to move them around like a painter preparing his palette. He then asked the desk officer for one of the medium-term projections tables, which he added to his collection on the table. Finally, he took some handwritten notes from his jacket pocket and placed them in the centre of his documents.

An official then burst in and announced the imminent arrival of the bank Governor. The team stood up. The Governor arrived with a flurry of officials and secretaries behind him. The Governor sat down directly opposite the chief, similarly surrounded by his cohorts.

After formalities, the meeting began. The chief stood up and commenced his oration. It was an oration in the sense that it had a formal structure, but more importantly it demanded a response or a reply as we shall see.

He began by complimenting the Arcadians on the work that had been achieved in the past year and the impressive performance in certain areas of the economy. He commented also on the continuing frailties in certain areas. He noted that there had been some practical difficulties in preparing the data during the mission as regards such things as the collection of the foreign debt figures and totals for credit to the government. But with the hard work of his team and the energies of the Arcadians themselves, the mission had been able to ascertain the basic features of the Arcadian economy. These were to be the basis of the discussions in the meeting. His concern was primarily with the monetary sector figures.

The chief then started to run through the team's figures, explaining that these indicated that there would be a growth in the money supply of 6.5% in the forthcoming year. Further, if government bonds were included in the figures, this would increase to 10.6%. As he explained this, he moved his hands over the tables in front of him, occasionally lifting one to read.

He then remarked on the fact that the team calculated certain figures differently to the Arcadians. For example, the Arcadians consolidated the figures for government credit from banks and other institutions, whereas the mission preferred to keep these banks and other institutions separated on their tables. One difficulty in respect of this related to the fact that there had been virtually no borrowing from non-bank financial institutions in the past, so the team were not expecting to find any this year. In fact, there had been. Amongst the issues that the team believed lay behind this new development was a desire by the authorities to avoid liquidity problems in the banks whilst satisfying the government's need for credit.

The chief then came to what the mission believed was the heart of the matter. For it was the team's view that the authorities were clearly exceeding their projected credit levels to the government. There were a number of reasons for this including lower than expected growth in some sectors and, most noticeably, an unexpected growth in expenditure in agricultural stocks, particularly for olives. Related to this, there was a reduction in the revenues from the sale of olives in export markets—all of this in a year where the harvest had been unusually good.

The chief explained that as a result of this situation, the Arcadian authorities would find their foreign reserves getting reduced to a very low level, little more than one week's imports, or even lower. This was, according to the chief, too little, and necessitated immediate corrective polices. Failure to adopt the correct policies could lead the Arcadians to seek assistance from the Fund in the near future.

When the chief finished his oration there was a long silence. Then the Governor turned to his officials and beckoned them to gather round his chair. For some minutes the Arcadians discussed matters quietly amongst themselves. All the mission could see was a wall of individuals with their backs facing outward. Gradually, officials started to peel off and return to their seats. Eventually, the Governor turned round to face the table again. There was some momentary discussions as to who should speak: the Governor instructed the official on his right to ask the first question. This individual, having looked either side, proceeded to say:

We are not sure of all the figures you have presented. Could you go over them again and this time in a little more detail? We want to make sure we agree with them all.

The chief proceeded to reiterate the key figures. Several of the Arcadian officials had by this time taken their pocket calculators out and had placed them on the table. As the chief went through the numbers so they keyed the figures in. At last the chief finished. Again a pause. The officials with the calculators read out their totals. They confirmed the mission's calculations. It was suggested that the chief run through for a third time during which process each number would be "checked" by the Arcadians. By this I mean that one of the bank officials had to agree or disagree with the numbers. The process involved calling out each number in turn and waiting for someone to accept it (or not). As with earlier stages, the numbers were all agreed to.

After this point the Governor and his staff formed a little group again and began to talk intensely amongst themselves. After a while, the officials turned round and asked the chief to explain where his team had received its figures. The chief responded by reporting on those individuals who had provided important numbers in institutions other than the bank. He asked his staff to help list these persons. The chief also explained how these figures had been consolidated with the figures his team had received from the Central Bank staff. The Arcadians then talked amongst themselves again.

After a few more minutes had passed, the Governor explained that his staff did agree with the figures that the chief had presented. They recognised the difficulties envisaged by the mission, and commented also on the fact that the team had been able to "consolidate some figures that we were expecting to receive shortly".

The chief then spoke up again and suggested that perhaps they should examine the olive and cereal stock figures in detail, and to begin to unpack the related issues. The desk officer quickly scribbled down the stock figures on a piece of paper and slid it in front of the chief who then read them out: the figures for the previous year had been 287.7 million for olives and 231 million for cereal (in the local currency denomination). This year the figures were 493 for olives and 214 for cereal. This meant there was a 71% increase for olive stocks[179] since the past year.

The chief then explained that the question for the meeting was: "How the costs of this, combined with reduction in revenues from the sale of olives, would impact upon the credit available in the economy". The chief explained that in the mission's view, the situation would have a significant impact in the allocation of credit in the economy. It would mean that there would be a substantial growth in credit to the government, and this in turn would have an impact on growth and GDP. An increase in credit to the government would also result in a continuing growth in money supply but without allowing a growth in investment and productivity. These would be "squeezed out". Accordingly, the chief went on, the authorities would need to revise their estimates for growth and reserves and revise their policy stance to achieve new projections. Otherwise, the government would take a larger share of credit in the economy, further adding pressures in the balance of payments.

Once the chief's oration was complete, the participants started investigations of the detailed implications of the credit issue and its potential impact on other figures. The problem they had to solve was where exactly those connections between credit and other issues, such as growth, inflation and the balance of payments, would show themselves. This was to be found out in the process of working up the monetary tables.

So, the next stage of the meeting involved varying certain figures (or variables) in the monetary tables to see "just what" the impact would turn out to be in respect of other variables. In the first "run through" the Arcadians suggested that their projections for inflation be slightly

---

[179] It should be added that costs for stocks were carried by the government since it had a policy of purchasing unsold stocks off the suppliers.

increased. The chief turned to his team and discussed what they would view as an acceptable alternative projection for inflation. Their concern was not to make up any inflation figure, but to determine what would be a *reasonable variance* in the inflation rate. After some discussion, both sides agreed to a variation that increased inflation by 1.3%. Once this had been determined, the impact of that variation upon other variables, such as government borrowing and balance of payments, could be calculated.

These investigations took some time. The meeting then proceeded to alter other variables to see what impact those changes might have on the economic situation. By the time they had done all this, they had spent nearly five hours together.

Comment

There was obviously much more involved in this meeting (and the others I have ignored) than is conveyed in these brief remarks. The investigative work, and the elaboration of the monetary projections, all required considerable skill, not so much in the mathematics of these tasks, but in the levels of expertise that were required to enable the participants to determine what levels of variation could be used. Ultimately this work led the team and the authorities to a position where they had produced a robust and well-reasoned account of the economy. It was not perfect, not 100% accurate, but as best as it could be with the materials at hand.

Just as the meeting I have described focused on one sector, so the other meetings dealt with the remaining sectors. By the time the team had completed the meeting cycle, all sectors had been covered.

There were a number of outcomes from these meetings. One was a finalised and jointly agreed set of key economic indicators. These would be presented in the *Selected Economic Figures Table* in the staff report (Table 8.2).

A second outcome was a specification of the salient factors in policy. For, once the basic figures had been agreed, investigations into the future were to be undertaken. These investigations involved making projections and varying different factors in these projections. The purpose of these investigations was not just to predict the future as to enable better understanding of the present. So in the monetary meeting, both sides came to an agreement as to what was of central concern to policy—namely, the current levels of government borrowing and the

Table 8.2 Arcadia: selected economic and financial indicators

	Yr 1	Yr 2	Yr 3	Yr 4	Yr 5	Yr 6	Yr 7 Prog.[a] Est.[a]	Yr 8 Proj.[a,b]
Annual percentage changes: unless otherwise specified								
National accounts (constant prices) and prices								
GDP	-1.1	6.7	0.1	3.7	7.6	4.0	6.9	8.0	3.0
Domestic demand	-3.5	0.7	-1.5	7.9	10.7	1.3	5.4	7.2	1.6
Consumption	1.1	1.3	1.3	4.0	6.1	3.4	4.5	5.7	3.2
Investment	-18.1	-1.8	-12.2	24.9	27.6	-5.2	8.4	12.6	-3.6
Gross fixed capital formation	-17.5	-10.1	-4.0	12.4	17.4	1.6	10.6	12.5	8.2
Exports of goods and non-factor services	5.2	13.4	21.5	5.0	1.8	-3.5	12.6	13.1	6.9
Imports of goods and non-factor services	-2.1	-3.5	16.1	14.6	8.9	-8.3	8.4	12.6	2.6
GDP deflator	2.6	6.8	8.5	7.3	5.7	6.6	6.2	5.8	5.7
Consumer price index (CPI), average	6.2	8.2	7.2	7.7	6.5	7.8	6.5	5.5	5.5
Consumer price index (CPI), December–December	7.1	7.0	8.4	6.7	6.8	7.1	...	5.0	...
External sector								
Exports, fob (in SDRs)	-11.6	9.7	7.9	28.2	13.4	4.6	6.7	5.6	9.7
Imports, fob (in SDRs)	-7.5	-7.2	19.7	24.4	19.1	-7.0	11.7	16.9	4.7
Export volume	11.4	8.9	8.7	18.8	4.5	4.7	2.6	5.8	5.2
of which: nonenergy	11.4	14.6	12.1	17.1	10.0	6.3	5.9	0.9	10.0
Import volume	...	-3.4	17.0	16.4	9.6	-7.0	7.8	13.0	1.8
Terms of trade (deterioration (−))	-13.3	2.8	-1.0	1.1	-0.4	-1.0	0.4	-3.7	1.5

Nominal effective exchange rate[c]	−15.6	−16.4	−5.2	−4.2	−4.6	−2.3	...	0.6	...
Real effective exchange rate[c]	−14.2	−13.6	−2.5	−1.7	−2.8	1.0	...	1.7	...
Central government consolidated operations									
Revenue	−0.8	4.5	7.1	7.9	12.2	6.3	13.3	14.7	10.4
Total expenditure and net lending	1.6	4.7	8.7	11.3	8.7	5.5	9.6	11.4	8.0
Current expenditure	1.1	11.0	8.2	19.4	6.3	10.2	10.0	11.0	7.5
Capital expenditure and net lending	2.8	−9.1	10.1	−9.7	17.1	−11.5	8.2	13.0	10.2
Money and credit[d]									
Domestic credit	8.3	7.9	1.9	7.2	10.4	9.8	11.9	11.8	7.0
Government	(13.2)	(15.0)	(−6.2)	(6.8)	(11.8)	(5.7)	(5.9)	(−13.4)	(−8.8)
Economy	(7.5)	(6.7)	(3.3)	(7.3)	(10.2)	(10.4)	(12.8)	(15.5)	(8.8)
Money and quasi-money	5.7	13.7	19.0	11.0	6.3	5.5	11.0	8.2	7.5
Velocity of circulation	2.15	2.15	1.96	1.97	2.11	2.21	2.25	2.35	2.37
Money market interest rate (percentage per annum; end of period)	10.25	9.50	8.63	11.31	11.81	11.81	...	11.31	...
Ratios: percentage of GDP unless otherwise specified									
Government revenue	34.6	31.7	31.2	30.3	29.9	28.8	28.7	28.8	29.1
Total expenditure and net lending	39.2	36.0	36.0	36.1	34.5	32.8	31.8	31.9	31.5
Current expenditure	26.7	26.1	26.0	27.9	26.1	26.1	25.4	25.3	24.9
Capital expenditure and net lending	12.4	9.9	10.1	8.2	8.4	6.7	6.4	6.6	7.0
Central government consolidated deficit									
(payment order basis) (−)	−4.6	−4.1	−4.5	−4.3	−3.9	−3.9	−2.5	−2.7	−2.0
(excluding grants) (−)	−4.6	−4.3	−4.8	−5.7	−4.6	−4.1	−3.1	−3.2	−2.4
Domestic bank financing	(1.0)	(1.2)	(0.5)	(0.5)	(0.3)	(0.4)	(0.4)	(−0.8)	(−0.4)

Table 8.2 (continued)

	Yr 1	Yr 2	Yr 3	Yr 4	Yr 5	Yr 6	Yr 7 Prog. Est.[a]	Yr 8 Proj.[a,b]	
Gross investment	23.5	20.6	19.4	22.6	26.6	23.8	23.4	25.9	23.8
Gross national savings	15.5	19.6	20.4	19.3	21.3	19.4	20.8	21.6	21.2
Gross domestic savings	16.2	19.6	19.8	18.6	19.3	19.0	20.4	20.4	20.4
External current account deficit (−)	−8.0	−1.0	1.0	−3.3	−5.3	−4.4	−2.6	−4.7	−2.6
External debt	63.0	58.9	60.4	58.0	54.2	54.4	52.7	50.9	50.2
Debt service/current receipts[e]	27.9	26.8	22.3	23.0	22.7	23.5	20.4	20.0	18.7
Gross official international reserves (in months of imports)	1.3	2.1	3.1	2.7	1.8	1.9	2.1	1.9	2.3
In millions of SDRs									
Overall balance of payment surplus or deficit (−)	−195	110	295	62	−74	−48	112	83	156
Gross official international reserves (at end of period)	257	378	676	739	565	559	703	673	825
External debt (at end of period)	4,305	4,267	4,336	4,713	5,007	5,355	5,530	5,625	5,814
In millions of local currency									
GDP at current prices	7,021	7,997	8,685	9,661	10,990	12,178	13,772	13,928	15,170

Sources: Data provided by the Arcadian authorities; and staff estimates and projections.

[a] Excludes operations related to trans-Arcadian gas pipeline.

[b] Annual percentage changes for Yr 8 are from the Yr 7 estimated outcome. Absolute levels of variables for Yr 8 are those discussed with the authorities in October of Yr 7. They have not been revised on the basis of the Yr 7 estimated outcomes and the current policy stance.

[c] Weighted by non-oil trade and tourism flows of 16 partner and competitor countries; (−) denotes depreciation.

[d] Starting in Yr 4, data reflect the addition of several new deposit-taking institutions.

[e] Debt service includes repurchases from the Fund.

levels of growth in the economy and what this would mean for the future.

More specifically, these investigations of the future resulted in the realisation that the current credit problems could lead the Arcadians to the Fund in the future. Alternatively, these current problems might be reduced by larger than expected revenues from export growth. Both possibilities looked plausible from the basic facts at hand. The team took this evidence to subsequent meetings on the last day of the mission, and used them to make persuasive arguments to the effect that the Arcadians should reduce structural impediments (manifest for instance in such things as complex and restrictive investment codes) to help ensure that the potential growth in the economy turned into a reality. These arguments were also presented in the staff report.

My concern here, however, is to focus on a number of features of these policy meetings and missions as a whole that underscore the *social organisation* of what that work involved. In particular, I want to focus on the fact that these meetings were meetings that *count*, as I noted at the outset. There are two aspects to this. On the one hand, they were about adding numbers; on the other, these meetings had particular and crucially symbolic aspects. Both issues are intimately connected. But one has precedence over the other, as I shall explain.

Meetings that count

The meeting consisted of two main parts, with a watershed in the middle. The chief's oration flowed across both stages. His oration commenced with a presentation not just of what the team had been working on, but what the team's view had reached at that point in time. Given that the team was invested by the Fund to act on its behalf, this view was effectively the Fund's view. Moreover, the relationship between the mission and the authorities was one wherein the team was instructing the Arcadians as to what were the salient issues. In this respect, they were in a subordinate role as regards the mission. This was symbolised in the oration: the chief reported on the conduct of the authorities; he offered correctives; he gave guidance. This was more of a paternalistic relationship than one of equals. Accordingly, it was presented with all the solemnity it deserved. This was not an opportunity for the discussion of opinions, or for jokes and levity.

Nonetheless, the Arcadians still had the power to reject the view offered by the chief. They had to respond to his oration. To this extent, this was paternalism without power. For though the Arcadians had been involved in the development of this view—some individuals more than others as we have seen—the Arcadian authorities had not officially accepted it and were under no obligation to do so. The period during which the Governor and his officials turned away and discussed the chief's remarks was the opportunity for them to decide whether to accept or reject it. It was therefore a moment pregnant with tension for the mission team. As it happens, in this process (i.e. being signed off) some of the figures could have been revised or amended, but none were in the meeting I described. But irrespective of that, the bottom line was that it was only once the Arcadians had announced acceptance that the next stage of the meeting could occur.

I would like to argue that in accepting the numbers the Arcadians transformed the meeting into a ritual one, or rather one that had ritual consequences. For their acceptance resulted in the numbers being ones that could be acted upon. They were transformed from being mere numbers into resources for policy. But, such changes cannot be guaranteed. If the Arcadians had rejected the numbers, this ritual transformation would not have occurred. This is why the mission team were so apprehensive when they waited in the hotel lobby that morning: they knew the meetings could turn out to have the desired ritual effect; but they could turn out otherwise.

This second stage also involved the chief standing up and making a speech—continuing his oration—but this time his remarks had a different character. If before they were descriptive, now they became an opportunity to outline issues to be investigated. It is in this respect that there was a watershed in the centre of the meeting. For after the Governor's acceptance, the chief's presentation became the common ground upon which both sides undertook subsequent analytical work. I shall say some more about that work in a moment but, before I do so, let me make some more remarks about how that transformation could occur.

For the "acceptance of the numbers" to matter, these meetings were organised in such a way that all those persons whose views counted were there. For though, say, the official in the Ministry of Planning may have been able to say "yes these figures are right", his status was not sufficient to have his signing off represent the authorities as a whole. Rather, those in charge needed to be there to have their say on matters. Hence it was that in the meeting I described that the Governor of the Central Bank had to be present. Up until that time he had had little to do with the mission, all of the analytical work undertaken at that bank involving more junior officials and his deputies. But for that work to count, this individual had to sign off the product of that work.

The reverse holds true as well. That is to say that, just as the fiscal economist was able to present what in effect were the mission figures to the official in the Ministry of Finance, his views were ultimately subordinate to the mission chief's. To be transformed into the official team's view, the chief had to present them as his own. This he did in his oration to the authorities. It was in this sense that power showed itself in the meetings.

One should not be surprised by the fact that the chief had to sanction his team's views or that Arcadians had to do the same. There is no news in pointing out that institutions are *hierarchical*. But there is much to be learned from drawing attention to what one might call the moral transformation in question. It is to expand on what is meant by this that I now turn.

The raw and the cooked

It might appear that I am proposing a view on missions that echoes the perspective of Lévi-Strauss[180]. Lévi-Strauss was an anthropologist who claimed (amongst other things) that what was essential to human society was the fact that objects in the world were transformed from their natural, "unsocial" status into social objects by the process of cooking. Lévi-Strauss' argument was that it was the miraculous transformation that cooking brought about that displayed man's (for it was mostly man in Lévi-Strauss' work) Godlike power over nature. Here it might be thought that I am suggesting that policy meetings involve a transformation of something that is, in a sense, *raw* into a thing that is *cooked*. In being cooked it is thereby touchable, clean and, in the Fund's sense, usable for analysis. Although this will allow some light-hearted remarks about how missions are involved in the process of "cooking the books", I think the comparison with Lévi-Strauss is useful. For it draws attention to the moral element in the work that gets undertaken on a mission—a moral element made conspicuous in the process of sanctioning numbers.

For the process of converting "raw numbers" into meaningful and

---

[180] See Lévi-Strauss (1962).

"usable" information constitutes, in part, a *moral transformation* and not just an arithmetical or econometric one. But I want to suggest that this does not just hold for the events within the policy meetings, albeit that they highlight the issues most clearly. I want to argue that mission work as a whole consists of a process of gathering data, subjecting these data to various assessments and sanctionings and, if the data pass these tests, using them in analytical tasks. This is in part a moral process because the data in question will often remain the same (i.e. the actual numbers at issue) irrespective of whether they are signed off, as in earlier stages of a mission, or ceremonially accepted, as in the policy meetings at the end. *Passing the test*, being signed off, being accepted, may make no difference to the number as a number (although sometimes it does). The difference made is to the moral status of the number.

As an aside, one might note that once data have been transformed (signed off), they come to exist in a moral field. By this I mean a field in the following sense: when a number is signed off, it can jostle other numbers, sometimes resulting in those other numbers being ejected or returned to a non-signed-off status (i.e. thrown out of the figures). In this regard, one might say that missions are to some extent in the business of creating a moral order, an order upon which the Fund's analytical apparatus can operate.

It is worth noting also that this process did not appear to involve a preference to seek agreement in the sense that both sides always try and agree with each other (as is the case with ordinary conversation). In this mission, there were distinct occasions when difficulties reaching agreement were confronted. These difficulties were solved through small, "intimate" meetings between the chief and his equals in the authorities, including the Governor of the Central Bank. The chief and the mission team believed that these meetings would be difficult, and so asked for them to be held *in camera*. The Arcadians too asked for certain meetings to held in the same private manner.

I was not able to understand what the difficulties in question were. One reason for this was that I could not participate in prior meetings that had led to the discovery of difficulties. These meetings had apparently also broached the various ways they could be solved. The meetings in question were those between the deputy chief and the official in the Ministry of Planning, one of the earliest of which I described. As I explained at that point, this individual was a key informant for the mission. Apparently the team knew that at a certain time in the mission,

difficult topics would have to be discussed with this individual. Therefore they were happy to let me observe some of the early meetings, less
so the later ones. The team felt that my presence might make these
discussions more difficult.

Thus, it is difficult for me to assess what impact my own presence (or
in this case absence) throughout the mission had. Doubtless it had
some kind of an impact. As I noted in Chapter 3, the chief remarked
that my cheerful countenance kept his team's spirits up. The Arcadian
themselves thought it amusing that the Fund would allow an outsider to
watch them at work. But beyond this I cannot determine what my
influence may have been. The meetings held in camera may be indicative of how certain tasks were undertaken in a way that made them
invisible to me. But as I have indicated, one might reasonably take the
view that this was a reflection of the fact that the mission team had hard
work to do, and they did not want a stranger breathing down their neck.

Be that as it may, all this discussion of the moral transformation of
economic facts could lead one to think that economic reality is
"merely" a social construct. It might lead one to believe that the
concern of a mission and their counterparts in the authorities was not
the real, hard, economic facts, but to ensure that the process of building
a picture resulted in agreement, the difficulties in achieving this notwithstanding. This would give the impression that the exact nature of
the picture does not matter; the main concern being simply that the two
sides, the mission and the authorities, agree to it. To be sure, certain
sociological commentators would delight in such a notion, but this
view is quite wrong[181]. The point I am making is that the business of
economic fact and the analysis of policy are immersed in considerations of the social. It would be wholly incorrect to separate them.

This leads me back again to the second stage of the meetings. I noted
in the vignette that the Arcadians wanted to add up the numbers for
themselves. I mentioned this not to point towards the possibility that
they did not trust the mission's numbers. I mentioned it because it drew
attention to how the Arcadians were cognisant of the practical fact
that people understand numbers better if they handle those numbers
themselves.

But behind this was something much more significant, and this
relates to what one thinks of as the economic reality of concern to
all parties in the meetings and the relationship of that reality to the

---

[181] Though, of course, those I have in mind would not formulate it this way.

process of determining it. For this apparently inconsequential running through of the numbers points towards the fact that for participants in these meetings, the objective reality could only be brought into view through extensive investigations of the numbers.

This process was both a hands-on econometric undertaking and a social one, wherein the various participants tested and corroborated their investigations with their colleagues. These testings and corroborations were crucial since the meetings were populated by those people whose status and business was to determine what was the right way and the wrong way of doing these things. These were the experts doing their work. It is in this sense that there was a moral basis to the policy meetings: that the activities in these meetings were being undertaken by the experts this field. It was their determinations that counted, their assessments of what was the right way of doing things that mattered.

This is a difficult point. It was not simply that in being there their views came to hold sway. What I am drawing attention to is that their views were the product of analytical work. This involved unpacking and investigating how the figures fitted together. That meant working through the figures, presenting views on the figures and investigating the numbers and their implications with calculators in hand, i.e. there and then. This was the way in which the economic reality came into sight. The facts of policy analysis were constituted in the methodical ways the mission team and the authorities jointly worked out an intelligent basis for their analysis.

But at the same time, and this is the difficult point, the adequacy of the methods used was attested to by the willing participation of members of those meetings in those investigations. By willing I do not mean that they were uniformly compliant to what was done—far from it. For they discussed and reasoned through together what were the appropriate ways of proceeding. The point is that these meetings were so designed as to provide the opportunity for *these* people to demonstrate, use and participate in the determination of facts in policy work. This was a group of experts doing their work, together. These were meetings that "counted" by dint of those who did the counting[182].

---

[182] As I say, this is a difficult point and one that is often lost in most sociological descriptions of experts at work. For a good exposition see Button & Sharrock (1993).

Conclusion

As I have remarked at several points within the book, each and every mission is unique. Furthermore, the pattern of relations between the Fund and particular members is also always unique, reflecting the kinds of problems a member has, its expertise, its institutional structures and so on. In this case, the member authorities were somewhat reliant on the Fund mission to guide and instruct them on policy work. As one of the Arcadians quipped toward the end of the mission:

We've been waiting for you (the mission) to come back again to help us solve these policy dilemmas. You should come back more often!

The specifics of the Arcadian institutions also showed themselves in the mission process and in particular in the character of the policy meetings. The desk officer explained to me that one of the reasons why the Central Bank staff took so long deliberating on the figures the chief presented was that they were trying to determine which of those figures were their responsibility and which were other departments' within the government. They were concerned to make sure that the numbers they had produced did not indicate that they had done a bad job.

These particularities aside, I have been wanting to highlight a number of general, key features of mission work. Specifically, I have wanted to note that there can be a paradoxical surfeit in information at the start of a mission and that this has to be sifted through and sorted out to make sure a mission has just what it needs. I say paradoxical because in Washington a mission team may not have enough information. Furthermore, getting to the right information involves both an analytic and social process—analytical in the sense that it requires the understanding of the representational apparatus that will given to a mission (the numbers, the tables, the national accounts, etc.). It is social in the sense that it means talking to those who devise this apparatus. This enables a mission to understand the motives and purposes behind these tools. It is social also in the sense that when a mission begins to develop an apparatus of its own (i.e. their own set of numbers, tables, etc.), they have to have it signed off by the authorities.

I want to reiterate, however, that mission work itself is fraught with the possibility of not coming to understand what the policy situation is, not in the sense that the two sides (the mission and the authorities) might not agree, but because determination of the facts of the case may be difficult to do. One of the reasons why the Arcadian team became more and more tired towards the end of the mission was not simply because they were trying to get all the work done in time. It was because the work was turning out to be very difficult. Of course they wanted to get the work done in time, but first and foremost they had to get the numbers right. This holds true for all missions. Mission work is, in other words, a hands-on empirical science, albeit bound up with and immersed in social practice. Finally, missions come to an agreement as to the numbers representing the policy situation not in a fashion that is "merely ritualistic" (i.e. an agreement that is inevitable). The numbers a mission team generates get ritual transformation only because the analytical work for the construction of those numbers is done success-fully. This may take more time, or it may take less.

All of these matters are the kind of things that my own way of looking—my own expertise—would naturally lead me to focus on. That is to say, I have focused on the social organisational aspects of mission work. As should be clear, these are absolutely central to this work. This work is essentially to do with social action—it is about meeting and talking; it is about understanding the intents and tech-niques of others; it is about working out collaboratively systems for representing a world. Such interactions are of course infected by the ceremonies of personal and interpersonal behaviour—codes of polite-ness, decorum and respect. But it is also infected by the institutional locales of the individuals in question—the relative status of the chief and the desk officer, the distance (organisationally speaking) between the junior officials in the Central Bank and the mightiness of the bank's Governor. It has been my goal in this chapter to report on how these facts of life, along with many others, show themselves in Fund missions.

CHAPTER 9
The use of a staff report

When the Arcadian mission team returned to Washington they had much to do. First, they had to submit a *back-to-office report*. Then they had various archival and departmental reporting activities to undertake: *minutes* of the various meetings had to be completed; *memoranda for the files* on the monetary and the fiscal sectors had to be prepared; and a draft *summings up* had to be composed. Above all, they had to complete the *staff report*. This was drafted within four weeks and was presented to the Board some two months after the mission had first set foot in Arcadia.

This particular process, the set of jobs that needed to be done between the mission's return and the Board meeting, is the concern of this chapter. My interest is not in the fate of the Arcadian staff report (and associated documentation), though I shall take some examples from it. Rather I am interested in what happens to staff reports within this stage of the Fund's processes. I want to elaborate further the claim that the stages through which such documents go (the reviews, the amendments, the iterations, the readings and the acceptances) are best understood with reference to the specific sets of concerns brought to bear by participants within those processes.

In particular, I want to outline the *interpretative schema* relevant at certain of these junctures. I am alluding to those things that reviewers of a staff report will bear in mind at one stage in the document's career, and the other things they will consider at a later point. I am interested also in how reviewers will at certain times merge these considerations so that they undertake their work at one stage to ensure that work at another stage can be carried out. In this sense, I am interested in how actions in the present are oriented to actions in the future.

I have already outlined some aspects of this in the previous chapters, particularly in Chapter 5. There I spoke about how the Fund's documents—or rather certain of its documents like briefing papers and back-to-office reports—can talk in a way that enables a mapping out of the past, the present and the future. Users of those documents work within a particular temporal matrix of action allowing them to move from one point in time to another. Now I want to deepen those arguments. My concern with how individuals orient their work to ensure that those in subsequent stages of the document career can do their work is not intended to draw attention to how altruistic the Fund's staff are to one another—as if I was interested in their display of organisational piety[183]—so much as each of the successive tasks in the later stages of the career of a staff report involves a gradual tidying up, a whittling away, a coming to an end. This can only be achieved by each and every participant within these stages being aware that this happens and allowing that whittling away to occur through the accomplishment of their own responsibilities. The work I want to describe is in this sense, cumulative, although it consists of various individual components.

Overview of the chapter

I shall organise my discussions in the following way. I start by quickly recapitulating how *back-to-office reports* are interpreted and making a brief contrast with the use of *minutes*. I then turn to the interpretative schema brought to bear on the document that will be my main focus, namely a *draft staff report*. I examine the bundle of activities related to that document by focusing, in the first instance, on how those documents are treated by Policy Development and Review (PDR). I briefly characterise the division of labour within that department and explain how that impacts upon the perspective of those who do the reviewing. I then draw attention to what PDR views as the kinds of problem it has to deal with, and in particular, how some of the materials it has to assess contain *normative* arguments. They are normative insofar as they involve assessment of the policy judgements and stance of the member authorities. This has significant implications for the kind of relationship the mission teams have with all reviewing departments and not just PDR. What is crucial here is that review is at once a technical enquiry (i.e. as regards the policies of the authorities) and a normative one insofar as the mission will have had to assess the motivations of the member authorities. At the same time, and at a more mundane level, I shall explain that the perspective brought to bear by PDR relates not just to the technical and normative issues embedded in a

---

[183] I am alluding to a remark made in Egon Bittner's *The Concept of Organisations* (Bittner, 1965).

staff report (and whether the mission has trustfully dealt with those issues), but also has to do with assumed responsibility of the authors of that report to get those details right. This too is normative.

Because the relationship between PDR and the mission teams turns around this particular complex of concerns, I shall argue that the reviewing process is a very intense affair. PDR economists (and indeed economists in the other reviewing departments) take their work very seriously. This shows itself in variety of ways. One is the concentration given to the kind of reading and analysis that PDR economists undertake. One measure of this is the extensive mark-up of documents within the review process. A by-product of this is the creation of personalised (i.e. marked-up) document repositories. This intensity of reading, combined with the fact that the reviewers' comments are themselves documented, will lead me to pause and consider how the Fund is fully a *literary* organisation.

Of more importance, I shall suggest, is how the existence of personalised document stores is the embodiment of various communities within the reviewing process. These communities are, in part, formally defined by the organisation, and in part constituted through the informal creation of these stores. In formal terms, these communities consist of the mission teams, the front offices, the reviewing departments, the Executive Directors, and the community of three, namely the Deputy Managing Directors (DMDs)[184].

Finally, I want to move on from the work of PDR and discuss how it is that by the time a report is presented to the Board, the mission chief's oration becomes an opportunity for Executive Directors to raise a host of non-technical and largely political matters. The chief is no longer responsible for the content of the report insofar as it is most unlikely that any changes will be requested by the Board. Furthermore, though the oration will be the chief's, that oration stands as the indication of the Fund's professional body's view and *not just the chief's*. In other words, by the time he or she speaks to the Board, the chief's personal involvement, his or her personal responsibility for getting it right will have been absolved.

It is in these ways then, that what is relevant changes as a staff report moves through the Fund's processes. My concern in this chapter is to show how this discourse shifts as staff reports are passed from the offices of the mission team, through the offices of PDR and the other

---

[184] As I said earlier, this community expanded to three during the research.

reviewing departments, to the DMD's department and finally up to the
Executive Directors' more commodious accommodation on the 11th
and 12th floors.

The review process

The first task then that the Arcadian mission had to undertake was to
write up a back-to-office report. As noted in Chapter 5, this report is
intended to be an opportunity to flag up unexpected outcomes of
mission activities. These need to be highlighted since the unexpected
can cause difficulties and delays in subsequent stages of the review
process. As it happens, the Arcadian mission had nothing untoward to
report, apart from the fact that the Arcadians' fiscal position was
somewhat worse than expected. Thus, the reviewers of this particular
back-to-office report were more or less pleased (or perhaps I should say
relieved!) by its contents insofar as it did not indicate that the draft
staff report, when it did arrive, would require any more reviewing time
than normal. The Arcadian back-to-office report was instead an indication that everything was running smoothly.

In this sense, the perspective, or the *interpretative schema* brought to
bear on the back-to-office report by those who received it (in the area
department front office, in PDR and by the DMD) was not so much one
that focused on the work it entailed for them at the time they received it
(i.e. what background reading, comments and discussion they would be
required to do when it turned up) as it was an interpretative schema that
drew attention to what that document implied about what those individuals would have to do in the future, when the Arcadian staff report
arrived on their desks. From this view, the back-to-office report was
not a document whose contents were the stuff of work (i.e. requiring
analysis, thought, consideration), rather, it was more of a workflow
device, indicating what work they would need to do in the future. In
this sense one might say that a back-to-office report is a document with
little in the way of content.

In contrast, some of the other documents that were completed soon
after the team returned were approached by those who read them more
or less solely in terms of their contents. Little concern was given to
what future jobs they might imply. For example, the *minutes* from the
various meetings attended were looked at for how thoroughly or accur-

ately they represented the meetings in question. From this view, minutes are not workflow tools so much as information repositories.

Minutes, however, are relatively inconsequential documents. Of far greater significance, of course, is a staff report or more specifically, a *draft staff report*. As I say, this particular document is the one I want to focus on. The particular interpretative schema brought to bear by those numerous parties involved in its review are considerably more complex than used in reference to back-to-office reports, minutes or indeed any of the other documentation that surrounds the post mission process.

The mechanics of the process

Before examining those complexities, one may be reminded of the actual process, or the mechanics, if you like. First of all, it consists of sending the draft report to the area department front office. Here the director of the department and specified others will make their comments. The mission team makes changes accordingly. It is then sent out to PDR and the other reviewing departments. These departments send written comments on the draft. Again the mission team makes changes. A revised version is then sent to the front office and PDR for final clearance. This is then sent to the DMDs, who sign it off before it is sent to the Board. The Board too revises or, more precisely, accepts or rejects the staff report. But as we shall see, this kind of transformation does not involve the same kind of concerns as those which characterise the earlier stages of review.

Each of these participants in the review process (the front office, PDR, the other reviewing departments, the DMDs and the Board) have their own perspective to bring to bear—their own interpretative schemata. I want, however, to focus primarily on those of PDR. In many respects, the perspective of this department is the most influential within the Fund, but in any case, examination of some of its elements will be, I would argue, sufficient to characterise at least some of the more important elements within the interpretative schema of all the reviewing functions.

The draft staff report

It is perhaps best to begin by reminding ourselves of the organisation of a staff report. This structure reflects a standard (although there is some practical variation). In the case of the Arcadian report, there were four main sections: an introduction, a description of developments in the previous year, a report on discussions with the authorities and, most important of all, a staff appraisal section. These totalled 24 pages[185], which were followed by 22 pages of tables and appendices.

More specifically, the *introduction* described the history of Arcadia, its relationship with the Fund over the years, and the auspices of the mission being reported. The *description of developments* noted such factual matters as the good weather impacting upon olive production (and the reduction in the international price for olives and olive oil), the rate of GDP growth, the reduction in the inflation rate and much else besides. The *report on the discussions* focused on what the authorities perceived as the major obstacles in achieving their medium term objectives. Particular foci included liberalisation of price codes, the phasing out of trade restrictions and a reduction in the "crowding out effect of the financing of the budget". The *staff appraisal* section considered how the Arcadians would be able to attain their objectives, and this included some duplication of the views of the authorities (i.e. because there was agreement over these policies). Staff recommendations included the rapid completion of the reform in regulations and a sharper than envisaged reduction in the budget deficit. Certain goals were listed with regard to growth rate, inflation rate and current account deficits. To achieve these goals, targets were outlined with regard to such things as the GDP investment ratio.

This then was the *object* sent out for review. Other staff reports will be more or less similar, and I shall not concern myself with variations between them. Instead, my main focus is to consider what this review process in general terms consists of and, in particular, what is brought to bear on any draft staff report at any particular juncture within its career.

One might start by noting that a draft staff report is not recognisable as a draft in terms of its contents (for a draft staff report will only exit the offices of a mission team if it is as "good as" a final version). It is intended to be something that will pass muster first time round, as I noted in Chapter 5. Thus a reviewer will not be able to pick up a draft staff report and observe anything intrinsic to its contents that makes it identifiable as a draft. For example, there will be no extensive typing errors or oddities in format, nor will there be substantive differences in

---

[185] This was somewhat longer than usual. I could not find out any particular reason why. "It was just longer", the desk officer said.

the contents of a report because it is a draft. A mission team does not write a staff report to address the reviewing function, as if it were to say: "the mission would like to say this". Rather, the report looks for all practical purposes the same as it would do when it arrives on the desk of the Executive Directors.

One consequence of this is that any changes that a report may have gone through in lieu of the review process will be invisible to those Directors. But another consequence is they will also be invisible to anyone outside the review process of that particular report. The contents of a staff report do not identify its position within its career.

What does identify this, however, is something external to the report itself. For staff reports are "tagged" with covering letters, and it is these which identify the career position of a staff report. A draft staff report will have a letter attached to the front stating that it is due for review and will include the name of the reviewers and the timetable for review. Once a staff report has been cleared by the reviewing functions, but before it has been sent to the Board, a different covering letter is appended with the relevant reviewers' signatures on it. It is these attachments that identity where a staff report is in its career.

I mention this not only because it is in reference to these attachments that the identity of a staff report is immediately see-able, but also because I want to underline the fact that the text within a staff report does not necessarily change through the stages of its career. It might change (and indeed in nearly all cases does change), but this is not necessary. Reviewers of staff reports, whether they be in PDR or any other reviewing function, know this when a report arrives in their in-tray. They look at it to see *if* they need to make contribution as regards reviewers' comments; not because they *have to* make a contribution. This then is the first element in the interpretative schema brought to bear in review.

The perspective from PDR

Once a staff report has been recognised as a draft, reviewers will approach it with a certain set of concerns. The particular interpretative schema within PDR actually consists of a set of schemata, for there is more than one reviewer within PDR, and each has his or her own specific set of interests. There are, first of all, those of the reviewing economists in the divisions (also called, like economists in the area departments, desk officers) and their respective division chiefs.

Second, there are the concerns of the chief reviewing officer (a PDR chief) who is responsible for collating all the responses from the divisional economists and drafting the official PDR review.

More specifically, divisional economists (disregarding the difference between the economists and their bosses for the moment) have specific concerns which reflect the PDR division they are part of. So an economist in the "trade division" will focus on how the Arcadian staff report dealt with the issue of how trade regulations were affecting economic growth. Those in another division, "development", will focus on issues of relevance to that. As a result of this division of labour, PDR desk officers are unable to make general comments on a staff report and instead their remarks focus on a specific domain:

We don't have a view on the whole thing. We just comment on our bit.

That they do so is not just a reflection of how they are concerned with just one area; this concern is bound up with what they understand is the concern of others. Or rather, one should put it this way: a reviewer in PDR will focus on his or her concerns knowing that others will consider the remaining outstanding issues in a report. This is important. A division reviewer will not be concerned with the relative importance of the issues he or she deals with against the issues others will deal with. He or she does not look through a draft report and see which are the most worrisome issues (if any). Concern with those overall measures is the job of another—namely the chief reviewing officer. But in knowing this, division reviewing economists can be confident that in doing their part of the job, the job as a whole will be done. They trust in the fact that in discharging their responsibilities, they will be contributing to the achievement of the work of everyone.

Individual reviewers are able to deliver on their own "patch" in large part because they will review the same issues for several other missions and not just the one they have in hand. Thereby they develop a comparative view on policy. This is key to PDR:

At first it is difficult, but after a while you cannot help but see the general picture [within the division's frame of reference]. You get to know what is the standard, the Fund way of dealing with things. The missions don't really get that perspective. They are too close to their own countries.

When they do look at the specific set of materials, there is another element to their focus:

Economist: We look at the products of the work, not the hard data.
Interviewer: What do you mean?
Economist: Well, I assume that the figures they send us are good. We might request some more, but we don't question them. We look at what the mission team recommends on the basis of them.

In this respect, the perspective of a PDR divisional economist doing a review of a staff report is not one concerned with empirical accuracy since that is taken for granted. Ensuring adequacy and thoroughness will have been PDR's concern when they reviewed the associated briefing paper, as noted in Chapter 5. By the time the work associated with a briefing paper has turned into a staff report, the concerns of a PDR divisional economist will have shifted towards interpretation of policy.

This in turn has a certain form:

We say the same thing, you know. Some people might call it an ideology. PDR has a view about that and everyone knows it. But what I find is that I tend to reiterate that view when I do a review. For example, PDR has a view about export taxes. It has a bias against them. So I end up saying that. This is to give you a simple example.

Such a perspective showed itself in aspects of PDR's review of the Arcadian report. In particular, one of the concerns expressed in the reviewers' comments had to do with the pace of regulatory reform and specifically price regulation. PDR wanted the mission to urge the Arcadians to intensify the pace of liberalisation. This was, the Arcadian desk officer put it (i.e. the mission desk officer), "Just what one would expect from PDR".

There is one last element I want to draw attention to. I mentioned earlier the importance of a back-to-office report as a workflow device. One may begin to appreciate just how important this is when one comprehends the workload of a PDR desk officer:

It can vary but I suppose I do about three a week [by this he meant any and all reports to review, and not just staff reports]. That doesn't sound like a lot. But it is. Each of those require close reading and then there is all the background reading. Another problem is the fact that you can't tell when these reports will actually arrive on your desk so you can't prepare yourself for them until they turn up. Then you have to respond within 24 hours. It is very intensive.

(Twenty-four hours is all the economists get, though PDR as a whole gets three days. This allows the chiefs to collate the economists' comments.)

The perspective of chief reviewers

The views of these economists are confined to their particular domain. They do not orient themselves to assessing a draft staff report in the general, though their assumption that the work as a whole will be done guides them in their own activities. Dealing with this overall concern is the business of the main reviewing officer. Or, more precisely, he or she has to collate the contributions of the individual economists and then add, as necessary, his or her own slant on the upshot. As one chief put it:

My task is to ensure that the (mission) chief has discharged his responsibility as outlined in the briefing paper. My task is to check that the chief has done what he is supposed to.

This task is not one that has a simple linear logic to it. They do not just read a draft report from beginning to end. They organise their reading so that, loosely speaking, they start off with where they will want to end. This "trick" is a resource to order the reading of the rest. This sounds rather complicated, but it is not. Consider the remarks of another chief:

I always read the staff appraisal first. That is the most important, and that guides me as to what to look at. I still read the lot—I have to—but I do the appraisal first. That tells you what you need to look for, what problems that you might be dealing with.

In other words, a reviewing chief will see what the problems are likely to be before he or she actually investigates those problems. The chief needs to construct his or her own frame of reference to organise the work effectively (divisional economists do the same of course, but with their own concerns to guide them).

This frame of reference consists of identifying in broad terms what any problems in a report might be. This provides a structure which identifies what will be the relevant details and what will not, and thus what needs to be examined carefully and what can be left aside.

Part of constructing this framework will mean bearing in mind the associated briefing paper. For the same reviewer (ideally) will have dealt with that paper as with the ensuing staff report. In this sense, a chief reviewing officer will be prepared for a staff report. But nonetheless, they will still need to organise their reading of the report that actually arrives on their desk in such a fashion as to re-investigate and structure their concerns. They do not assume that what they understood as the import of the relevant briefing paper will hold true when the actual staff report turns up. They hope so, but as I made clear in Chapter 5, they assume that in practice any staff report may need reading afresh, i.e. with the possibility that it does not hold to the briefing paper. Key to this is the back-to-office report, which as I have previously noted, flags up any discrepancy between what was planned in a briefing paper and what is documented in a staff report.

Amongst the problems that a chief reviewing officer will focus on are those already mentioned, including, for instance, whether the analysis with regard to some particular area of policy is in accordance with PDR's perspective, and so on. But it is also more than that. Consider these remarks made by a senior member of PDR when I asked him what PDR was concerned with when it reviewed staff reports:

Reviewer: The worst thing, the biggest problem we can have, is when a young chief gets complained about by the member authorities.
Interviewer: Are they always young? Don't older ones get into difficulties?
Reviewer: No, what I should have said is that we can get problems with chiefs that are not familiar with the authorities and who haven't been able to appreciate their situation. Young chiefs are most often the ones who lack that familiarity and so cause the problems.

These complaints have to do with whether a draft staff report reflects too greatly the perspective of the mission itself and not what one might describe as the "objective"or the "right view"; the one that, crudely speaking, PDR is able to recognise as adequate.

Part of an adequate view has to do with the various assessments that the team makes about the member authorities' policies. This is the crux of the problem: whether a mission team has made a correct assessment of the situation the authorities find themselves in and therefore a correct assessment of their policies. This is not simply a question of understanding the present situation of some member country; it is also wrapped up in implications for the future.

To illustrate with problems found in the Arcadian staff report: the chief reviewer raised concerns about the language that was used in the *staff appraisal* section: he felt the tempo was "too upbeat" (and the area department front office felt the same). He also did not approve of the word used to describe the Arcadians' change in membership status a year or two before ("graduating" from Article XI status to Article VIII[186]). This language was, to paraphrase, "all too complimentary". His concern was that it might give the impression that the Arcadians were on the right track and unlikely to face any difficulties in the near future, and that their past policies had always been appropriate. The reviewer wanted this language toned down to express what he described as "the Fund's concern" that the Arcadians should not become too complacent in their policy stance.

There are two issue of relevance here. First, the perspective of the Arcadian team was treated by the PDR chief as essentially *normative*. When PDR examines the materials in front of them, they are not just looking for the right numbers. They are after the right as against the wrong perspective on the policies of the Arcadians. More precisely, the questions that PDR ask are whether a certain set of policies are appropriate, effective, weak, substantive, in need of further development, and so on. This too contains a prospective element (i.e. what differences these judgements will make in the future). Chiefs that are unfamiliar with the authorities may misjudge these issues.

That reviewers of staff reports are concerned about these matters indicates, then, how they treat the relationship between the Fund and its members as not merely one wherein one side reports on the other's activities. Rather, this is a situation where the Fund is viewed as reporting on the *conduct* of the member authorities. This is why PDR reviewers of a staff report are not too concerned with the facts; the adequacy of the facts are assumed. What is of concern is how these data are related to the doings of the authorities. The doings of the

---

[186] In simple terms this is related to whether a member country has foreign currency exchange restrictions. Full status, under Artivle VIII, requires free exchange of currency.

authorities, their policies, their regulatory changes, their plans for the future and so on, are what PDR needs to assess.

Second, the remarks on the Arcadian staff report point toward how the chief reviewer was orienting to later stages of the career of the staff report (i.e. stages after the one in which he was involved). He was particularly concerned with how such things as phraseology could be consequential in those later stages. In this sense, he too was taking account of a division of labour just like those economists who worked for him. But whereas those economists are concerned with the division of labour within PDR, his interest in the division of labour has to do with what his work implies for the outcome of the Board's activity. In the case of the Arcadian report, the reviewer was concerned that the use of certain phraseology at the stage of the career he was concerned with would eventually lead to the Board using the same phraseology at a later stage. That would be a concern for them.

In other words, the concerns of PDR involve combining an understanding about what one may label generally applicable policies with those that are appropriate for the unique circumstances of a member, and it involves judgements about the nuance of language as used in the staff appraisal and how these may play out through time. This results in the work within PDR having an intensive character. It is not just workload that is at issue, at issue is the *kinds of concerns* borne in mind when a report is read, analysed, thought about and reviewed.

That this work is so intense is attested to in a number of ways. Consider the following remarks:

Reviewer: Well, we have complete sets of all the mission papers in PDR and I just ask for whatever I need. They have everything you know. I always make copies for myself though.
Interviewer: Do you mean in addition to the ones that you have requested?
Reviewer: Yes, I like to mark them up. You know I make all sorts of jottings on them. Once you have done that you can't really send them back. You are supposed to send copies back since they are confidential which I do, but I make extra copies. This is one of the reasons why I have so many documents here. It is all the copies I have made and scribbled on—look.

At which point he turned to look at the stacks of papers behind him. He then picked up one of the papers and flicked through it. He soon found a page to demonstrate his point—he wagged a finger towards a

table with some figures scribbled in pencil beside it; just below some
remarks in the margins beside some text.

The making of copies of documents, the marking of them with notes
and remarks, the personalising them if you will, would not necessarily
seem so consequential. But I would like to suggest that within PDR it is
indicative of the kind of *engagement* of the reviewing economists and
the reviewing chief with the documents at hand:

This is not the kind of work you can do on screen, even if we got all the draft
staff reports electronically. You've to print them out to do it properly. You
have to settle down behind your desk and get into it. You like it or you don't. I
love it in PDR. The pressure gives me a thrill. But it is not for everyone.

So, given the nature of the relationship between PDR and the missions, it is imperative that PDR reviewers get deeply involved in the
texts they deal with. Marginalia, personalised stores of documents, are
various measures of this.

One consequence of this marking up of copies is as follows. In many
instances, including the Arcadian one, PDR will send back to a mission
team a marked-up copy of a draft report. This is not the marked-up
copy of the PDR division economists, this is a copy annotated by the
chief reviewing officer.

This (marked-up) copy is used by the mission team to guide it in its
response to the officially documented "reviewers' comments". This
marked-up copy, it is important to note, is not abandoned once the
review process is complete, but kept for future years. A good desk
officer will keep this and others from previous years and use the "texts
on texts" as a resource when he or she is preparing for the next mission
cycle.

These marked-up copies are not made generally available, however,
nor are they stored in the official archives. The enriched text remains
within the hands of those who originally received them. These persons
are those within the centre of a mission team, not those who participate
in the periphery. So it was with Arcadia: the desk officer was proud of
the fact that he had copies of the marked-up texts going back several
years. These were not made available to the EP when he undertook to
"read up" for the mission. This was not because the desk officer was
trying to exclude the EP from getting the extra richness from the
marked-up copies. Instead it reflected different complexes of meaning.
These are bound up with the diverse modalities of understanding

within a division of labour constitutive of mission work, as I described. The desk officer could do his job better if he had these resources; but they would have made no difference to the EP. They do not preclude each other, however. The point here is that the marked-up texts would have served only to increase the amount of reading the EP had to do. He had enough already. The result of this is that there is a differentiation of the kinds of materials available to different persons within the mission and review processes. Some persons have more documents than others, and some have documents with marginalia, creating a text within a text. In this respect there are communities within communities, those within and those without. I shall come back to this.

A digression: some remarks on Fund culture

That one finds marginalia, and, related to this, finds such an intense form of reading, is something I would like to pause on. In particular, I want to consider what implications this has for what one might think of as Fund *culture*.

Consider the following remarks made to me in one of the first interviews I undertook:

You are a sociologist. Are there papers on culture in organisations? Ones that deal with how an organisation becomes obsessed with its writing? I mean this place is obsessed with its writing, everything we do goes through draft and draft and draft. Of course substantive matters are changed but, do you know, when I first came here I couldn't believe how much time was given to getting the right phrase.

And another:

Do you know (the director of the area department)? No? Well I was amazed. When I joined the department, one evening he came into my office to discuss my writing. He was very helpful. But I couldn't believe that someone in his position would read everything. And he clearly had read them (the papers) closely. I mean, it was like he had examined me for English. The thing is English is my first language.

A third:

Oh yeah, you would be interested in this. Do you know one of the initiations of this place (the Fund) is when you get a paper sent back by DPU [document preparation unit] with red lines all over it. It's like being at school. X (the head of the DPU) sends it back if you don't use the right phraseology. These are not big matters—things like the numbering of the tables and figures. It happened to me with my first report. I was furious. It made no difference to the paper. My chief seemed to think it was funny.

Staff within the Fund are then sometimes scolded for not writing up to standard. Some complain, like the last economist, that they are treated like school kids. But this economist's experience notwithstanding, the point I am making is that Fund economists live and breathe texts and words; but not numbers, data and spreadsheets—the stuff of economics. As a result, Fund economists and especially newcomers complain that the Fund is too literary. The comments from members of PDR would appear to confirm the basis of these complaints—that there is indeed microscopic examination of phraseology and word-smithing that absorbs considerable time, all of which does seem like an intense literary endeavour.

This has a number of implications. They can be brought into relief by reference to an essay by George Steiner. As the reader will shortly see, I do not hold with all that Steiner argues. But his essay makes a delightful contrast between different types of readings and I would like to suggest that these point towards the sort of reading that PDR undertakes and indeed the kind of relationship between text and user that exists in the policy function of the Fund.

In *The Uncommon Reader* Steiner suggests that the nature of reading has altered over the past few centuries[187]. He illustrates this by examining the depiction of reading in eighteenth-century painting, *Le Philosophe*, by Chardin. This painting depicts a handsomely dressed scholar studying the pages of a thick folio with ink and quill at hand. It shows also an hourglass and medallions of some kind placed beside the book. Having explained that there is much within this painting to comment on (especially so since the iconography of an eighteenth-century painting is subtle and complex), Steiner suggests that only certain things are of interest. In brief, his claim is that the painting

---

[187] See Steiner (1996).

depicts a reader *totally engrossed* and *absorbed* with the text. He argues that the hourglass, the quill and even the reader's clothes, are symbols that indicate that the reader is not passively accepting the text, but is actively learning from it. Through the process, the reader is creating an interaction which transforms both the text-as-understood and the reader's understanding. Such a contrast between an active reading and a passive reading is of course one that does not hold water, especially in the light of investigations by Dorothy Smith amongst others, as the reader will recollect from Chapter 2. But disregarding that, Steiner goes on to make an interesting contrast.

More specifically, he contrasts this kind of engrossed absorbed reading with that done with a paperback. Here Steiner claims (wrongly, but that is beside the point) that the reader passively listens to the author but does not wish to improve or to push the arguments in the text further on. The reader simply takes from the text. He says that this is of course precisely the point of paperbacks: to entertain, to distract readers from hard thought; to provide leisure, not to teach. Steiner goes on to suggest that the distance between what he calls scholarly reading and the kind of lay reading one does with a paperback is becoming increasingly small in the modern world. He remarks that not only is less value being placed on deep, intellectual readings, but any attempt at such reading is interrupted by modern technology—concentration is undermined by telephones ringing, peace is disturbed by the sound of music from personal stereos. Steiner laments: the art of reading is being lost.

Whether this is true or not in general (i.e. whether there is much less serious and intellectual reading throughout society) is something I cannot comment on here. I would also dispute the suggestion that there is ever a completely passive reading, but I would happily go along with the claim that there are less active readings and more active ones.

These quibbles aside, what I want to suggest is that the kinds of comments I heard during my interviews in the area departments, the kinds of work practices described to me in PDR and elsewhere, led me to understand that the concerns of the reviewing economists in PDR result in the readings they undertake having a deeply intellectual or scholarly character. This seems equal to the absorption, the intensity, the intellectual work that Steiner claims Chardin's painting depicts.

To pursue the point: Steiner argues that during the eighteenth century (and before), the process of engaged reading would typically involve the scribbling of marginalia on the side of the text:

The writer of marginalia . . . is creating an impulsive, perhaps querulous discourse or disputation with the text (Steiner, 1996: 6).

Steiner explains that during that period, many libraries consisted of texts that were marked up with such marginalia. This personalised these libraries, making the owner and user of the books not only manifest in their physical location (i.e. in that person's house) but also in the margins of the book. In addition, the process of creating marginalia was a demonstration of how engaged the readers were with the texts in question. These readers did not only listen to what the author said, they repudiated and debated, they wrote a critical commentary.

I would like to suggest that the fact that PDR annotate the texts for review, that they create personalised document stores—libraries if you will—indicates that the economists in PDR are like the eighteenth-century readers: immersed in the texts they read, not so much in the physical sense of the volume of documents that surround them, as in the nature of their interaction with those texts. PDR economists read a draft staff report and create, if you like, a text in response: not just in the literal sense that a compendium of reviewers' comments is pre-pared and returned to the area department, but insofar as their concerns lead them to create an intellectual response, a text on a text, a docu-ment on a document.

The practices of PDR are not unique; all the reviewing functions involve similarly intensive readings. It is only that the activities of PDR are the most conspicuous by dint of the status of the department. At the same time, I would contend that authors of the Fund's key text(s)—most importantly mission teams—are also engaged as deeply, if not more so. They are engaged not just in the original creation of a text, but in their reference to it, and in the endless revisiting of what they said they would do to ensure that they do it. The relationship between a mission team and its briefing paper is perhaps most illus-trative of this.

Taken as a whole, the practices I had described to me in my inter-views, those I observed on mission and elsewhere, would confirm the comments I heard at the start of my research: namely, those comments that complained about the Fund's concern with text. For many mem-bers of the Fund are certainly engaged in a kind of reading, annotating and note-making that is quite distinct. If Steiner is anything to go by, this would make the Fund arcane, because it is a literary institution in a world where literary concerns and literary practices are ever diminishing. The ironies of this, with regard to both the nature of macroeconomics as a late-twentieth-century science, my own concern with the role of new document technologies, hardly needs expounding[188].

Responsibility for change

I now want to draw attention to how the reviewers in PDR formulated their descriptions of the problems they had to deal with. Though they did say they were concerned with how the *missions* had done their work, often they would slip into a mode of speech which implied a concern with whether a *chief* had done so. I want to suggest that this mode of expression indicates that, although a mission consists of a team, in *practice* responsibility for the work of that team resides with the chief. Of course, one should not be too surprised by this, since this reflects the patterns of all hierarchical organisations: someone takes responsibility; someone is the boss. Indeed, this colloquial term was used for the chief on the Arcadian mission (although not all chiefs appreciate such a term, needless to say).

There are two sides to responsibility: the accolades that come with success, and the flak that comes with failure. Hence, any fault that is generated by a mission is the responsibility of the chief. Of course, mission teams work hard to ensure that no difficulties arise for the chief (or indeed anyone else involved on the mission). As I have described, mission work is essentially team work. Nevertheless, it is the chief who puts his or her head above the parapet during the review cycle.

But more than this. It is not just that the chief is accountable. The chief is also responsible for making any changes urged by PDR.

Interviewer: Why don't you simply rewrite the sections (of a staff report) you want changed?
Reviewer: It's not our report. It's not our job.

---

[188] Through this irony will not be lost on those who have been claiming for years that economics is essentially a literary discipline. See McCloskey (1983).

Another member of PDR:

You need to understand that the Fund is at times a conflictual organisation. The area departments produce, we criticise. They revise, we critique again. We are at opposites. This is to put it baldly. You have to realise that this is generally speaking amicable although it can be very robust. Our job is to check on the work of others. We don't do that work.

But, at the focus of this intercourse and these robust disputations is the chief. To quote from a review of a briefing paper:

You mention a fear of balance of payments pressure leading to a retreat on convertibility. We share this . . .

At a later point:

Could you please put in the customary real effective exchange rate chart . . .

The relationship between PDR and the mission is then one in which a chief is viewed as accountable for the mission as a whole (i.e. it is a chief's mission and no one else's) and it is the chief's responsibility to revise and amend a staff report as it goes through the review process.

A mission chief is not obliged to make changes as a result of reviewers' comments, though a chief will need to bear in mind that if he or she does not make requested changes, PDR may refuse to sign off a report. A chief may also dispute "robustly" as to what changes are necessary and what are not. But the willingness of a chief to do so, his or her *complaisance* to the demands of PDR (and indeed the other reviewing departments), is something that is remembered year in and year out. As the PDR staff remarked, they remember those chiefs who cause them problems. In this respect, a chief may get a reputation that will burden him or her in the future.

The chief's reputation aside, the point I am making is that a chief is treated as *responsible* for any changes that are made and he or she alone makes them. If a chief does not make changes, then from the reviewers' perspective, the chief is culpable for this, not the reviewing function. Similarly, if only some of the changes requested by reviewers are made and this results in a staff report that is unsatisfactory to say, PDR, then that is the fault of the chief. The reviewing function will not get the blame for this.

This is to exaggerate somewhat this division of responsibilities. In practice, if a chief and PDR cannot agree, both sides will meet and "thrash it out". But my point here is that the tenor, the character of the division of labour, is a reason for authorship to be important in the review process. The chief's presence is conspicuous insofar as the review process consists of a cycle of revision, amendment and a specific pattern of associated responsibilities for undertaking such tasks.

In some ways this is a mundane point. When documents are still evolving and being worked up, someone needs to be in charge of the document; someone needs to be its author. But this is worth drawing attention to since authorship (in this sense) is also wrapped up with how authorship is important on missions. Here I am thinking of how a chief needs to be involved in such things as the discussions with the authorities undertaken at the end of a mission. As I described in the previous chapter, a chief needs to participate in these events (along with senior officials from the authorities) to make them significant. In this sense, agreement as to the basic facts of a country's macroeconomic situation and appropriate policy stance is at once an economic matter (based on analysis of numbers) *and* a social one, based on the participation of particular persons. From this view, a chief is also an author of the materials used in policy analysis.

This is interesting in a number of ways, not least of which has to do with how bureaucratic documents have been shown to be anonymous kind of artefacts where the views of some real (i.e. flesh and blood) person are displaced by those of anonymous officials, as I noted in Chapter 2. I am not saying that the Fund is completely unlike other bureaucracies. My point is that if one examines the career of documents within the Fund, one will find the flesh and blood of the author is very much there, at least at the start of the reviewing point in the career of a staff report. As I shall discuss in a moment, the presence of the author does eventually disappear from view as a staff report reaches the last stage of its career.

The last stages in the career of a staff report

Once departing the reviewing functions and the area department front office, a staff report will go across the desks of the DMDs. It will then appear in the in-trays of the Directors of the Board and their Assistants.

I want to make some brief remarks about what is undertaken when a staff report is presented at the Board. I shall take materials from interviews with just two *Assistant Executive Directors*. Executive Directors (EDs) themselves were in fact one step beyond the remit of my research, so I did not have free access to them. They are organisationally speaking outside of the professional body, and to get access would have required a great deal of negotiating. One particular concern was that it might have required an agenda item on the Board's own meetings. Members of the Board might not reject an interest in research but, it was thought by senior officials in the Fund, they might baulk at being asked to give valuable agenda time to such a "trivial" matter.

Be that as it may, my interest is not to use these limited materials to describe the full range of activities on the Board, however, so much as to use this as an opportunity of highlighting the last component of the career of a staff report through the Fund's professional body. I want to do so by appreciating the role, purpose and significance of *a summings up*. This is the last document produced by a mission team related directly to its staff report.

So, here are the comments of one of the two Assistant Executive Directors I met. I asked him to explain how he read a staff report: what were his concerns, how did he approach it?

How do we read it? [a staff report]. I do not read them all. I only read those relevant to me. That is to say my country, the neighbours and also ones in similar circumstances. I read the staff appraisal first. If it looks as if I need to I will then read the rest. I always read the whole thing for my country though. There isn't much to say, I mean we don't have much to say by the time a report reaches us. Let me put it this way: by the time it comes up here most of the difficult work has been done. We more or less agree with what is said in them by this time.
Interviewer: So what do you say?
Assistant: Well, normally the kinds of things we have to say have to do with, well the politics of the case. Sometimes my authorities will want me to make a comment about a member. It is difficult to give an example. Here is an example—last week we had a Board meeting about (a member). They are in arrears. My government wanted the Fund to express a strong opinion about that country, so I outlined something to that effect in a memo for the ED. He rewrote it for himself. It wasn't quite that simple. It gives you the idea. But anyway, it was essentially not about the report itself. It was about my authorities being heard at the Board. They were making a point by making

the statement. If that makes sense. Normally we just agree, I would write a memo that goes to the Director who either submits that to the Board or merges it with comments from his other Assistants. The ED normally prefers to get this drafted out beforehand and submitted as a Board paper so that it is circulated before the meeting. He doesn't often like to make an oral statement.

Interviewer: Are there no substantive concerns that might arise? That might make you want to discuss the report with say the mission chief?

Assistant: No. All of that should have been sorted out by then. Look, I would consider it unethical to talk to the mission chief directly. I mean I will do so sometimes but one has to be careful since I cannot be said to be impartial since I am my country's representative here. If I were to contact the chief it might be seen as an attempt to pull strings. I do contact them sometimes just to get some things clarified. The mission will normally send up a memo asking for our comments and questions. They use that for the draft summings up.

Interviewer: What about the chief's oration? Does that provoke discussion?

Assistant: It depends. It is rather ceremonial. Most of the things that we want to say we know before the meeting anyway. The chief's oration is an opportunity for some of the EDs to make a statement. Some of them like to. Especially some for the big countries. [the name of a member] always says something. I think that EDs with those constituencies feel as if they're obliged to say something.

Here are some remarks from an interview with the other assistant:

Interviewer: [The approach you take to the staff reports] makes this sound like a ritual process, a rubber stamping.

Assistant: Well, you have to realise that what we do is based on trust. But you have to realise also that many of us are deeply familiar with the kind of work that the Fund does. I did the same thing for my country. So we know what it involves, we know how it is done. So therefore we know what is being trusted, and that is what it comes down to. We have to trust the Fund.

In Chapter 5, I remarked that texts are able to talk in certain kinds of ways. To be heard, members of an organisation need to know how to listen to the voices of these texts. This requires that they understand the purpose and context in which those texts exist. In this case, Assistants to the EDs approach the staff reports delivered to them already knowing how they are produced and the kinds of implications they might have for their own courses of action.

In some respects, these understandings enable them to make very mundane determinations as to those courses of action: for example they can be sure enough about what a staff report will say to distinguish between a report that they need to read and one that they do not. Such a distinction can be made because staff reports will stick to the main business at hand—describing Arcadia for example, rather than its trading partners. This much is obvious, however.

More significantly, their understanding of staff reports is such that they assume when they get one on their desk that they will not need to dispute the facts and associated policy recommendations in it. They pick up a staff report more or less assured that they can take on trust its contents, as the remarks of the Assistants indicate. That they do so is not merely a reflection of the fact that some of the EDs' Assistants have done similar tasks to those of the Fund's policy workers. It has to do with their assumption that the staff reports they see have been "successfully reviewed". The stage at which it arrives on their desk is one where the work of sorting out the contents has already been done. This work will have resulted in the fact that anything stated or implied about a member's current circumstances, and anything remarked on the present and future policies of a member, has been agreed and determined as adequate. In a phrase, this work results in enough being said.

Members of the Board and their Assistants will then not approach a staff report to see what they can say *about* that report, since all those sorts of talkings (about the need for rephrasing, further evidence, specification of detail, present and future implications of policy, etc.) will have been completed. What the report provides for members of the Board is an opportunity to talk about *other things*. As the Assistants indicated, those other things can include political issues, the relationship between the Fund and a member that another member wants to comment on, and more. My point is that such discussions are not about the contents of a staff report, rather a staff report provides the opportunity for such discussions.

I am not interested in those broader discussions: for one thing, I had no access to them. What I do want to focus on is the other side of this—how being able to talk about other things turned around the fact that there was nothing to say about the report itself. For this I want to explicate the stages associated with and the nature of *summings up*. These documents are linked to the last stage in the career of a staff report.

Summings up

The interviews with the ED Assistants were undertaken toward the end of my research. Up to these interviews I had not heard mention of a *draft summings up*. I went back to one of the chiefs I had interviewed several times before and asked him to say something about them.

Chief: You've never heard of a draft summings up? I am amazed. I thought you would have come across that straight away. It's extraordinary that you've missed that for so long. It's the most important thing we do. No, it isn't. What I mean is that the fact we can do them is demonstration of how effective we can be. You are a sociologist so you would understand. We are a bureaucracy. We work by being able to predict decision making. If we couldn't do that we would never get things done. The draft summings up is our attempt to predict what will be the outcome of the Board's decision making. The key fact of it is that we do get it spot on. If a draft summings up did not reflect what the Board actually said in response to a staff report then whoever drafted it would be in trouble. In principle it should be the chief but it is normally the desk officer who drafts it. It is in my division.
Interviewer: You are telling me that the draft summings up is written before the discussion on the Board but that it actually reflects what is said on the Board?
Chief: Yes. The DMD uses that for his own remarks summarising the discussions. There will be some changes in expression but it shouldn't require any substantive changes. Essentially it is only a very brief document, a page or two. It is a summary of the main arguments on the staff report—essentially the rub of the staff appraisal—and what the Directors will say about it. But we know what they say because we will have asked them what concerns they might have beforehand. In any case, we can predict what they are going to say. If we couldn't we wouldn't be doing our job.
Interviewer: So if that is the case, what is the point of a chief making an oration? I mean, doesn't that cause debate, discussion?
Chief: No. It is essentially ceremonial. The chief can also answer some questions. Sometimes you do get asked on or two technical questions. The chief will normally take his team or least his desk officer with him to make sure he has the data he needs. But basically it is a chance for the chief to stand before the Board and say that this is his work. It was his staff report after all.
Interviewer: So nothing changes the report. I mean the discussions don't lead to revisions in the report?
Chief: No. Not normally.

Comment

What I learnt during these last interviews was that the ease with which a draft summings could become an official summings up was a demonstration of how effective the Fund's professional body is at achieving its goal. This goal is to be able to specify the kinds of talk a staff report will generate on a Board meeting. But in saying this, I am not saying that they can specify *all* the things that get spoken about in a Board meeting, but only those which are directly related to a staff report—for example, to do with its contents, its recommendations, its specifics, if you like. This is the heart of the matter in the Fund's policy work.

Let me recapitulate the career of a staff report to highlight what I mean. At the start of the review process, the matters of concern are at once specific and broad. As a result, a mission team can predict *some* of the comments they will have to deal with in review, but not all. But, as a staff report makes its way through the review process, there is a gradual whittling away of what is relevant until it is quite tight and predictable—indeed documentable. This is key to the Fund's operations. The *draft summings up* is symbolic of how the Fund's staff are able to bring together the heterogeneous materials that mission teams gather in such a way that when those materials are used to make decisions, those decisions can be made in a social setting (namely the Executive Board) where matters of relevance to the report in question can be encompassed in a single statement. A key feature of this is that this statement can be written before the events in question. In other words, the matters of relevance—with regard to a staff report—are not just whittled away with regard to what any group dealing with it might say (as it moves from, say, the front office to the DMDs). Rather, for the last stage of review, those parameters of relevance—and hence those comments that will be made about a staff report—can be *predetermined*. The boundaries of relevance are then at once *organisational*, reflecting the various parties involved in the process, and *temporal* insofar as certain of those boundaries can be predicted to hold through time.

It has been my main purpose in this chapter to explain this phenomenon—the transformation of an object that is a focus for a number of partly unpredictable doings (e.g. unpredictable insofar as an area department desk officer cannot always predict what PDR will say) into an object whose associated doings are more or less entirely predictable (e.g. the predictability of the Board's response to a report as demonstrated in a summings up).

I have wanted to highlight a number of features of this process. First, when the materials that constitute a staff report enter the review process, they are demonstrably authored by the mission team. By the time the summings up is presented to the Board, all issues of ownership of those materials have vanished. By then, the materials that constitute a staff report have become the Fund's responsibility, or rather the responsibility of the Fund's professional staff as a whole. This achievement, I suggest, embodies the Fund's ability to process the stuff of policy analysis into the digestible facts of decision making. This is a transformation of a set of materials essentially based on professional judgement (i.e. the missions chief's, the reviewer's in PDR, and so on) into a set of materials that become the sanctioned, objective product of an institution.

Second, within this transformational process, users of reports (whether they be, say, reviewers in PDR or Executive Directors), bring a variety of concerns to bear on the process of reading. Staff reports are subject to schema of interpretation which are bound up with an understanding of how the Fund works and what it is about, as well as interpretations of specific materials presented in the report itself. Therefore one should not think of a user's perspective on documents as being unitary, but rather as bound up with a temporal matrix that supports a division of labour.

At the same time, users of documents are not operating in a world where they know little or nothing about the perspectives of other users. Rather, their perspective is constituted partly in reference to what they know about the concerns of others. In some cases, this construction is somewhat loose (for example, an area department desk officer may be only able to predict some but not all of the concerns of PDR reviewers), but at other times it is much more accurate and tight (as in the case of determination of the concerns of the EDs). In this respect, the organisation consists of a community of users who orient their actions partly in terms of their specific terms of reference (or organisational remit) and partly as a consequence of their understanding of the tasks of others who at some later point depend upon them.

One issue that one can note from this is that it is precisely the lack of understanding about the tasks of others that is likely to make newcomers to the Fund poor at their work. This was the case with me. As I noted in earlier chapters, when I first arrived at the fund I could not make out what was significant in a staff report. In large part this was because I had little understanding of the labour that went into that report, as well as how that labour was divided between authors, reviewers and those who ultimately accept the report, the Board.

Third and finally, bound up with this fact is how selection of the appropriate interpretative schema is undertaken within parameters of what is practical and what is ideal. I have only briefly alluded to this during my discussion, but what I have in mind here is how participants within the process do not just interpret a staff report as a function of their organisational location, they also bear in mind what one might call, following Gerson and Star, *due process*[189]. By this is meant, in part, how they bear in mind the need to fulfil their obligations not only to themselves but also to others. Put simply, reviewers in PDR do their job not only because it means they have achieved their goals, but also because it enables others, such as the EDs, to achieve theirs.

Conclusion

These then are the matters that consist of the interpretative schema used in the review process. These are the kinds of material brought to bear when reviewers see a draft staff report lurking in their mail boxes. These reports are the physical embodiments of their responsibilities insofar as the location of those reports implies what has been done, what these individuals will do, and what others are going to do in the future.

This is also the conclusion of my discussions. I have not described in detail all of the post-mission process, though I have focused on what I consider to be the most important. I have wanted to show how the matters that are treated as appropriate at any point within the post-mission process create what one might think of as borders. I have argued that these borders are constitutive of what one may loosely describe as the *communities of use*. By this I mean those groups of people who are involved at any stage within the cycle. There are a number of these, including the mission team itself, the front office directors, PDR and the Executive Directors. Taken together, these communities consist of a society, or, more exactly, an *institution*.

---

[189] See Gerson & Star (1986).

Being a member of these communities is constitutive of membership of the Fund itself.

This particular point is made complicated by that fact that although each community has a border, what is *relevant* to each community is intimately bound up with what is relevant for other communities. Each identifies itself in part by structuring its concerns with due regard to what are the concerns of other communities later on in the process. This mapping of relevance involves a moving back and forth between temporal locations such that what was planned in the past can be seen to be achieved in the future, and such that the present can be used as a resource to justify the past.

Key to all of the work of the communities I have described is how what is documented becomes tighter and tighter as the documents in question—staff reports—move through their career. In this sense, the process I have been examining is cumulative. Or, to put this another way, the changing perspective of users relates to how this perspective is broader and looser at the start of the review process than at the end. This looseness does not reflect vagueness in the boundaries of the communities of users, so much as the breadth of topics that are bought to bear by any community of users at any particular time. If, when a back-to-office report is submitted, a reviewer in PDR picks it up somewhat tentatively, being fearful of the possibilities it might contain, then, in contrast, when the chief makes his or her oration to the Board, very little is unexpected in the discussions about the staff report that follow, though there might be considerable discussion about matters that are parenthetical.

This achievement constitutes the final stage of the processes I am interested in. For though there is much more that happens at the Fund, this provides a natural conclusion to my concerns. In Chapter 5, I commenced my empirical discussions with a description of the tentative schedule process. That process determined the dates of missions and the date of the relevant item on the Board's agenda. Having followed a mission, considered the materials that derive from it, investigated the process of review that ensues, and made some brief remarks about the doings associated with an agenda item itself, I have reached the terminal point of the Fund's routine surveillance activities under Article IV.

CHAPTER 10
Conclusion

The main purpose of this book has been to describe the working life of the Fund. This has involved mapping out the organisational goals and structure of the institution as well as characterising the activities undertaken within those parameters. My slant has been, naturally, the *social organisation* of the activities in question, and this has led me to focus on such things as how desk officers organise their work through time, the social process and rituals of missions and the division of labour that coheres the review process.

The Fund is virgin territory with regard to investigation into these matters: no one has looked at these concerns before. This has been one of the reasons why I have wanted to eschew elaborate or arcane sociological and anthropological arguments about the role of organisations, the patterns of Text within them, or the nature of ethnographic reportage, though I have had to allude to these matters, and some more than others. What I have focused on are empirical materials.

Related to this has been a concern to provide a description of documents that those outside of the usual audience for ethnographic reportage might find useful. In particular, I have wanted to sketch out how certain documents within the Fund are essential to that institution's life, and how that may be illustrative of the role of documents elsewhere.

To do so has required a certain approach. This has consisted of three elements.

First, I have focused on how the relationship between text and user is always *active* and *transformational*.

Second, unpacking the transformations in question has required that I specify *the context* of the relationship between user and text.

Third, understanding that context has required following key documents through the Fund's various processes and examining the modalities of organisational action in each stage. The notion of the *document career* was central to this.

In this chapter I want to review the materials this approach has uncovered and make some remarks about the relationship between organisational action and the technologies of documents. Here I shall be concerned not just with the current form of documents at the Fund, but also with what those might be in the future both in that institution and elsewhere.

Overview of the chapter

I organise my discussions in the following way. First, I reiterate the claim that the document career reflects the Fund's organisational *problematics*. Appropriate patterns of documenting within each of these problematics are distinct. Two aspects of these problematics will concern me. First, I want to explain how in one problematic the production of documents that are suited to generalised, public sharing is precluded and how in the other, the reverse holds true. Reference to the role of relational databases in the respective work of the statistical and policy functions of the Fund is used to clarify this argument.

Second, I discuss the role of time in the two problematics and its implications for documenting practices. This is illuminated by reference to certain document management tools, namely workflow technology. I note that within the policy branch of the Fund, what keeps document processes together is not their linear organisation or sequential unfolding, but rather the reciprocal interplay of temporal perspectives within a division of labour. This may be contrasted with the temporal organisation of work in the statistical function.

I then turn to various stages of the career of documents within the policy function of the Fund. This career commences in the offices of the area department desk officers. I consider how various sources of information are accessed and marshalled at this point (or stage) and how new electronic media may alter this. Web type technologies that increase access to information will clearly be important, but there are issues to do with distinguishing between what one might call Web surfing (when information is being gathered playfully) and the use of the Web for practical, needs-driven purposes. This distinction is bound up with the distinction between the work done outside the mission cycle and the work done within that cycle. I will draw attention to how the utility of information—wherever it comes from—is bound up with issues of authority and the rituals of "signing off". Information off the Web may lack the appropriate "authority" desk officers may need and furthermore may be difficult to sign off in ways that can allow it to be transformed, as I have described within the context of mission work.

This naturally leads me on to the middle stage of the document career: missions. Here, documenting takes a different form, having more to do with the social process of meetings and the ritual transformation of numbers into "talking texts". This allows me to further elaborate the issues to do with the use of the Web already alluded to, but will lead me also to consider the role of audio-visual technologies that may support some of the interactional practices of documenting that is requisite in mission work. In particular, I discuss the use of video technology to support certain elements of mission activity.

I then turn to the post-mission career of documents. I begin by remarking on the modalities of documents that facilitate smooth articulation between post-mission stages. I illustrate this with reference to the delivery of a draft staff report from an area department division to PDR. This will provide background to a discussion of how document technologies need to support practices of intense reading. This is associated with rich patterns of document annotation.

I then move to the last stage of the career of Fund documents—their use by the Executive Board. I will discuss how new modalities of documents might alter the relationship between the Board and the professional body of the Fund. This relationship consists of that juncture where the officials of the professional body are held accountable to their political masters. Hypertext will be of particular interest here, since its capacity to allow new, diverse forms of information draws attention to what might or might not be pertinent in questions of accountability.

This will lead me to revisit how the use of documents is bound up with particular interpretative schemas. These schemas distinguish what is and is not relevant at any point in a document career. This will take me back to the beginning of my arguments and the claim that to understand documents is to understand the context of their use. Without reference to context, the documents in question cannot speak in a fashion that will be heard, or to put this more simply, outsiders will misunderstand what they read, mistaking the materials in a staff report for a rich version of the *International Financial Statistics* (*IFS*), and editions of the *IFS* as materials for the Fund's policy work.

Documenting practices and the Fund's organisational problematics

My argument has been that the organisation of the Fund's work has two main forms: the organisation of policy activity and the organisation of statistical activity. This reflects what I have called the problematics of these activities. There are a number of distinguishing characteristics to these activities, two of which concern us now.

The first has to do with how, in one element of the Fund, information is processed and agreed through complex and elaborate negotiations and agreement. In the other, information is processed by individuals working more or less autonomously. That is to say, in one area, policy work, information is produced through collaborative work. In the other area, statistical work, it is produced individually.

The two different ways of organising information, one a social process, the other more individualised, have important implications for the kinds of technologies that may support the work. Consider multi-user relationship databases. By this I mean systems that are used by various individuals to store and process alphanumeric information. One will find many thousands of such systems in organisations; the Fund's Economic Information System (EIS) is a good example. What is of concern is the role such systems will have in the Fund's work.

I suggest that one will find something of a paradox: in the part of the Fund that requires individuated work, that is to say in its statistical domain, one will find a role for such "collaborative" systems. In the area of the Fund that requires collaboration, in policy work, one will not. I say this is paradoxical because one might assume that to the extent that work is collaborative, then a multi-user system would support that work; in individualised work, such a system would not. But this is the reverse of what happens.

In Chapters 5 and 6 we saw why: in the Fund's Statistics Department, individuals can work by themselves because methodological criteria ensure that what they produce is "objective". This objectivity is recognisable to anyone familiar with the methods in question. Hence there is no need to check, negotiate, corroborate and agree. What is entered onto a system like the EIS is just that which any one expert in the methods would enter. Thus, other individuals can use that information without necessary reference to the producer of that information.

The information can exist and be used independently of the person who authored it.

In contrast, though economists working in the area departments are responsible for maintaining databases on their member countries, they do not have all the data they need when they want it and in the form they need it. Instead, they are required to make professional judgements about where to fill in missing figures and inconsistencies, and to clarify areas where the data seem muddled, and so on. This is a natural feature of policy information. It is never complete, never certain, and always subject to revisions and amendment (sometimes years after the period in question). Because this work involves judgement, there are checks and balances to ensure that the judgements are correct. This is the review process. One consequence of this is that these economists do not create the resources suitable for a multi-user database. They are unable to document their work in the same way as those working in the Statistics Department.

The EIS is of course a currently operational system. My view is that something like it will continue to support the work of the Statistics Department for many years to come. Advances in the technology will not alter the form of documenting, but will gradually make data entry and data access easier. One noticeable change is likely to relate to the broadening of access rights to data to those outside the Fund's walls. Indeed the Statistics Department has recently set up a *Bulletin Board* on the Internet that has allowed anyone with access to the Web to download Fund statistical data for a limited range of countries. If my characterisation of the nature of documenting in statistical work is correct, then this will be only the first step in various new ways in which documented information will be made more widely available.

By the same token, the kinds of documenting practices within the area departments—and the mission teams particularly—will mean that such generalised access would be unlikely. But this work could still be supported by new forms of technologically mediated documentation. For example, something like a Lotus Notes application that provided a shared repository of data could be useful on mission. More specifically, these repositories might come into their own as a mission team progresses towards the end of its work, when the data that each individual economist has been collecting has become increasingly "worked up". As economists reach this latter point, so they start needing to share their data more and more often. This enables them to finalise their "working up". A shared repository would be particularly useful if it could operate over a hotel telephone network, enabling economists to access each other's data sets late at night without disturbing each other. However, more detailed examinations of these carefully managed "sharing practices" would need to be undertaken to specify the ideal and exact form of such a Lotus Notes like application. My research has only served to identify the organisational context within which such an application would be suitable.

What is of greater concern in this text is that one should not assume that this contrast between the two elements of the Fund's organisation is unique to the Fund as an institution; the lesson is that it is in the nature of documented information that its suitability for generalised sharing both *across people* and *across time* will vary. One of the problems with the introduction of applications that are intended to support new forms of sharing is that they are all too often introduced without due regard for these differences.

The flow of work

The second aspect of the organisational problematics I am concerned with has to do with the differences in temporal arrangements in the two parts of the Fund. In one, these arrangements are flexible and the time when information is delivered may—and indeed does—vary. In the other, these arrangements are strict and constantly adhered to. This difference is fundamental, as should be clear. To remind ourselves: in *policy work* not only is it in the nature of balance of payments problems that they can arise unexpectedly, but it is also a feature of policy work that the time of information delivery has enormous bearing on the information itself. In *statistical work*, it is essential that information be produced on a regular basis if that information is going to be used for comparative purposes. Time delays are not allowable, and indeed would be treated as inimical to the job at hand. In one, those who make the information need to have some control over timeliness; in the other, issues of time dictate to the workers. One can put this more strongly: whereas in statistical work time creates a frame in which work can be organised—a schedule, a temporal plan; in policy work, time appears to be a problem— upsetting plans, demanding reworking of schedules, forcing a halt to one sequence of activities and a commencement of another.

Such difficulties might point towards tools that are intended to help deal with the management of document work through time. These tools are typically called "workflow tools". There are numerous such tools on the market and the differences between them need not concern us here[190]. In simple terms, they provide the capacity for document production work to be sequentially represented in and controlled by the system. Thus a workflow tool will represent the whereabouts of a drafted document in the work process and will automatically notify individuals when a document moves through a phase of the work process. An alternative scenario is that the tool draws attention to some delay or some movement of a document through a specified process to managers or administrators.

However, the utility of a workflow tool is more difficult to determine than it might appear. For though it might be clear that policy work has a "workflow" problem, the solution to that may not be of the kind provided by workflow technologies. Consider: with such a tool administrators in charge of linking the documents to organisational processes (such as the Executive Board agenda) could be provided with information about when documents will reach certain stages. With this they could alter the schedule. But it is precisely by allowing this that the tool could undermine effective working. As I have shown, being able to control the "just when" of information delivery is very much part and parcel of providing effective policy information. Although in many cases, alterations in the "just when" of information delivery may be little more than tweaking of the system, at other times it is far more dramatic and consequential. If decisions about timelines got into the hands of people who were not familiar with the circumstances of policy information work—namely administrators of such things as the tentative schedule—then staff reports and associated recommendations could reach the Executive Board at the wrong time.

Workflow tools may find a much more suitable role in statistics. Here the makers of information do not need to have control over the timing of information delivery since this is not flexible. Their task is to get the work done in the specified period irrespective of other matters. But, as noted, manpower problems may make this difficult for them to do. For example, judicious use of a workflow tool could enable administrators of the information production process to shift manpower

---

[190] See, for example, Abbott & Sarin (1994), Agostini et al. (1993), Georgakaopoulos & Hornick (1994) and Medina-Mora et al. (1992). For a discussion of workflow at the IMF see Sellen & Harper (1996).

around in such a way as to ensure that these difficulties are avoided: thereby what needs to get done will be done on time.

At a superficial level, the issue here would appear to be a political one: a question of who has the right to control what. The Fund's professional staff, its policy workers, would naturally want to retain their rights over the scheduling of their own work. But as the contrast with the Statistics Department was meant to make clear, the issue is much deeper than that. It is not only that policy workers need to understand that they work within time constraints. They need to understand how, at certain junctures, they will plan for the future; how at a later moment they will need to account for the past. And further, they have to bear in mind how others within the Fund's division of labour will be doing the same. So for instance, when a staff report leaves an area department division for review by Policy Development and Review (PDR), members of the mission will be looking forward to the review. But in contrast, PDR will looking back at the briefing paper. They will be using that as a resource to measure whether what was said by the mission team in the past is what they have delivered in the present. The mission team will have borne this in mind when they wrote their briefing paper (i.e. they would have taken into account the prospect of a retrospective examination of that paper).

It is for these reasons that I have wanted to claim that policy work is undertaken within a division of labour that enables a complex movement between temporal locations. Workflow tools would fail in policy activity not because they might shift political power within the organisation, but because they cannot support the subtlety and complexity of these temporally organised working relations.

It seems unlikely that workflow tools will ever be able to deal with such complexity. Nor is it likely that policy work will radically alter in the future to reduce this complexity. It is worth mentioning that policy work is so organised not just because it will continue to be so organised in the future, however. All "policy analysis"—it does not have to have anything to do with economics—will have similar forms. But, just as with the Fund, it is likely that such activity is undertaken alongside other tasks that have a much more linear and sequential pattern. What is crucial for any organisation is to continue acknowledging the important differences between each and not to select technologies which support one of these at the expense of the other.

The document career

These discussions have been intended to reiterate the context in which the Fund's documents exist. This has led me to say something about the various junctures in the career of Fund documents. I now want to say some more about this career, starting where it starts (more or less): in the offices of the area department desk officers.

In Chapter 7, I noted that desk officers gather articles from the *Financial Times* and *The Economist* as well as from the press for their member country. They receive papers from the World Bank and other organisations, and many receive *quarterly statements* of foreign currency holdings and *estimates of government fiscal revenues*. All of this arrives in a variety of forms: in personally addressed letters, parcels, faxes, telex, email and occasionally telephone messages.

But these modalities of information are changing. Email of course is creating some of the most well-documented changes in organisational life, and those changes are affecting the Fund like everywhere else. During the time of this research, email had only begun to make a difference. This will surely change. Given the research on the impact of email in other organisations, I will not make any comment about that here[191]. However, during the research period other new forms of electronic access to external sources were beginning to show themselves and these I do want to discuss.

For example, one set of area department divisions were being provided with access to on-line news services such as Reuters. These services offer daily and sometimes hourly updates on certain financial data (market prices, international currency exchange rates, base lending rates and so on) which the desk officers in the divisions found very useful. They were finding this useful not only in the period immediately before a mission, but throughout the year. In addition, some member country authorities were also beginning to allow direct access to their own statistical databases. Desk officers would download from these on a regular basis. This too was proving very useful to desk officers.

In the future it is likely that the use of news services will increase, and there will be more direct electronic access to member authorities'

---

[191] See for example, Sproull & Kiesler (1992).

databases. The spread of the Web, too, will further enhance desk officers' ability to access and download information.

All of this will have a number of advantages, of course. First, and perhaps the most obvious, is that these changes will increase the range of "up-to-date" data desk officers have available. What is meant by up-to-date needs some explication, which I shall come to in a moment. Second, desk officers will be able to increase the amount of electronically sourced information they have to hand. This may reduce the time they had previously given to trying to mix and match between various physical documents: newspaper articles, journal papers, statistical bulletins, and so on. Instead of engaging in a kind of "hands on" bricolage, they might do so within the electronic domain via a keyboard and mouse. This may be easier. Ultimately their black books may shift into their workstations, although it is very doubtful that the media they use will be electronic only. It is more likely that the balance between electronic and paper media will shift towards the electronic.

Such changes are likely to show themselves in all organisations, needless to say. But within the Fund's policy work, any technologies that allow more rapid access to information and which increase the breadth of access will be strongly welcomed—indeed one might say that the Fund has to welcome them—it is after all in the business of "knowing" about the world as a surveillance institution.

Its efforts to do so, to broaden and improve its information-gathering techniques, must be understood with reference to the relative importance of this work, however. Surfing the Web for the latest financial data is certainly something that desk officers would like to do on a regular basis, but this will most definitely take a second place to mission work. Surfing is a casual activity, something that is done when there is a little bit of spare time. But as I have shown, such spare time rarely shows itself.

Nonetheless, mission work itself will require desk officers to be interested in what data they can get off the Web. It is only then that desk officers will use the Web *in anger*, i.e. for practical and immediate purposes. There are a range of further qualifications one needs to consider, however, before imagining that the emergence of technologies like the Web will radically alter desk officers' work, in particular their mission-related work. These have to do with what one might call the related problems of appropriate use and authentication. By this I mean whether desk officers can be sure of the authenticity of the information they have taken from the Web, and related to that whether they can have that information "signed off" in the ways I have described.

To elaborate: one of the problems that is beginning to emerge with Web documentation is that it is difficult for users to be sure of the exact provenance of the information they download and, bound up with this, how to appropriately interpret and use that information. As Numberg has noted[192], the Web offers a kind of anarchic information world. Some commentators—Web propagandists if you like—claim that it is precisely this that makes the Web so exciting: those who access Web sites are themselves defining what counts as good information and what is not and furthermore anyone can set up a Web site.

But what Nunberg is drawing attention to in his *Farewell to the Information Age* is how all information is bound up with broader systems of use that are not limited to the precise point of use at any moment in time. So, for example, to understand what it "means" to use an article in an academic journal cannot be defined by what happens at the point of reading (i.e. the cognitive processes of understanding the contents of the article). Instead it is to understand that activity as one that occurs within broader institutional practice. That is to say, an academic journal article does not just convey information, its meaning is wrapped up in such things as what is known about the status of the journal; whether articles in that journal are reviewed; the status and expertise of those reviewers; and finally what the reader knows about the general impact of the article (i.e. whether it is viewed as an article that is expected to or has had a major impact in the relevant academic community). It is knowledge about these kinds of things that provides the context for "reading"[193].

---

[192] See Nunberg (1996), pp. 103–139.

[193] By way of an aside, some elements of this context are more subtle than they might appear at first consideration. One of particular relevance to the Fund's policy work and its concern with timeliness is worth noting. Numberg points out that in relation to articles in academic journals timeliness is not really an issue. This is because by the time an article appears in the journal it is probably many months if not years since the research in question was done. And he suggests that in any case most if not all the key researchers in the field will know about the findings in the article well before that article appears. They will do so by dint of participating in the review process, by hearing preliminary versions of the findings at workshops and conferences, and through informal communications beforehand. But this does not mean that having an article published has no value. Doing so embodies and signifies the status of the research in question.

Now, with the Web, similar "systems of interpretation" have not been developed yet, though of course with time they might evolve. At the moment the existence of informal ratings of Web sites that are freely available on various Bulletin Boards is an indication of how Web surfers are trying to create for themselves what one might call institutional processes that enable people to determine what is or is not of value. The fact that these ratings are informal is viewed as one of the things that makes the Web so exciting: for here is an information world in which the participants are defining for themselves the institutional processes of use. Nonetheless, it may be that the institutional processes of using Web documentation will slowly merge with already existing institutional patterns of information use. Thus it might be that the reading of a Web site will become analogous to the reading of, say, an article in an academic journal. Readers will assume that the Web site they have downloaded has been through processes of review; that the findings in question have been previously disseminated elsewhere and that the research is "out-dated". This seems unlikely, however. A more probably scenario is that the institutional practices that will give meaning to and a context for the use of Web documentation will be diverse, supporting a whole range of different systems of use. Time will tell.

In any case, what these remarks are leading me to is the question of how the Fund's desk officers will be able to differentiate between the information on the Web that they can and cannot count on in their work. Two examples of how the Fund's desk officers currently place information within a context of use will illustrate my point. These examples are related to Arcadia.

I have noted earlier that area department desk officers often receive copies of the newspapers for the country they are responsible for. This held true for the Arcadian desk officer. He received (via the embassy in Washington) copies of two "dailies" from Arcadia. But, as he explained to me, the utility of the information that these newspapers conveyed was quite limited:

You've got to understand, Richard, that in Arcadia there is no real opposition. This paper (he pointed to one) is the official party paper. That tells the official party line. This one (he pointed to another) is meant to be the opposition paper but it isn't really.
Interviewer: So what do you do with them?
Desk officer: Oh, I still read them. You get some feeling for events in Arcadia.

Also you can get a feel for the views of the authorities. That can be useful in policy discussions. You can't trust the figures in them though.

So this desk officer knew enough about the institutional context of these particular newspapers to know how to use the information they conveyed. Similarly, if the desk officer was to surf the Web to get to sites purporting to present information about Arcadia, he would want to know who produced those sites. In particular, he would want to know things like whether the sites in question were official party sites or genuine opposition sites. Knowing these differences would enable the desk officer to determine what would be the appropriate use of the information he found.

Of course, in relation to the kinds of materials one finds in newspapers—official party ones or otherwise—it may be objected that they do not convey a great deal of macroeconomic data and that therefore desk officers would not be too interested in what they find in them. The contents of newspapers may just be too inconsequential—though useful for getting a "feel" for a country. A second example can illustrate how the need for understanding the appropriate processes of interpretation and use is relevant even for information that looks, at first glance, directly relevant to the macroeconomic concerns of desk officers.

This example is taken from the Arcadian mission itself. During the mission, a meeting with one of the Arcadian officials led to a discussion of an economic analysis institute that had been recently set up. Thereafter, the desk officer and the EP arranged a visit to the institute to find out what it had been doing. This visit led them to discover that it had undertaken a range of studies on recent macroeconomic developments in Arcadia. The desk officer and his colleague reported this in the meeting they had with the rest of the mission the following evening. During this meeting, the team discussed whether they might be able to use information generated by the institution in their own analytical work. They decided that it would be inappropriate to do so since that institute's views were not taken on board by the Arcadian authorities. The chief concluded the discussion by remarking that it may be that in the future the institute would get a higher profile in Arcadia and that its views and economic analysis might therefore become more relevant to future missions. Accordingly, he instructed the desk officer to keep a note of what the institute did in the future and to track whether it started to have any influence with the authorities.

What is to be learnt from this example is that it is not the *contents* of information that defines what is or is not relevant to the work of desk officers. It is how the information in question is placed within a broader context that gives that information its "meaning". In this case, the information the institute produced did not count, but with time perhaps that would change.

Now my point is that when it comes to the Web, a desk officer may be able to locate a great deal of information that might look directly relevant to his or her concerns. But the problem for desk officers is to distinguish between the information they can use and that which they cannot. This in turn relates to such things as whether that information is viewed as counting by the authorities of the member countries themselves. Of course, it may well be that in some cases the authorities disregard some information that the missions would prefer they took heed of. Here there are issues to do with the various pressures that a mission can bring to bear on the authorities and what resistance the authorities can offer to such pressure. As I noted in Chapter 8, in the Arcadian case the relationship between the authorities and the mission was in part a didactic one. Therefore the mission was in a position whereby it could direct the authorities to take account of information the mission thought appropriate. As I say, the mission decided to let the Arcadian authorities make the decision about the new economics institute.

So by way of concluding this section, my view is that, while the World Wide Web will make a difference to the work of desk officers, how this happens will need to evolve. This not because desk officers will need to familiarise themselves with the technology of the Web— its various browsers, informal standards and so on—so much as they will need to build up knowledge of how the information they can download is institutionally relevant to their particular organisationally situated task.

The use of the Web by other organisations will, I suggest, be bound up with a similar path of evolution. But this evolution will take diverse forms depending upon the tasks and concerns of the organisations in question. The Fund is in a particular sort of business; other organisations will have their own quite dissimilar concerns. But whatever those concerns, each and every organisation will need learn how to use the Web to deliver information that they can use "appropriately".

As should be clear, within the Fund what is key to the appropriate forms of use is the mission process itself. I have wanted to argue that it is this process that is at the heart of the Fund's policy activity. This is also central to its documenting practices. Having said something about the ways in which new technology might impact upon the work up to and surrounding missions, I now want to turn to missions themselves.

Missions

On the face of it, mission activity would appear to be the kind of work where new technologies might have the most consequential impact. One might think, in particular, that computer networks and the ability to transmit, access and process data remotely might remove the need for mission work, allowing member countries to make available the kind of up-to-date information the Fund is interested in. But as I hope to have shown in Chapter 8, mission work involves more than just gathering pre-existing data. To be sure, mission teams start with some kind of data—some missions with more data than others—but the teams use the first part of the mission to "work up" these data along with other materials they gather on the mission to create an *analytical perspective*. This perspective is the outcome not so much of "mere" arithmetic or econometrics, as it is the product of certain social processes of uncovering interpretation and meaning, and then coming to agree to these interpretations, sanctioning them, and having them *signed off*. In other words, the data that missions end up using does not exist out there waiting to be gathered up. Rather, information has to be *transformed* into the suitable stuff of policy work. Such transformations require a certain social process that validates the interpretations that can be placed on the numbers in question.

With this in mind, one can revisit the possible benefits that such things as the Web might provide. For it should be clear that the materials gathered via the Web will need to be transformed in the way I described: through the agreeing of interpretations and through the rituals of "signing off" which are at the heart of mission work. Certainly, once use of the Web has evolved in the ways I have described, it may broaden the amount of data a mission team starts off with; the Web may also make that data more up-to-date. This may ease the preparatory work that goes into a mission: the briefing paper may be more thorough; the team may be more accurate in their determinations of the outcome of a mission. But missions will still need to occur because the agreeing of interpretations, the mapping out of a jointly shared view of the policy situation, all of which I have argued are essential to missions, will need to continue.

This does not mean that the actual events that get undertaken while on a mission cannot be supported by new technology. It is just that this new technology might support activities that at first glance would seem less well suited for technological tools. Take, for example, the meetings that occur at the end of the mission. During these, the taking of turns at talk is massively bound up with status. The mission chief's presentation is an oration that demands a response, and this response has to come from the chief's equivalent in the authorities. In the meeting I described, this person was the Governor of the Central Bank. Such a semi-ritualised occasion would seem quite unsuited for technological support. But consider, *video conferencing technology* might support and indeed bolster some of the structures of interaction in such meetings. For many multi-person video conferencing systems allow strict protocols for turn taking, and these might enhance the controls that chiefs and their equivalents in the local authorities might want to exercise during these meetings. One might contend that the turn taking monopolies that are manifest in these meetings could be embedded in the control of the "floor" in video systems. The exact technique through which this control is exercised may vary[194].

However, it is important to recognise that the control of talk within the meetings I am alluding to is normative, meaning that it is not hard and fast so much as something that participants orient to as best they can. Sometimes these meetings break down into fragmented talk with several persons competing to hold the floor at the same time. In such situations, a system that controls the turn taking may become too inflexible. One result of this may be that participants in the meetings would start to avoid such fragmentation and this in turn may make the meetings even more structured than they already are. I do not know whether this would be better. It may be that a fully "duplex" video conferencing system that allows everyone to talk and see each other at

---

[194] One such system that might suit these requirements is Toronto University's *Livewire*. This is a system that uses voice activated switching to determine who sees and hears who. With this system, whoever is talking is effectively the focus of the audio visual environment. When another person starts talking, the system automatically switches to that person, shifting the focus of all participants accordingly. See Buxton et al. (1997) esp. pp. 390–391.

the same time would ultimately be easier to manage[195]. As it happens, such unstructured multiparty video conferencing systems would appear to be becoming the norm. One reason for this may be that they allow participants more flexibility in the social constraints imposed upon the organisation of the video conference.

My concern however, is not to necessarily claim that one kind of video conferencing system would be better than another but to under-line the apparent paradox that the activities that would appear least amenable to computation—the orations, the responses, the ritual trans-formation of numbers and so on—are the very tasks that may well be supported technologically. All the more so, I suggest, when one con-siders that the meetings I have in mind are planned for days if not weeks in advance, ensuring that the persons of high status who need to attend will attend. By the same token, a video conferencing system might justify its costs simply by the reduction in the travel expense saved for those high status persons.

Of course, there may be a host of reasons why video may none-theless be rejected. Perhaps most importantly, video technology may be unsuited to supporting those aspects of end-of-mission meetings that are analytical: i.e., after the ritual transformation of numbers has occurred. Here, the "talking head model" of social interaction, which appears to be the basis of most video technology, is antithetical to the flexible sharing of work objects (spreadsheets, lists of numbers and so on) in the ad hoc, pragmatic, unpredictable way that I have described is constitutive of how the policy "experts" do their work together[196].

Finally, there may be considerable unwillingness on the part of member authorities to accept Fund recommendations for how those authorities might put "their house in order" when the Fund's senior staff have not even bothered to visit the house in question. This is to put it glibly, but points towards the delicate balance of symbolic power between the Fund and its members. As I have noted, such a balance will vary between different members and the Fund. Part of how this balance of power is played out is also through the informal social activities that Fund missions and the member authorities undertake. These are not just opportunities for the member authorities to show hospitality, but are also opportunities for the two sides to get to know

---

[195] In simple terms duplex means that the system allows two-way traffic on the lines that connect that participants.

[196] See Heath et al. (1995) for more detailed comments on these issues.

one another. As it happens, I have said very little about this particular aspect of missions.

These social activities are, however, only one other element in the social practices of mission work. Another which I would suggest is much more important (and which I have spent some time describing) relates to those ad hoc meetings undertaken by mission members when they gather raw data at the start of the mission. But, rather like the post transformation stage of the end-of-mission meetings, these ad hoc analytical meetings are document centred. Therefore, here again the talking head model of video support may be unsuitable. Furthermore, these meetings are not only many and varied, but they are in their very nature unpredictable and often of only short duration. For video systems to support such activities, member authorities would have to have many dozens of video "nodes" in their institutions. At the current time, it is difficult to imagine that such costs could be justified for such brief, ad hoc and unpredictable activities.

Issues of cost justification notwithstanding, the important issue I am trying to convey is that when it comes to mission work, new technologies—once suitably developed and improved—could be used to support the interaction of experts doing their collaborative work. Video technologies would have a role here rather than systems that support the computation of alphanumeric data.

The importance of the kind of collaborative activities I have in mind is, needless to say, somewhat particular to the Fund and its concerns with economic policy. Other organisations will have quite different concerns and requirements. Consequently, the balance between supporting face-to-face work and supporting remotely processed alphanumeric information may be different. In this section, what I have wanted to illustrate is how one might analyse the particular requirements of an organisation such that one does not disregard the social processes that one might think, at first glance, are unsuitable for technological support.

The post-mission process

I now want to turn to some of the things that are undertaken in the post-mission period. and in particular I want to focus on the role of paper. One of the images that the success of the World Wide Web has revived is that of the *paperless office*. The possibility that desk officers may be able to use the Web to access and download electronic data may well lead to a reduction of paper in their offices but not, I suggest, to its complete disappearance either in their offices or in those of many others in the Fund. I do not want to say anything more about the work of desk officers, however, but want instead to look at some of the work that is undertaken by the reviewing departments, and especially PDR. I want to look at how paper is so central to that. But I want to approach that in a slightly teasing way—the same way that members of mission teams normally approach PDR—with paper in hand.

For, it will be recalled from Chapter 3, that when an important document like a briefing paper or a staff report needs to go from an area department division to PDR, it is often personally carried there. I listed some of the reasons why. I noted that some chiefs (or their deputies) like to go down to PDR to give a quick "run through" of the main issues in their document. Sometimes they prefer to deliver documents to PDR by hand to reflect the importance of the documents in question. Hand delivery is also a way of "making sure it gets there" and by the same token "making sure it gets dealt with". The physical presence of a staff report on a reviewer's desk is a method whereby the document draws attention to itself and serves as a continuous reminder that action needs to be taken.

Of course, and as should be clear, briefing papers do not slip off the desks of PDR by mistake, nor do they get forgotten about. The plonking of such things as staff reports on the desk of a PDR economist serves to reiterate what those economists already know—that they have an important, urgent job to do.

But there is another reason why division staff deliver hard copy to PDR, and that is because paper is preferred by PDR. Further, because PDR wants paper and not an electronic copy, one thing one might say here is that the delivery of paper is therefore a sign of politeness on the part of the division staff—trying to help out their colleagues down the corridor by providing documents in the medium they prefer. But why is it that PDR want paper? I think I have pointed out many of reasons for this, and these have considerable implications for the future.

One will recollect that the kind of work undertaken by PDR is particularly intense. Reviewers have to get engaged with the documents at hand. One particular manifestation of this is the extensive marginalia and annotations that many PDR economists make on the reports they review.

This kind of activity resonates with findings from other settings which are beginning to show that paper offers better support for such intense reading and note-making practices, or at least better support than is currently offered by electronic document technologies.

The issues here are not related to such things as screen resolution, contrast or viewing angle of electronic displays against paper. Rather, they have to do with the ability of an individual to work their way around a document, to navigate through it, and to lay it out in space. Part of this has to do with annotation and marginalia: these are ways in which PDR reviewers document their own reasoning, creating as they do a text on a text, a document on a document. It is in these ways that members of PDR "get to grips" with their documents.[197]

In the future it is likely that more effective stylus entry techniques will go some way toward offering the kinds of support that reviewers in PDR might desire. Stylus input techniques might increase the extent to which they offer variegated, idiosyncratic marks through the use of pressure-sensitivity to vary line thickness, or the use of texture and colour. Digital technologies could offer advantages over paper by allowing users to choose whether their annotations are to be permanent or temporary, or by offering selective processing capabilities according to whether they want some set of annotations converted into typescript for collation in the official reviewers' comments. There might also be considerable improvements to be gained by improving the portability and flexibility of electronic document reading devices through advances in lightweight, wireless display technologies.

But these improvements may make no difference to PDR's preference for paper. As the previously mentioned Nunberg notes, with paper, perception of content and the physical volume are inextricably intertwined[198]. As long as documents in the electronic world are essentially two-dimensional objects they will not support the intensive reading activities that paper documents do. Waller too notes that the physical properties of paper support people's reading strategies and their ability to comprehend text[199]. Christina Haas has reported similar research as well as my colleagues O'Hara and Sellen[200].

Most of this research derives from experimental and laboratory studies. The materials I have provided here are of a different nature, and I am unsure whether the two sorts of approaches to empirical

---

[197] See Haas (1996) and also O'Hara & Sellen (1997).
[198] See Nunberg (1996).
[199] See Waller (1986).
[200] See Haas (1996) and O'Hara & Sellen (1997).

phenomena sit side by side very well. One unpacks the composites of social action to specify its variables (namely, the laboratory approach), and the other seeks to preserve that complex (namely, ethnography). But what is certain is that the kind of intensity and engagement to documents that I have described within PDR (and other places in the Fund) will continue. That it does so will continue to be a measure of the kind of analytical work that gets undertaken. Such work surely shows itself elsewhere. But wherever it shows itself, future document technologies must support that engagement.

The end of the document career

I want to conclude my discussions by considering the last stage in the career of a staff report: the stage at which it is presented to the Fund's Executive Board. As I made clear in Chapter 9, the Board's activities were one step beyond the remit of my field work investigations, though the materials I gathered allowed me to outline the general parameters of those activities and to detail all of those undertakings that precede and provide a context for them.

I want to consider this last stage in the career of staff reports with reference to hypertext. As the reader will recollect, hypertext has been the focus of considerable discussion with various commentators arguing that its introduction will make for revolutionary changes in organisational life. My own review of those discussions drew attention both to the main benefits predicted to derive from the introduction of hypertext as well as problems that I perceived in those claims. Despite these problems, I contended that the debates surrounding hypertext are of interest since they point toward the relationship between user and text and, in particular, to the question of whether a user wants to take on board what a text says or whether the user wishes instead to dispute what a text is intended to convey. I noted that the different ways a reader will treat a text will vary depending upon the particular stage a document has reached in its career. Whether a user will want to accept or reject a text is, I will suggest, particularly pertinent when considering the relationship between Executive Directors and staff reports.

One can approach the issues of concern by returning once again to the Fund's policy problematic and how this shows itself in the nature of documents. So, we have seen that a staff report documents the present state of an economy, based on currently available data and analysis.

This present state is precisely what it implies: in the here and now, in the very weeks that the analysis is done. From this view, a staff report presents a snapshot in time. As time passes, so the relevance of a report declines. After a certain while, a report simply becomes out of date. In this sense, a staff report has a certain "shelf-life".

I have noted also that to understand a staff report—and hence the Fund—one needs to realise that such a report will go through various organisational processes, the most important of which are the processes of its review. These guarantee the adequacy of the professional assessments and judgements used. Currently these processes are supposed to take no more than 60 days (i.e. this is the maximum period between a mission returning to the Fund and the delivery of a report to the Board). In this sense, one might say that if a staff report takes a snapshot in time, then the Fund treats that snapshot as an adequate representation of the economy in question throughout the period of time normally given to processing a report.

Now consider what might happen if staff reports were reconstituted in hypertext. The issues that need to be considered are at one level rather facile—reflecting the superficiality of some of the claims made by those I called the hypertext protagonists—and at a second level, much deeper, pointing toward not only *what* is involved in the Fund's policy work but *who* is involved in it. Let me begin with the first set of issues.

In very simple terms, the view of Landow, Bolter and others is that with hypertext the borders of a narrative can be dissolved and new borders constituted by the reader in the process of reading. By border is meant the beginning and end of a narrative structure. With hypertext, these borders can be dissolved by the reader starting and ending at different points. Similarly (the hypertext protagonists claim), the middle of texts also has borders and with hypertext the reader will be able to dissolve these by linking to other texts. According to this view, with a *hypertext staff report*, members of the Board would be able to replace the narratives created by the mission team with their own narratives. Thus, a document that hitherto was meant to convey the voice of the chief and his or her team would now present the voices of the Executive Directors and their interpretation of the materials at hand.

In some ways this might seem appealing. It suggests the possibility that the Fund's Directors themselves undertake more analytical work than they currently do. Given that the Board are the political appointees discharged with the role of overseeing the work of the professional body of the Fund, this may have the advantage of increasing the effectiveness of accountability.

But one needs to consider how the process of accountability is bound up with how an organisation is organised. So, for example, one possible outcome of introducing hypertext staff reports at this juncture in their career is that the time taken to "review" a staff report (by the Board) would become longer. For one thing, the Directors would have to discuss amongst themselves which of their various "readings" is the most acceptable. For another, it will surely take longer for the Directors to work out for themselves the correct readings of policy since they will no longer take on trust the contents of the *staff appraisal* section.

Taking longer to review a staff report does not sound such a radical thing. But consider, this could have the consequence of *stretching* that snapshot in time that staff reports represent. A question that needs to be asked is: at what point does that stretching become too great? As I have just noted, it is currently about 60 days or eight weeks. If it is stretched to ten weeks would that start to become too long? Would fourteen weeks be too long? It should be borne in mind that as it currently stands the time frame given for the production and review of a staff report is already viewed as rather long. Indeed, there are some concerns that the Fund currently does not squeeze the time period enough.

The fact that hypertext may impinge upon the temporal constraints on the Board are, I think, of little significance however. The idea of hypertext allowing a cacophony of voices and thus (in this context) creating a situation where the Managing Director (or his Deputies) find themselves wringing their hands trying to get the Board to agree to one particular view is simply unrealistic. Apart from anything else, the weighted voting system would ensure that one view would more or less always prevail.

Of much greater significance, I suggest, is that with hypertext, the structure and process of producing staff reports would need to change. For whereas now they are structured to provide the grounds for an elaboration of a policy position, with hypertext they would need to be constructed to make available all the information that would be needed to do policy analysis. This may be impossible to do. As I have argued (especially in Chapter 8), policy analysis does not just turn around the production of certain information. It requires mission teams to sit down and work out, hand in hand with the member authorities, what is a reasonable view on the policy circumstances. This is a collaborative affair that requires their joint working. If it were the case that staff reports were going to allow members of the Board to make the policy analysis, then according to my analysis, those same members of the Board would have to participate in these meetings with the member authorities. In other words, members of the Board would have to form missions of their own. This of course would have even greater implications for the time frames in which the Board operates.

But a more important question here is whether this is what the Directors would want. For what we have seen (in Chapter 9) is that the documents that are delivered to the Directors are so refined, so effectively polished by the review process, that the Directors do not have to talk about the contents directly, preferring instead to talk about only related matters (politics, for example). I suggest that the Directors do not begrudge this, as if they have been deprived of the opportunity to jostle with the reviewing departments about what should and should not be said in a staff report. My argument has been that they do not want to participate in that kind of talk. Rather, they want a staff report they can rely on. Crudely speaking, the Directors want exactly the opposite to what the hypertext protagonists desire. That is to say, the Directors want to hear what the text has to say, and they want to know what the author(s) is/are telling them. This is what the Fund's professional body is discharged to provide—not to deliver the raw materials of policy work, but the product of policy work; not rough stuff that needs sorting, but the materials that enable the Board to see their way through to a decision.

Now my thesis throughout the book has been that the preferred courses of interaction within any stage of a document's career are not idiosyncratically decided by a document's users, nor are they arbitrary. They are bound up with the organisational location in which document users find themselves. It is these locations that provide both the context for and the framework through which appropriate modalities of document use are determined by users themselves. In this case, it is my view that the approach of Directors to staff reports reflects their organisational location within the Fund's processes. It is proper that they take on Board what a staff report "says"; it makes organisational sense for them to do so.

Now this begs all sorts of questions about whether the Board is effectively overseeing the work of the Fund. Indeed, it points towards the possibility that accountability is something that needs to be thought about not in relation to the role of the Board, but in relation to earlier stages in the career of staff reports. The fact that the Board typically accepts the views of a staff report may indicate that some other group have undertaken the task of evaluating the work that has gone into the production of a staff report. And, indeed, as should be clear, this is precisely the case. The process of review that operates both before, during and after the mission process is designed to ensure the adequacy of staff reports. It is staff in PDR and the other reviewing departments who are effectively the overseers of accountability at the Fund; not the politically appointed officials on the Board.

Now I have stated again and again that the approach I have taken in this book has not allowed me to discuss whether this is ideal or may need reforming. My purpose has been to sketch out the current organisation of the Fund. The materials I have presented would, I hope, enable others to undertake such investigations into the nature of accountability if they wish to do so.

In any case, my concern here is to point out that to properly understand the relationship between the Fund's Board, staff reports and the technological medium of those reports, requires appreciation of the nature of that relationship not just at this particular point, but at every stage of the Fund's processes. That is to say, that how members of the Executive Board approach a staff report—their preferred courses of action with it—can only be understood by appreciating the distinct courses of action that those participants in earlier stages of the career have oriented to. Each of these stages has consequences for each subsequent stage, allowing a staff report to become an artefact that is used in certain types of ways by the Board. In effect, each stage is part of a *plenum* that reaches its final production with the acceptance of the report by the Board.

The specific interaction between the various stages of the career of a staff report are unique to the Fund, of course; but the importance of understanding the full complement of a document career is, I would argue, important in determining the role of new technologies in any organisation. Failure to do so can lead to misunderstanding the nature of relationship between documents and action within an organisation as well as the role of new document tools in an organisation.

In recognising this, one can return to the question of whether hypertext will have a role in the Fund. For what I have argued would seem to imply that those who believe hypertext offers radical change and improvement in organisational life are wrong. Far from it; my argument is that this last stage of the career of a staff report may not be the place where the benefits they have in mind will show themselves. Instead, one should consider other junctures within the career of a staff report. So, for example, although I have noted that PDR will probably continue to use paper for the foreseeable future, I have also noted that reviewers in PDR like to have a great deal of information at hand when they work. They do not just read a staff report but refer to a range of documents from the past and the present to inform them while they read. These include the ones they have collected themselves as well as those they have retrieved through more official channels. They are, if you like, very much interested in questioning the authority of the author. This is their job. For this they may find hypertext functionality particularly useful, providing them with access to a range of documents that paper-based filing systems would have made just too difficult to locate.

Having said that, I would not want to claim that hypertext would be the unique tool that would enable PDR staff to question the text of (draft) staff reports. One of the problems of the hypertext protagonists is their failure to recognise that such questionings have always gone on and that a variety of tools and document media have been used to support it. Hypertext would add to the toolbox; not create a tool for a task that has never been carried out before.

In any case, a further problem with the arguments of the hypertext protagonists is that they leave one unsure as to what exactly they mean by such things as texts without borders. For a text without a border is rather curious idea. The use of hypertext to create navigational techniques that allow the movement between texts with fixed borders would seem a much more realistic formulation and this leads one to think of the World Wide Web. I have already discussed how the use of this technology would need to evolve. I suggest that the same sort of evolution would probably be required to ensure that *hypertextuality* enhances or deepens the systems of accountability currently operational in the Fund.

Conclusion

In this book, my elaboration of the relationship between technology, documents and organisational action has been necessarily selective: I have enquired into only some aspects of this relationship and looked at only one part of the Fund's activities (albeit the most important). I have had to focus on some things and ignore others. But what I have wanted to do is not provide a comprehensive description of *doings with documents* but to illustrate how such a concern can provide an analytic focus for organisational ethnography and a resource for the design of new technologies.

On both counts, what I have been attempting is something new. Traditional ethnography tends to focus on what one might call the classic concerns of anthropology and sociology—namely power, hierarchy, culture, community and gender—while the traditional approach to the design of document technologies has been based on either laboratory studies of usability or simply entrusted to the inventiveness of designers themselves. As I noted in Chapter 2, this latter approach has often led to technologies that no one seems to want, while laboratory studies have also led to technologies that do not always fit as expected into the complexities of organisational life.

With regard both to my approach to ethnography and to my claims to provide resources for designers, I am sure I will be criticised. With regard to ethnography, I will be rebuked for focusing on the tools of organisational power rather than on the more sinister results of that power; with regard to design I will be criticised for not providing any particular design solutions. My riposte to the first set of criticisms is that to understand the nature of organisational life one needs to understand the mundane artefacts that allow organisations to function. Documents are crucial to this. These criticisms are then wholly misplaced.

As for my response to the second set of criticisms—from designers—I would agree with them wholeheartedly. Indeed, I would suggest that I have added to the concerns that designers need to think about rather than offering solutions. For, I have drawn attention to how diverse the requirements placed on technologies are at different points in the organisational career of documents. As I argued in Chapter 3, I do not believe ethnography provides design solutions. It maps out the context in which technologies might be used; it does not specify what those technologies might be. Other approaches and other methods need to be used alongside ethnography to do that. But in mapping out this context, I think I have achieved something very useful and powerful: here at last is an investigation into what documents do in organisational life that designers can use to ground their flights of fancy; here those who use laboratory techniques have a resource to inform their experimental designs.

To be useful for this I have attempted to ensure that though my investigation has been long and rather rich in detail, it has not been too difficult to follow. Furthermore, I have structured it to exemplify how similar investigations may be undertaken in the future. Such investigations may lead to the revisiting of my own work and the discovery that much of it needs correcting, of course. Irrespective of this, if my work does provoke anyone else to undertake something similar then, in this book, I will have achieved what I set out to do.

References

Abbott, K. & Sarin, S. (1994). Experiences with workflow management: Issues for the next generation. *Proceedings of CSCW '94* (Chapel Hill, North Carolina). New York: ACM Press, pp. 113–120.

Agostini, A., De Michelis, G., Grasso, M. & Patriarca, S. (1993). Reengineering a business process with an innovative workflow management system: A case study. *Proceedings of Organizational Computing Systems* (Milpitas, CA). New York: ACM Press, pp. 154–165.

Altheide, D. (1995). *An Ecology of Communication: Cultural Formats of Control*. New York: Aldine De Gruyter.

Anderson, P.B., Holmqvist, B. & Jensen, J.F. (1993). *The Computer as Medium*. Cambridge, England: Cambridge University Press.

Anderson, R.J. (1994a). Beating the bounds: Who's the community? What's the practice? *Human–Computer Interaction (Special Issue on Context in Design)*, 9(1), 42–46.

Anderson, R.J. (1994b). Representations and requirements: The value of ethnography in system design. *Human–Computer Interaction*, 9(1), 151–182.

Anderson, R.J. (1997). Work, ethnography and system design. In *Encyclopaedia of MicroComputers*, 20, 159–183.

Anderson, R.J., Hughes, J.A. & Sharrock, W.W. (1989). *Working for Profit: The Social Organisation of Calculation in an Entrepreneurial Firm*. Aldershot, England: Avebury.

Atkinson, P. (1990). *The Ethnographic Imagination: Textual Constructions of Reality*. London, England: Routledge.

Bandow, D. & Vasques, I. (1992). *Perpetuating Poverty: The World Bank, The IMF, and The Developing World*. Oxford, England: Oxford University Press.

Bannon, L. (1985). The pioneering work of Douglas C. Engelbart. In Z. Pylyshyn & L. Bannon (Eds), *Perspectives on the Computer Revolution*. Norwood, NJ: Ablex, pp. 301–306.

Bannon, L. & Schmidt, K. (1992). Taking CSCW seriously: Supporting articulation work. *Computer Supported Cooperative Work: An International Journal*, 1(1/2), 7–40.

Barron, D. (1989). Why use SGML? *Electronic Publishing*, 2(1), 3–24.

Bittner, E. (1965). The concept of organisations. *Social Research*, 32, 239–255.

Blau, P. (1955). *The Dynamics of Bureaucracy*. Chicago, IL: University of Chicago Press.

Block, F. (1977). *The Origins of International Economic Disorder: A Study of United States International Monetary Policy from World War II to the Present*. Berkeley, CA: University of California Press.

Blomberg, J., Giacomi, J., Mosher, A. & Swenton-Hall, P. (1992). Ethnographic methods and their relation to design. In D. Schuller & A. Namioka (Eds), *Participatory Design: Principles and Practices*. Hillsdale, NJ: Lawrence Erlbaum Associates.

Boden, D. (1994). *The Business of Talk: Organizations in Action*. Cambridge, England: Polity Press.

Bodker, S. (1989). A human activity approach to user interfaces. *Human–Computer Interaction*, **4**, 171–195.

Boje, D.M., Fitzgibbons, D.E. & Steingard, D.S. (1996). Storytelling at Administrative Science Quarterly: Warding off the Postmodern Barbarians. In D.M. Boje, R.P. Gephart, Jr. & T.J. Thatchenkery (Eds), *Postmodern Management and Organization Theory*. Thousand Oaks, CA: Sage, pp. 60–92.

Bolter, J.D. (1991). *Writing Space: The Computer, Hypertext and the History of Writing*. Hillsdale, NJ: Lawrence Erlbaum Associates.

Bowers, J.M. & Benford, S.D. (1991). *Studies in Computer Supported Cooperative Work: Theory, Practice and Design*. Amsterdam, The Netherlands: Elsevier.

Bowker, G.C. (1994). Information mythology: The world of-as information. In L. BudFrierman (Ed.), *Information Acumen: The Understanding and Use of Knowledge in Modern Business*. London and New York: Routledge, pp. 231–247.

Bowker, G.C., Timmermans, S. & Star, S.L. (1995). Infrastructure and organisational transformation: Classifying nurses' work. In W.E. Orlikowski, G. Walsham, M. Jones & J. Degross (Eds), *Information Technology and Change in Organisational Work*. London: Chapman and Hall.

Brancheau, J.C. & Brown, C.V. (1993). The management of end-user computing: Status and directions. *ACM Computing Surveys*, **25**(4), 437–482.

Braverman, H. (1974). *Labour and Monopoly Capital: The Degradation of Work in the Twentieth Century*. New York: Monthly Review Press.

Brown, J.S. & Duguid, P. (1995). The social life of documents. *Release 1.0*, New York: EDventure Holdings, Inc. 11 October, 1–18.

Brown, P.J. (1996). The Stick-e document: A framework for creating context-aware applications. *Electronic Publishing*, **9**(1), 1–14.

Bryman, R. (Ed.). (1988). *Doing Research in Organisations*. London: Routledge.

Bucciarelli, L.L. (1988). An ethnographic perspective on engineering design. *Design Studies*, **9**(3), 159–168.

Bucciarelli, L.L. (1990). Reflective practice in engineering design. *Design Studies*, **5**(3), 185–191.

Bucciarelli, L.L. (1994). *Designing Engineers*. Cambridge, MA: MIT Press.

Bud-Frierman, L. (Ed.). (1994). *Information Acumen: The Understanding and Use of Knowledge in Modern Business*. London and New York: Routledge.

Bush, V. (1945). As we may think. Reprinted in Z. Pylyshyn & L. Bannon (Eds) (1989) *Perspectives on the Computer Revolution*. Norwood, NJ: Ablex, pp. 49–62.

Button, G. (1993). The curious case of the vanishing technology. In G. Button (Ed.), *Technology in Working Order: Studies of Work, Innovation and Technology*. London: Routledge, pp. 10–30.

Button, G. & Harper, R.H.R. (1996). The relevance of "work practice" for design. *CSCW: An International Journal*, **4**, 263–280.

Button, G. & Sharrock, W. (1993). A disagreement over agreement and consensus in constructionist sociology. *Journal for the Theory of Social Behaviour*, **23**(1), 1–25.

Buxton, W. Sellen, A.J. & Sheasby, M.C. (1997) Interfaces for Multiparty Videoconferences, in Finn et al. (Eds), *Video-Mediated Communication*. New Jersey. Lawrence Erlbaum: pp. 385–400.

Callon, M. (1990). Society in the making: The study of technology as a tool for sociological analysis. In W. Bijker, T.P. Hughes & T. Pinch (Eds.) *The Social Construction of Technological Systems: New Directions in the Sociology and History of Technology*. Cambridge, MA: MIT Press, pp. 83–107.

Card, S.K., Robertson, G.R. & Mackinlay, J. (1991). The information visualizer: An information workspace. *Proceedings of CHI '91*. New York: ACM Press, pp. 195–197.

Clarkson, M.A. (1992). The information theatre. *BYTE*, 145–152.

Clifford, J. & Marcus, G.E. (Eds). (1986). *Writing Culture: The Poetics and Politics of Ethnography*. Berkeley, CA: University of California Press.

Copeland, D.G., Mason, R.O. & McKenney, J.L. (1995). Sabre: The development of information-based competence and execution of information-based competition. *IEEE Annals of the History of Computing*, **17**(3), 30–57.

Dalton, M. (1950). *Men who Manage*, New York: Wiley.

Dandeker, C. (1990). *Surveillance, Power and Modernity: Bureaucracy and Discipline from 1700 to the Present Day*. Cambridge, England: Polity Press.

Davenport, T.H., Eccles, R.G., & Prusak, L. (1992). Information politics. *Sloan Management Review*, Fall, 53–65.

De Vries, M.G. (1986). *The IMF in a Changing World, 1945–85*. Washington, DC: International Monetary Fund.

Douglas, J.Y. (undated). What hypertexts can do that the print narrative cannot. *The Reader*, **42**, Autumn, 1–27.

Douglas, J.Y. (1992). Gaps, maps and perception: What hypertext readers (don't) do. *Perforations*, **3**(1).

Douglas, J.Y. (1993). Social impacts of computing: The framing of hyper-text—revolutionary for whom? *Social Science Computer Review*, **11**:4, Winter, Duke University Press, pp. 417–428.

Driscoll, D. (1992). *What is the International Monetary Fund?* Washington, DC: International Monetary Fund.

Dunlop, C. & Kling, R. (Eds). (1991). *Computerization and Controversy: Value Conflicts and Social Choices.* San Diego: Academic Press.

Easterbrook, S. (Ed.). (1993). CSCW: *Cooperation or Conflict?* London: Springer-Verlag.

Ehn, P. (1988). *Work Oriented Design of Computer Artifacts.* Stockholm: Arbetslivscentrum.

Ehrlich, K. & Cash, D. (1994). Turning information into knowledge: Information finding as a collaborative activity. *Proceedings of the Digital Libraries Conference, Texas.*

Fayol, H. (1949). *General and Industrial Management.* London: Pitman.

Feldman, M.S. (1989). *Order without Design: Information Production and Policy Making.* Stanford, CA: Stanford University Press.

Ferguson, (1990). *The Anti-politics Machine: "Development", Depoliticisation and Bureaucratic Power in Lesotho.* Cambridge, England: Cambridge University Press.

Feyerabend, P. (1975). *Against Method.* London: New Left Books.

Finn, K.E., Sellen, A.J. & Wilbur, S.B. (Eds) (1997). *Video-Mediated Communication.* New Jersey: Lawrence Erlbaum.

Furata, R. (1992). Important papers in the history of document preparation systems: Basic sources. *Electronic Publishing*, **5**(1), 19–44.

Gardner, K. & Lewis, D. (1996). *Anthropology, Development and the Postmodern Challenge.* London: Pluto Press.

Garfinkel, H. (1967). *Studies in Ethnomethodology.* New York: Prentice Hall.

Garfinkel, H. (undated). *A Parsons Primer.* manuscript.

Gasser, L. (1986). The integration of computing and routine work. *ACM Transactions on Office Systems*, **4**(3), 205–225.

Gaver, N. & Lee, S. (1994). *Derrida and Wittgenstein.* Philadelphia, PA: Temple Univeristy Press.

Geertz, C. (1973). *The Interpretation of Cultures.* New York: Basic Books.

Geertz, C. (1983), *Local Knowledge: Further Essays in Interpretive Anthropology.* Basic Books, USA.

Georgakaopoulos, D. & Hornick, M. (1994). An overview of workflow management: From process modeling to workflow automation infrastructure. *Distributed and Parallel Databases, An International Journal.*

Gephart, R. (1996). Management, social issues and the postmodern era. In D.M. Boje, R.P. Gephart, Jr & T.J. Thatchenkery (Eds), *Postmodern Management and Organization Theory.* Thousand Oaks, CA: Sage, pp. 21–44.

Gerson, E.M. & Star, S. L. (1986). Analyzing due process in the workplace. *ACM Transactions on Office Information Systems*, **4**, 257–270.

Goffman, E. (1959). *The Presentation of Self in Everyday Life*. Harmondsworth, England: Penguin Books.

Goffman, E. (1961). *Asylums*. Chicago, IL: Aldine.

Goodman, P.S., Sproull, L.S. & Associates (1990). *Technology and Organizations*. San Francisco and Oxford: Jossey-Bass Publishers.

Goody, J. (1987). *The Interface Between the Written and the Oral*. Cambridge, England: Cambridge University Press.

Grudin, J. & Grinter, R. (1995). Ethnography and design. *Computer Supported Cooperative Work: An International Journal*, **3**(1), 55–59.

Guitián, M. (1992). *The Unique Nature of the Responsibilities of the International Monetary Fund* (IMF Pamphlet No. 46). Washington, DC: International Monetary Fund.

Guitián, M. (undated). *Fund Conditionality: Evolution of Principles and Practices* (IMF Pamphlet No. 38). Washington, DC: International Monetary Fund.

Haake, J. & Wilson, B. (1992). Supporting collaborative writing of hyperdocuments in SEPIA. *Proceedings of Computer Supported Cooperative Work* (Toronto, Canada). New York: ACM Press, pp. 138–146.

Haas, C. (1996). *Writing Technology: Studies in the Materiality of Literacy*. Hillsdale, NJ: Lawrence Erlbaum Associates.

Hammersley, M. & Atkinson, P. (1983). *Ethnography: Principles in Practice*. London: Tavistock.

Harper, R.H.R. (1988). Not any old numbers: An examination of practical reasoning in an accountancy environment. *Journal of Interdisciplinary Economics*, **2**, 297–306.

Harper, R.H.R. (1991a). Review of "The ethnographic imagination: Textual constructions of reality". *Sociology*, **25**(1), 140–141.

Harper, R.H.R. (1991b). The computer game: Detectives, suspects and technology. *British Journal of Criminology*, **31**(3), 292–307.

Harper, R.H.R. (1992). Looking at ourselves: An examination of the social organisation of two research laboratories. *Proceedings of CSCW '92* (Toronto, Canada). New York: ACM Press, pp. 330–337.

Harper, R.H.R. (1996a). Why people do and don't wear Active Badges: A case study. *CSCW: An International Journal*, **4**, 297–318.

Harper, R.H.R. (1996b). *Requirements Analysis in Support of Organisational Work* (RXRC Technical Report). Cambridge, England: Rank Xerox Research Centre.

Harper, R.H.R. & Newman, W. (1996). Designing for user acceptance using analysis techniques based on responsibility modelling. *Proceedings CHI '96* (Vancouver, B.C.). New York: ACM Press.

Harper, R.H.R. & Sellen, A.J. (1995). *Paper-supported Collaborative Work*

(RXRC Technical Report No. EPC-1995). Cambridge, England: Rank Xerox Research Centre.

Harper, R.H.R., O'Hara, K., Sellen, A.J. & Duthie, D. (1997). Toward the paperless hospital? A study of document use by anaesthetists. *British Journal of Anaesthesia* **78**, 762–767.

Harper, R.H.R., Hughes, J.A. & Shapiro, D.Z. (l989a). *The Functionalities of Flight Data Strips* (CAA report). London: Kingsway.

Harper, R.H.R., Hughes, J.A. & Shapiro, D.Z. (1989b). Working in harmony: An examination of computer technology in air traffic control. *Proceedings of The First European Conference on Computer Supported Cooperative Work*. Gatwick: Kluwer, pp. 73–87.

Harper, R.H.R., Hughes, J.A. & Shapiro, D.Z. (1991). Harmonious working and CSCW: Computer technology and air traffic control. In J. Bowers & S. Benford (Eds), *Studies in Computer Supported Cooperative Work: Theory, Practice and Design*. North-Holland, Amsterdam: Elsevier, pp. 225–235.

Harper, R.H.R., Hughes, J., Randall, D., Shapiro, D. & Sharrock, W. (In press). *Order in the Skies: Sociology, CSCW, and Air Traffic Control*. London: Routledge.

Heath, C. & Luff, P. (1991a). Disembodied conduct: Communication through video in a multi-media office environment. *Proceedings of CHI '91* (New Orleans, LA). New York: ACM Press.

Heath, C. & Luff, P. (1991b). Collaborative activity and technological design: Task coordination in London Underground control rooms. *Proceedings of the Second European Conference on Computer-Supported Cooperative Work*. Amsterdam, The Netherlands: Kluwer.

Heath, C., Sellen, A.J. & Luff, P. (1995). Rethinking the virtual workplace: The need for flexible access in video-mediated communication. *Proceedings of ECSCW '95*. Stockholm, Sweden: Kluwer, pp. 83–100.

Heclo, H. (1977). *A Government of Strangers: Executive Politics in Washington*. Washington, DC: Brookings Institute.

Heclo, H. & Wildavsky, A. (1974). *The Private Goverment of Public Money: Community and Policy inside British Politics*. London and Basingstoke: Macmillan Press.

Hendry, D.G. (1995). Breakdowns in writing intentions when simultaneously deploying SGML-marked texts in hard copy and electronic copy. *Behaviour and Information Technology*, **14**(2), 80–92.

Hirschheim, R. (1985). *Office Automation: A Social and Organisational Perspective*. Chichester and New York: John Wiley and Sons.

Hockey, J.C. (1986). *Squaddies: Portrait of a Subculture*. Exeter, England: Exeter University Press.

Hughes, E.C. (1937). Institutional office and the person. *American Journal of Sociology*, **43**, 404–413.

Hughes, J.A., Shapiro, D.Z., Sharrock, W.W., Anderson, R.R., Harper, R.H.R. & Gibbons, S. (1988). *The Automation of Air Traffic Control* (SERC/ESRC Grant No. GR/D/86157).

Hughes, J., King, V., Mariani, J., Rodden, T. & Twidale, M. (1993a). Paperwork and its lessons for database systems. *Proceedings of the 12th Schaerding International Workshop on Design of Computer Supported Cooperative Work and Groupware Systems.* (1–3 June) Springer-Verlag.

Hughes, J.A., Randall, D. & Shapiro, D. (1993b). From ethnographic record to system design: Some experiences from the field. *Computer Supported Cooperative Work*, **1**, 123–141. (Kluwer, Amsterdam)

Hughes, J., King, V. & Rodden, T. (1994). Moving out of the control room: Ethnography in systems design. *Proceedings of CSCW '94* (Chapel Hill, North Carolina). New York: ACM Press, pp. 429–440.

Jirotka, M. & Goguen, J.A. (1994). *Requirements Engineering: Social and Technical Issues.* London: Academic Press.

Jirotka, M., Gilbert, N. & Luff, P. (1992). On the social organisation of organisations. *Computer Supported Cooperative Work*, **1**(1–2), 95–119.

Karsten, H. (1995). Converging paths to Notes: In search of computer based-information systems in a networked company. *Information Technology and People*, **8**(1), 7–34.

Karsten, H. (1995) It's like everyone working around the same desk: Organisational readings of Lotus Notes. *Scandinavian Journal of Information Systems*, **7**(1), 31–32.

Kling, R. (1980). Social analyses of computing: Theoretical perspectives in recent empirical research. *Computing Surveys*, **12**(1), 61–110.

Landauer, T.K. (1995). *The Trouble with Computers: Usefulness, Usability and Productivity.* Boston, MA: MIT Press.

Landow, G.P (1992). *Hypertext: The Convergence of Contemporary Literary Theory and Technology.* Baltimore, MD: The Johns Hopkins University Press.

Latour, B. (1987). *Science in Action.* Cambridge, MA: Harvard University Press.

Latour, B. (1988). *The Pasteurization of France.* (trans. A. Sheridan & J. Law). Cambridge, MA: Harvard University Press.

Latour, B. (1990). Drawing things together. In M. Lynch & S. Woolgar (Eds), *Representation in Scientific Practice.* Cambridge, MA: MIT Press, pp. 19–68.

Latour, B. & Woolgar, S. (1986). *Laboratory Life: The Construction Of Scientific Facts* (2nd edn.). Princeton: Princeton University Press.

Lave, J. (1986). The values of quantification. In J. Law (Ed.), *Power, Action and Belief.* London: Routledge, pp. 88–111.

Lévi-Strauss, C. (1962). *The Savage Mind.* London: Weidenfield and Nicolson.

Lofland, J. (1971). *Analyzing Social Settings: A Guide to Qualitative Observation and Analysis*. Belmont, CA: Wadsworth.

Luff, P., Gilbert, N. & Frohlich, D. (Eds). (1990). *Computers and Conversation*. London: Academic Press.

Lynch, M. (1982). Technical work and critical inquiry: Investigations in a scientific laboratory. *Social Studies of Science*, **12**, 499–534.

Lynch, M. (1985a). *Art and Artifact in Laboratory Science*. London: Routledge and Kegan Paul.

Lynch, M. (1985b). Discipline and the material form of images: An analysis of scientific visibility. *Social Studies of Science*, **1**(5), 37–66.

Lynch, M. (1988). The externalized retina: Selection and mathematization in the visual documentation of objects in the life sciences. *Human Studies*, **11**, 201–234.

Lynch, M., Livingstone, E. & Garfinkel, H. (1983). Temporal order in laboratory work. In K.D. Knorr-Cetina & M. Mulkay (Eds), *Science Observed: Perspectives on the Social Study of Science*. London: Sage, pp. 205–238.

McAlpine, K. & Golder, P. (1994). A new architecture for a collaborative authoring system: Collaborwriter. *Computer Supported Cooperative Work: an International Journal*, **2**, 159–174.

McCloskey, D. (1983). The rhetoric of economics. *Journal of Econmomic Literature*, **21**, 481–517.

McGrath, J. & Hollingshead, A. (1994). *Groups Interacting with Technology*. Thousand Oaks, CA: Sage.

March, J.G. (1987). Ambiguity and accounting: The elusive link between information and decision-making. *Accounting, Organizations and Society*, **12**, 153–168.

March, J.G. (1988). *Decisions and Organizations*. Oxford: Basil Blackwell.

March, J.G. (1991). How decisions happen in organizations. *Human–Computer Interaction*, **6**, 95–117.

March, J.G. & Simon, H.A. (1958). *Organizations*. New York: John Wiley.

Marvin, C. (1988). *When Old Technologies Were New: Thinking about Electronic Communication in the Late Nineteenth Century*. Oxford: Oxford University Press.

Medina-Mora, R., Winograd, T, Flores, R. & Flores, F. (1992). The action workflow approach to workflow management technology. *Proceedings of CSCW '92* (Toronto, Canada). New York: ACM Press, pp. 281–288.

Merton, R.K. (1957). *Social Theory and Social Structure* (revised edn.). New York: Free Press.

Monk, A.F. & Gilbert, N. (Eds). (1985). *Perspectives on HCI: Diverse Approaches*. London: Academic Press.

Mooney, J.C. & Reiley, A.P. (1931). *Onward Industry*. New York: Harper Row.

Morgan, G. (1986). *Images of Organization*. London: Sage.

Morton, M.S. (Ed.). (1991). *The Corporation of the 1990s: Information Technology and Organisational Transformation.* Oxford: Oxford University Press.

Mumford, E. & Henshall, D. (1979). *A Participative Approach to Computer System Design: A Case Study of the Introduction of a New Computer System.* London: Associated Press.

Nardi, B. (1993). *A Small Matter of Programming: Perspectives on End User Computing.* Cambridge, MA: MIT Press.

Neuwirth, C.M., Kaufer, D.S., Chandhok, R. & Morris, J.H. (1994). Computer support for distributed collaborative writing: Defining parameters for interaction. *Proceedings of CSCW '94* (Chapel Hill, North Carolina). New York: ACM Press, pp. 145–152.

Newman, P. & Newman, J. (1993). Social writing: Premises and practices in computerised contexts. In M. Sharples (Ed.), *Computer Supported Collaborative Writing.* London: Springer-Verlag, pp. 29–40.

Newman, W., Eldrige, M. & Harper, R. (1996). Modelling last-minute authoring: Does technology add value or encourage tinkering? *Proceedings CHI '96* (Vancouver, B.C.).

Nielsen, J. (1993). *Hypertext and Hypermedia.* London and San Diego: Academic Press.

Nonaka, I. & Takeuchi, H. (1995). *The Knowledge Creating Company.* New York and Oxford: Oxford University Press.

Nunberg, G. (1993). The places of books in the age of the electronic publication. *Representations*, **42**, 13–37.

Nunberg, G. (1996). Farewell to the Information Age. In G. Nunberg (Ed.), *The Future of the Book.* Berkeley CA: University of California Press, pp. 103–138.

O'Hara, K. & Sellen, A.J. (1997). A comparison of reading paper and on-line documents. *Proceedings of CHI '97.* Atlanta, Georgia: ACM Press, pp. 335–342.

Olerup, A. (1989). Socio-technical design of computer-assisted work: A discussion of the ETHICS and Tavistock Approaches. *Scandinavian Journal of Information Systems*, **1**, 43–71.

Olson, M.H. (Ed.). (1989). *Technological Support of Work Group Collaboration.* Hillsdale, NJ: Lawrence Erlbaum.

Orlikowski, W.J. (1992). Learning from notes: Organisational issues in groupware implementation. *Proceedings of CSCW '92* (Toronto, Canada). New York: ACM Press, pp. 362–369.

Orlikowski, W.J. (1995). *Evolving with Notes: Organizational Change around Groupware Technology.* Cambridge, MA: MIT Press.

Plowman, L., Rogers, Y. & Ramage, M. (1995). What are workplace studies for? *Proceedings of ECSCW '95* (Stockholm, Sweden). New York: ACM Press, pp. 309–324.

Porter, T.M. (1995). *Trust in Numbers: The Pursuit of Objectivity in Science and Public Life*. Princeton, NJ: Princeton University Press.

Pylyshyn, Z. & Bannon, L. (1985). *Perspectives on the Computer Revolution*. Norwood, NJ: Ablex.

Randall, D., Rouncefield, M. & Hughes, J. (1995). Chalk and cheese: BPR and ethnomethodologically informed ethnography on CSCW. *Proceedings ECSCW '95*. Dordrecht, The Netherlands: Kluwer, pp. 325–340.

Randall, D., Twidale, M. & Bentley, R. (1996). Dealing with uncertainty: Perspectives in the evaluation process. In P.J. Thomas (Ed.), *CSCW Requirements and Evaluation*. London: Springer-Verlag, pp. 141–155.

Rouncefield, M., Hughes, J. & Rodden, T. (1994). Working with "constant interruption": CSCW and the small office. *Proceedings of CSCW '94* (Chapel Hill, North Carolina). New York: ACM Press.

Rule, J. & Attewell, P. (1989). What do computers do? *Social Problems*, **36**(3), 225–241.

Russell, D.M., Stefik, M. J., Pirolli, P. & Card, S.K. (1993). The cost structure of sense-making. *Proceedings of INTERCHI '93* (Amsterdam, The Netherlands). New York: ACM Press, pp. 308–314.

Salerno, L. (1985). What ever happened to the computer revolution? *Harvard Business Review*, **63**(6), 129–138.

Salton, G. (1989). *Automatic Text Processing*. New York: Addison-Wesley.

Scheil, B.A. (1983). Coping with complexity. *Office, Technology and People*, **1**, 295–320.

Schuller, D. & Namioka, A. (Eds). (1992). *Participatory Design: Principles and Practices*. Hillsdale, NJ: Lawrence Erlbaum Associates.

Schutz, A. (1962). *The Problem of Social Reality: Collected Papers I*. (Edited by M. Natanson). The Hague, The Netherlands: Martinus Nijhoff.

Schwartzman, H.B. (1993). *Ethnography in Organizations*. Newbury Park, CA: Sage Publications.

Sellen A.J. & Harper, R.H.R. (1996). *Can Workflow Tools Support Knowledge Work? A Case Study of the International Monetary Fund* (RXRC Technical Report No. EPC-1997). Cambridge, England: Rank Xerox Research Centre.

Shapiro, D. (1994). The limits of ethnography: Combining social sciences for CSCW. *Proceedings of CSCW '94* (Chapel Hill, North Carolina). New York: ACM Press, pp. 417–428

Shapiro, D.Z., Hughes, J.A., Randall, D. & Harper, R. (1991). Visual re-representation of database information: The flight data strip in air traffic control. *Proceedings of the 10th Interdisciplinary Workshop on Informatics and Psychology: Cognitive Aspects of Visual Language and Visual Interfaces* (Scharding, Austria, May) Springer-Verlag.

Skolnick, J. (1966). *Justice without Trial: Law Enforcement in a Democratic Society*. New York: Wiley.

Smith, D.E. (1982). *The Active Text*. Paper presented at the 10th World

Congress of Sociology (Mexico City, Mexico). International Sociological Association.

Smith, D. E. (1990). *Texts, Facts, and Femininity: Exploring the Relations of Ruling*. London and New York: Routledge.

Solomon, S. (1995). *The Confidence Game: How Unelected Central Bankers are Governing the Changed Global Economy*. New York: Simon & Schuster.

Sproull, L. & Kiesler, S. (1992). *New Ways of Working in the Networked Organisation*. Cambridge, MA: MIT Press.

Stafford-Fraser, Q. & Robinson, P. (1996). BrightBoard: Video-augmented environments. *Proceedings of CHI '96* (Vancouver, BC). New York: ACM Press, pp. 134–141.

Star, S.L. (1995). *Ecologies of Knowledge: Work, and Politics in Science and Technology*. Albany, NY: State University of New York Press,

Steiner, G. (1996). *No Passion Spent: Essays, 1978–1996*. London: Faber and Faber.

Suchman, L. (1983). Office procedure as practical action: Models of work and system design. *ACM Transactions on Office Information Systems*, **1**(4), 320–328.

Suchman, L. (1987). *Plans and Situated Actions: The Problem of Human–Machine Communication*. Cambridge, England: Cambridge University Press.

Suchman, L. & Wynn, E. (1984). Procedures and problems in the office. *Office: Technology and People*, **2**, 133–154.

Taylor, F. (1911). *Principles of Scientific Management*. New York: Harper and Row.

Taylor, J.R. & Van Every, E., with contributions from Akzam, H., Hovey, M. & Taylor, G. (1993). *The Vulnerable Fortress: Bureaucratic Organisation and Management in the Information Age*. Toronto, Canada: University of Toronto Press.

Thain, C. & Wright, M. (1996). *The Treasury and Whitehall: The Planning and Control of Public Expenditure: 1976–1993*. Oxford: Clarendon Press.

The Economist. A Survey of the IMF and the World Bank. 12–18 Oct, **321**, (7728), 88–89.

Thomas, P.J. (Ed.). (1995). *The Social and Interactional Dimensions of Human–Computer Interfaces*. Cambridge, England: Cambridge University Press.

Thomas, P.J. (Ed.). (1996). *CSCW Requirements and Evaluation*. London: Springer.

Trigg, R., Suchman, L. & Halasz, F. (1986). Supporting collaboration in NoteCards. In *Proceedings of the Conference on Computer Supported Cooperative Work*. Austin, Texas: ACM Press, pp. 147–153.

Trist, E. (1981). *The Socio-technical Perspective*. London: Tavistock.

Turner, R., Douglas, T. & Turner A. (1996). *README.1ST: SGML for Writers and Editors*. Englewood Cliffs, NJ: Prentice Hall.

Turrell, M. (1995). Learning through experience: How companies are using groupware. *Proceedings of Groupware '95*.

Van Maanen, J. (1988). *Tales of the Field: On Writing Ethnography*. Chicago, IL: University of Chicago Press.

Van Maanen, J. (Ed.). (1995). *Representation in Ethnography*. Thousand Oaks, CA: Sage.

Waller, R. (1986). What electronic books will have to be better than. *Journal of Information Design*, **5**(1), 7275.

Walsham, G. (1993). *Interpreting Information Systems in Organisations*. New York and Chichester: Wiley & Sons.

Weber, M. (1947). *Theory of Social and Economic Organisation*. New York: The Free Press.

Weick, K. (1985). The significance of corporate culture. In P.J. Frost, L.F. Moore, M.R. Louis, C.C. Lundberg & J. Martin (Eds), *Organizational Culture*. Beverly Hills and London: Sage, pp. 381–391.

Weick, K. (1995). *Sense Making in Organizations*. Thousand Oaks, CA: Sage.

Wieder, D.L. (1974). *Language and Social Reality: The Case of Telling the Convict Code*. The Hague, The Netherlands: Mouton.

Wiener, N. (1948). *Cybernetics, or Control and Communication in the Animal and the Machine*. New York: John Wiley and Sons.

Woolgar, S. (1991). The turn to technology in social studies of science. *Science, Technology and Human Values*, **16**(1), 20–50.

Woolgar, S. (1993). What's at stake in the sociology of technology? A reply to Pinch and Winner. *Science, Technology and Human Values*, **18**(4), 523–529.

Wright, S. (1994). *Anthropology of Organizations*. London and New York: Routledge.

Yates, J. (1989). *Control Through Communication: The Rise of System in American Management*. Baltimore and London: Johns Hopkins University Press.

Yates, J. & Benjamin, R.T. (1991). The past and present as a window on the future. In M.S. Morton (Ed.), *The Corporation of the 1990s: Information Technology and Organisational Transformation*. Oxford: Oxford University Press.

Zuboff, S. (1984). *In the Age of the Smart Machine: The Future of Work and Power*. New York: Basic Books.

Index